This book explores the process of popular mobilization in contemporary Mexico through the experience of the country's most important popular organization – the teachers' movement. It provides a new perspective on Mexican politics by demonstrating that popular political organization is far more important to the political changes occurring in this country than previously thought. It also makes an original contribution to the literature on popular or "social" movements by providing a detailed look inside the movement, as well as linking its development to its changing political context.

# POPULAR MOBILIZATION IN MEXICO

# POPULAR MOBILIZATION IN MEXICO

## THE TEACHERS' MOVEMENT 1977–87

JOE FOWERAKER

*University of Essex*

CAMBRIDGE
UNIVERSITY PRESS

PUBLISHED BY THE PRESS SYNDICATE OF THE UNIVERSITY OF CAMBRIDGE
The Pitt Building, Trumpington Street, Cambridge, United Kingdom

CAMBRIDGE UNIVERSITY PRESS
The Edinburgh Building, Cambridge CB2 2RU, UK
40 West 20th Street, New York NY 10011–4211, USA
477 Williamstown Road, Port Melbourne, VIC 3207, Australia
Ruiz de Alarcón 13, 28014 Madrid, Spain
Dock House, The Waterfront, Cape Town 8001, South Africa

http://www.cambridge.org



First published 1993
First paperback edition 2002

*A catalogue record for this book is available from the British Library*

*Library of Congress Cataloguing in Publication data*
Foweraker, Joe.
Popular mobilization in Mexico: the teachers' movement, 1977–87 /
Joe Foweraker.
p.      cm.
Includes bibliographical references (p.   ).
ISBN  0 521 44147 1
1. Teachers – Mexico – Political activity – History – 20th century.
2. Teachers' unions – Mexico – History – 20th century.   3. Mexico –
Politics and government – 1970-   I. Title.
LB2844.1.P6F68   1993
371.1′04–dc20   92-33165   CIP

ISBN  0 521 44147 1  hardback
ISBN  0 521 52334 6  paperback

To
my sister Dinah,
my sons Jack and Max,
my nieces Jane and Karen
(family friends)

# Contents

## PART IV   POPULAR MOVEMENTS AND POLITICAL CHANGE

# Preface

I wish to thank the friends and colleagues who have encouraged and helped me throughout the research and writing of this book. I could not have done it without them.

It was Laurence Whitehead who introduced me to the Center for U.S.–Mexican Studies in San Diego. Wayne Cornelius, the director of the center, has provided solid support and a warm welcome ever since. Peter Smith and Paul Drake have often cheered me up and cheered me on. Miguel Centeno's good humor helped me keep mine during the writing of the first draft, and long talks with Gerry Munck helped me get a better grip on some key concepts. Ann Craig and Neil Harvey have always been ready with creative advice and loyal criticism, especially in the rewriting of the first draft. Alan Angell and Ian Roxborough have given me constant encouragement over many years.

So many people helped me in Mexico that I cannot mention them all. But my research might never have prospered without the kindness of Francisco Suárez, Luis and Graciela Santander, Graciela Paredes, and David and Cristina Torres. Luis Hernández gave me invaluable contacts at the beginning of the fieldwork, as well as free access to his remarkable personal archive. Alberto Arnaut also provided a mass of primary research materials. Both Sergio Zermeño and Juan Molinar have been provocative critics at key moments. Above all, the book could not have been written without the generous help of the teachers of Chiapas (and elsewhere), who were always willing to talk with me in their effort to educate me to the meaning of their movement.

I also wish to acknowledge and thank the Economic and Social Research Council, which provided the financial support for the research and writing through two research grants in 1986–7 and 1989–90. Equally, I wish to recognize the research commitment of my colleagues in the Department of Government at the University of Essex, who have accepted my recurrent leaves of absence with good grace and good humor. My thanks especially to David McKay and Ivor Crewe.

It is often said that scholarship is made up of 95 percent hard work and 5 percent imagination (which may be an optimistic estimate). The point is that long days of sometimes lonely work will always precede the delights of serendipity. So without the friends who stay close and keep faith, nothing can be said, nothing will be written. Among those whom I have not yet mentioned are Hama Agha, Amalia Chamorro, Jim Primm, Julie Reeves, Dave Sanders, Eric Tanenbaum, Rigo Vasquez, Chuck Wood, and Ruben Zamora. But more than anyone else Clare Dekker accompanied the rewriting of the manuscript and helped in so many ways to get the job done.

I first went to Mexico almost twenty-five years ago, and I have returned many times since. One of the many joys in making this book is in giving something back to a people and a culture that have given and taught me so much. But even if Mexico is its main inspiration, the book makes an argument about popular (or "social") movements and political change that may apply more broadly to Latin America, and beyond. In the Introduction I first sketch in the context and content of the inquiry, before staking out its analytical claims and previewing its overall organization. The argument itself is designed to be easily accessible, and the book aspires to entertain as well as enlighten. I hope you enjoy it.

Great Bentley, Essex
July 1992

# Glossary of acronyms

| | |
|---|---|
| ANOCP | National Popular Assembly of Workers and Peasants |
| ACR | Revolutionary Peasant Alliance |
| ARS | Revolutionary Syndical Alliance |
| ATE | Alliance of Workers in Education |
| BANRURAL | National Bank of Rural Credit |
| CCI | Independent Peasant Union |
| CCL | Central Struggle Committee |
| CFE | Federal Electricity Commission |
| CIOAC | Independent Union of Agricultural Workers and Peasants |
| CLPEZ | Emiliano Zapata Committee for Popular Struggle |
| CME | Municipal Education Committee |
| CNC | National Peasant Confederation |
| CNMCT | National Commission of TV-Secondary Teachers |
| CNOP | National Confederation of Popular Organizations |
| CNPA | "Plan de Ayala" National Coordinating Committee |
| CNTE | National Coordinating Committee of Workers in Education |
| COCEI | Coalition of Workers, Peasants and Students of the Isthmus |
| CODEMA | Democratic Teachers' Tendency |
| CONAMUP | National Coordinating Committee of the Urban Popular Movement |
| CONASUPO | National Company for Popular Subsistence |

| | |
|---|---|
| CONPA | Permanent Agrarian Congress |
| COSDE | Democratic Syndical Tendency |
| COSID | Independent and Democratic Syndical Tendency |
| COSINA | National Syndical Coordinating Committee |
| CT | Labor Congress |
| CTM | Confederation of Mexican Workers |
| CUD | Sole Coordinating Committee of Earthquake Victims |
| ETAs | Agricultural Technical Schools |
| FDN | National Democratic Front |
| FAT | Authentic Labor Front |
| FMIN | National Independent Teachers' Front |
| FNAP | National Popular Action Front |
| FNCR | National Front Against Repression |
| FNDSCAC | National Front for the Defense of Wages and Against Austerity and Need |
| FRTECH | Front for the Demands of the Teachers of Chiapas |
| FSTSE | Union Federation of Workers in the State Sector |
| INMECAFE | Mexican Coffee Institute |
| ISSSTE | Institute of Social Security & Services for State Employees |
| MAS | Movement Toward Socialism |
| MRM | Revolutionary Teachers' Movement |
| OCEZ | Emiliano Zapata Peasant Organization |
| PAN | National Action Party |
| PARM | Authentic Party of the Mexican Revolution |
| PCM | Mexican Communist Party |
| PEMEX | Oil Industry of Mexico |
| PPS | Popular Socialist Party |
| PRD | Party of the Democratic Revolution |
| PRI | Institutional Revolutionary Party |

| | |
|---|---|
| PRONASOL | National Solidarity Program |
| PRT | Revolutionary Workers' Party |
| PST | Socialist Workers' Party |
| PSUM | Unified Socialist Party of Mexico |
| SITUAM | Independent Union of Workers in the Metropolitan University |
| SNTE | National Union of Workers in Education |
| STUNAM | Union of Workers at the National University |
| SUTERM | Sole Union of Electrical Workers of the Mexican Republic |
| SUTIN | Sole Union of Workers in the Nuclear Industry |
| TABAMEX | Mexican Tobacco Institute |
| UOI | Independent Labor Union |
| USEDs | Units to Decentralize Educational Services |
| UTE | Union of Workers in Education |

# Introduction: The character and context of popular mobilization in contemporary Mexico

This is the story of the most important popular movement in modern-day Mexican politics – the teacher's movement. From small beginnings in the state of Chiapas in the late 1970s, the movement became a major force in the national politics of the 1980s. At a time when many union organizations faced defeat and despair, the teachers took the lead in combatting the corporatist controls and austerity policies of an increasingly unpopular government. Through their novel forms of organization and their audacious tactics, they captured the national imagination, as well as provoking the opprobrium of government leaders and political bosses; and through their mass mobilizations on the streets of Mexico City they challenged the government's claims to be the revolutionary and democratic representative of the Mexican people.

Teachers are not usually so important, but the special political and cultural legacies of the Mexican Revolution gave Mexico's teachers a central role in the political life of the country. The official teacher's union, the SNTE (The National Union of Workers in Education), is the largest and possibly the most powerful union in Latin America. The teachers organized within it have traditionally acted as one of the principal "transmission belts" of the political system overall, and in their community roles they are the living links the government uses to reproduce the kind of consensus and consent that has been called "hegemonic." The SNTE is thus one of the key corporate players of the system, and its ubiquitous presence gives it real political muscle. Unlike other syndical corporations, its strength does not derive directly from the federal administration. Most important of all in the contemporary context, the SNTE is strategically central to Mexico's "corporatist democracy" (Aziz 1987) insofar as SNTE machinery and SNTE cadres have run electoral campaigns, mobilized the vote for the dominant party, and controlled the voting booths. In short, the SNTE binds together the two main operational fields of the system, the corporative and the electoral, at an historical moment when their mutual influence and mutual incursions are becoming decisive for the future of the system. For these reasons the teachers' struggle to win democratic control of their union impinges directly on the destiny of Mexico's political regime.

Thus, the teachers' movement is of special interest because it has succeeded

in advancing into the strategic core of the political system. But it is also important because it has come to epitomize a complex process of popular struggle
involving many different movements. This struggle has increased the intensity
and multiplied the forms of popular mobilization in contemporary Mexico, so
that no aspect of Mexican politics can now be considered impervious to popular
influence. Such is the dynamism of this development that many commentators
are debating (prematurely in my view) the likelihood of a "democratic transition." Whatever the prognosis for the future, it is undeniable that this mobilization has already had a marked impact on the performance of the political
system. In this study the teachers' movement serves as proxy for the phenomenon of popular mobilization writ large.

Popular mobilization began to characterize contemporary Mexican politics
in the watershed year of 1968. This was the year of the first of the modern
popular movements, the students' movement. This movement astonished the
political authorities by the impetus of its organization, which was only reversed
by the political massacre of Tlatelolco on October 2, 1968 (Hellman 1982;
Zermeño 1978). The immediate result was the return to orderly streets required
by the government, but the longer term legacies included increasing popular
combativeness against a progressively less legitimate government. In analytical
terms it can be argued that 1968 marked a general shift from the politics of
class antagonisms to the politics of popular and democratic struggle. Before
1968 Mexican civil society found political expression largely through class conflicts, the majority of which were successfully mediated through the sectoral and
syndical organizations of the ruling party (or were repressed). After 1968 the
struggles of civil society were also directed to a broader and implicitly democratic set of demands, and they assumed organizational forms and developed
strategic capacities that have been more difficult to counter and contain.

## The changing character of popular organization

The government's violent response to the students' movement impelled many
student activists into popular grass-roots organizing, and this "generation of
1968" provided new leadership for popular movements that emerged in the
following years. According to seasoned observers these new leaders have participated in all the popular movements of the past twenty years and in every
attempt to build new parties. They have acted as advisors and leaders of insurgent unions and have moved on to become party organizers or nonpartisan
activists in urban popular movements (Pérez Arce 1990). In this way the middle-level cadres of the students' movement acted as the seeds of a new popular
political culture, and through their leadership they provided continuity to
diverse movements in different regions and sectors. Moreover, although nearly
every popular movement in contemporary Mexico has its historical forerunners,
it can be argued that the very accumulation of movements in recent years has

worked a qualitative change in their character, especially insofar as they have achieved a national political expression, first in the syndical arena of the 1970s and then in the electoral arena of the 1980s. This sea change in popular politics finds a striking metaphor in the explosive occupation of the Zócalo (the historic central square of Mexico City). These occupations began in 1968 and have recurred as popular mobilizations have increased, providing a measure of the (re)appropriation of public and political space by the people.

Popular movements are not only national in scope but also very diverse in their social composition. They are not confined to any one class or class fraction, but, on the contrary, have involved workers, peasants, slum dwellers, students, teachers, and even the middle classes. Yet more striking is the salient role of women in post-1968 popular organizations, especially in the urban and teachers' movements. Women clearly have played the key part in organizing low-income neighborhoods in the cities (even if the leadership of the urban movements is still mainly male), and they have become increasingly active in pressing a broad range of political demands (Carrillo 1990; Logan 1990). Hence, it seems plausible to suggest that popular politics have come to encompass more of the Mexican people, as more numerous popular movements have succeeded in mobilizing "new," or previously passive, political actors.

Just as the contours of popular mobilization have been changing, so, more importantly, has its political content as this is expressed through popular demands and popular political practices overall. In illustration, whereas some movements at some times continue to appeal to political leaders to resolve conflicts with their adversaries in civil society, many more call on the government itself to respect peasants', workers', teachers', and more generically, citizens' rights. By asserting that labor, land, and human rights are "universal," these demands represent a principled opposition to the traditional ways of doing politics in Mexico, which have been condensed in the particularistic relations of clientelism and of the very Mexican version of political bossism called *caciquismo*.[1] Thus, it is not simply the accumulation of movements, nor even a changing balance of social force, that is changing the character of popular mobilization; rather, it is the political and cultural shift from making petitions and asking for benefits to making demands and insisting on rights. This is tantamount to challenging the prerogative of the government to rule arbitrarily. Today's popular movements want to see the Constitution made real and the

---

1 *Caciquismo* is derived from the historical figure of the *cacique*, the Indian chief or headman, who kept his people subservient in return for political support or favors from the Spanish colonizers. Modern *caciques* manipulate their social and political clienteles through their special access to superior and often State resources. By extension, *caciquismo* has come to describe an informal system of political control and exchange, which is personal, particularistic, and often arbitrary. Where the practices of *caciquismo* have become institutionalized in some degree, or have come to form a relatively stable pattern of political power, they are said to form a *cacicazgo*. Such *cacicazgos* may be found in State-chartered union corporations, municipal and regional governments, and, indeed, throughout the Mexican political system.

government made accountable. Before anything else they aspire to the rule of law.

Nonetheless, popular demands are rarely political in the first instance, nor are they ''democratic'' in the sense that democracy has been imagined as a general aim. On the contrary, initial demands tend to be more concrete and more circumscribed, focusing on wages, social security, and services of all kinds including housing, education, and health provision. In short, they are immediate and pragmatic demands, and in this sense popular movements play a role analogous to that of trade unions at an early moment in liberal State welfarism in Western Europe. But where the political environment offers no response, or no effective means of making demands, the popular agenda expands to include the conditions for getting demands met. In this sense, contemporary popular movements are democratic insofar as they aspire to achieve more autonomous control over the political conditions of the social lives of the people they organize (Rubin 1987).

Similarly, it is worth insisting that most popular actors do not initially see their own struggles in terms of such high-flown notions of political control and self-determination. But a more conscious affirmation of citizenship can emerge where the movement is seeking to vindicate its ''rights,'' or where the issue of political representation has become central to its political practice. Both professional rights and representation were clearly relevant to the teachers' movement, and the struggle to defend them led one of its first regional leaders to declare from his prison in Cerro Hueco, Chiapas (see Chapter 6), ''We are not political actors and no longer political objects.'' Manuel Hernández was one of the main protagonists of the struggle in Chiapas, and his long years of militancy had convinced him that the change had come because of the organizational efforts of the movement, which had made of every committee and assembly a ''school of democracy.''

Making demands may set the popular political agenda, but the demands themselves fall far short of describing popular political practice, which is a complex combination of organization, strategic choice, and tactical deployment. To talk only of strategy for a moment, the movements have often chosen to organize within the syndical corporations or agencies of the government, the better to advance their demands through legal forms of representation. At the same time they have sought horizontal alliances in civil society, the better to protect their organizational autonomy from absorption by the State. In effect, negotiation and participation coexist with mobilization and direct action in modern grass-roots politics in Mexico, with novel results. The challenge to the pervasive patterns of clientelistic control has already been mentioned, and by aspiring to form competing and autonomous organizations the popular movements also challenge the main political premise of the corporatist system, which is its monopoly of representation through State-chartered institutions. In addition, their internal practices of mass consultation, collective decision making, and rotating leadership can further undermine traditional mechanisms of political control.

These initial observations simply serve to suggest the widespread changes that have been occurring in popular organization and mobilization in Mexico. In my view, all of these changes have found their fullest expression in the teachers' movement. Although organized within a syndical corporation of the government, the movement is rooted in rural communities and urban neighborhoods, and in both social composition and political practice it is a popular movement par excellence. Its organization is assembly-based and directly democratic, and its leadership is collective and accountable. The teachers' movement achieves sophisticated strategic choices and deploys an extraordinary range of tactical devices to reap maximum political benefit from mass mobilization. And at the heart of its practice is an insistence on professional rights that has carried the movement from syndical and community demands to a struggle for political control of the union and democratic representation.

Yet despite the scope of the changes in popular politics in Mexico, in reality very little is known about the political processes that either underpin or directly configure these changes. In a perceptive recent essay, Ann Craig (1990) remarked that little or no research has been done on questions of identity and leadership, or on "how strategic decisions are taken within popular movements." She assumes that leadership emerges and identities are constructed through "experience of struggle and interaction with the (legal and institutional) environment," but argues that research must begin with the "internal practices ... for discussing demands, selecting leaders, making strategic choices, and forging alliances." It is precisely in response to such concerns that this account of the teachers' movement delves in detail into forms of organization and factional strife, into leadership and identity, and into moments and modes of strategic choice. The account certainly does not stop there, but it is my hope that its first and intrinsic virtue is that it tells the "inside story" of the movement (at the regional level) before proceeding to reconstruct its interaction with the political system at large.

The political environment of popular movements is important because their characteristic political practices make it so. Whereas popular movements in Western Europe are said to seek a noninstitutional style of politics because of the growing perception that the conflicts and contradictions of advanced capitalism can no longer be solved by *étatism,* increasing political regulation, and a lengthening bureaucratic agenda (Offe 1985), quite the opposite is true in Mexico, where all these things are still seen as necessary and inevitable for demands to be met and needs satisfied. In other words, Mexico's popular movements seek institutional recognition in order to get material improvement, and despite a sometimes radical or revolutionary rhetoric, they pursue these ends through political exchanges and gradualist strategies that usually require some sort of negotiation with the government. The political outcome is a range of particular and differentiated forms of linkage between popular movements and the political system, which the movements will then seek to fix and validate in law. This "institutionalism" (see Chapter 10 and passim) is the hallmark of popular political practice, and there is no real alternative to this quest for what the movements call a *capacidad de gestión,* or enough political purchase to resolve their problems and possibly get their demands met.

## The changing political context of popular organization

The only way to understand the political practices of popular movements in general is in their relation to the political system. The literature has been remiss in this regard and has been correctly criticized by Boschi (1984) for consistently overlooking the links between popular movements and the State structure, which "is ignored both in its repressive potential and in its ability to endure and adapt to changes," let alone in its importance for "the movements' emergence and raison d'etre." In a similar vein, Touraine (1987) argues rotundly that any analysis of these movements must include "the form of their participation in the political system." Hence, this study of the teachers' movement aims to address its engagement with its political environment.

The broad assumption here is that the political system will shape, but not entirely determine, the discourse, demands, and even the organizational form of popular movements. This is a result of government policies that bear on popular organization, and even of those that do not; but more importantly, it is a result of complex interactions between popular movements and the accretion of State laws and institutions that compose the shifting terrain where popular political struggle takes place. The law, in particular, can "recognize" certain groups and encourage certain practices while denying and rejecting others, but there are limits. The State does not itself create popular movements, which may themselves develop strategies "positively and opportunistically" (Craig 1990) for taking advantage of the law and of divisions within and between State institutions. In short, it is not the political system alone that shapes forms of linkage. Yet it must be clear that legal and institutional changes will impinge on popular organization, and that government policies and priorities will create both opportunities and constraints for specific movements at different times.

The State has changed the legal context of popular mobilization since 1968, and the political trajectory of popular movements corresponds to these changes in some degree. The "democratic opening" of President Echeverría (1970–6) seemed to encourage these movements as a response to the apparent failure of the State to mediate a new order of conflicts in civil society (Rubin 1987), and many new local and regional organizations began to emerge. In particular, the labor law revisions of 1970 opened the door to independent unions (Pérez Arce 1990; Cook 1990), and changes in agrarian reform law and policies pressed some peasant organizations into credit and marketing agendas (Harvey 1990a;

Fox and Gordillo 1989). Then, beginning in 1977, the several political reforms provided opposition groups with limited incentives for electoral competition and subsequently catalyzed the difficult development of alliances between popular movements and political parties. Moreover, organized labor and the middle classes had mainly managed to defend their living standards in the 1970s, and the "union uprising" had created a number of independent and parallel unions; but the onset of the acute phase of Mexico's economic crisis in 1982, combined with the impact of an aggressive entrepreneurial reform project and with the initial success of the political reforms, appeared to restrain the more radical union and urban popular movements (Carr 1987). Yet, at the same time, important shifts in other areas of the legal and institutional terrain had created a favorable conjuncture for the dynamic emergence of the teachers' movement in many states of the federation.

The complexities of the interactions between popular organization and the political system seem to find no place in analyses of this system as it existed prior to 1968. In the "standard account" (Roxborough 1984) the State appeared to respond only to organized actors who were effective in pressing class demands, and the success of its corporatist strategy led to a characterization of the system as "inclusionary corporatist," even though it was recognized that the government's efficacy in limiting, discouraging, and manipulating the demands of the majority of the population made the system mainly exclusionary. In short, in the impeccable logic of this account, what could not be included was indeed excluded (which appeared to take care of all the possibilities), and exclusion often meant violence. Thus, the system was sustained by a politic admixture of cooptation and coercion, concession and repression, and such a comfortable result was more possible because the majority of the Mexican people were seen as unwilling to change the system, or incapable of doing so (Fagen and Tuohy 1972; Gonzalez Casanova 1970; Hansen 1971; Smith 1979). Since 1968, however, it has become increasingly apparent that the "people" do want to change the system, or at least the terms of their own representation within it, and are prepared to organize and mobilize to bring this about (Gómez Tagle 1987).

For the past sixty years and more this system has been dominated by its ruling party, the Institutional Revolutionary Party, or PRI, which was successful in imposing an enduring political order on a notoriously unruly nation. Yet Mexican civil society was never so quiescent before 1968 as it was often supposed to be. Historians point out that the period they ironically refer to as the *paz priista*[2] was relatively short, possibly only fifteen or twenty years, and then

---

2 This simply translates as the "peace of the PRI" or the "peace of the ruling party," by reference to the regimes of the *pax britannica* or *pax romana*, which achieved peace by force of arms and extension of empire. Many commentators have also pointed to the ironies implicit in the name of the PRI itself, where the "institutional revolution" composes a perfect oxymoron.

only very partial (Knight 1990). Stevens's (1924) work was seminal in this respect, recalling the railroad strikes of the late 1950s and the mass movements of those years in the telephone, oil, and especially the teachers' unions (see Chapter 3); the doctors' strike in Mexico City in the mid-1960s; and, above all, the student movement of 1968, which achieved "a magnetic influence on the conscience of the people" (Paz 1985). And Roxborough (1984) was successful in arguing that such popular combativeness was not merely episodic and that corporatist controls were always more uncertain than most studies allowed. Moreover, he saw the progressive weakening of such controls leading to a qualitative change in Mexican politics, with "civil society now seeking a place in the sun" (Roxborough 1984, p. 175).

Since 1968 the relations between popular organization and the State have been accorded a much higher profile, and there is no longer any doubt that these relations are now problematic. In the first place, this has to do with the rapidly expanding social base of popular demands. The industrial workforce grows, and so do subsidiary technical and administrative sectors in universities, schools, and the nuclear and electrical industries; slum districts swell within the cities, fed by the economic and social crisis in the countryside; and severe economic downturns in the mid-1970s, and especially the early 1980s, have left larger numbers from an increasingly young population unemployed or underemployed. Traditional rural demands for land and water moved into the city, where low-income groups agitated for the provision of public services; while in the countryside itself demands expanded to include jobs, wages, access to credit and markets, guaranteed prices, and sanctions against *caciques* and municipal authorities (Cornelius and Craig 1984). Furthermore, during the 1970s the number of teachers in Mexico nearly doubled.

At the same time the State was also expanding. Federal government agencies and apparatuses moved to control water resources and urban planning, public housing and social services, and agricultural credit and marketing mechanisms (Craig 1990). This control was highly centralized (and, as I argue in Chapter 11, is certainly becoming more so), and the provision of services and access to funds often appeared subject to arbitrary legal and bureaucratic criteria. As a consequence the State became a direct party to an increasing number of social and political conflicts (Craig 1990); and as legal and institutional initiatives designed to assuage these conflicts multiplied, it was drawn into further disputes over land tenure, syndical prerogatives, and electoral rules. In short, the expansion of the State's political domain through an increasing range of social regulation and economic responsibility meant that the main adversary for the emerging popular movements was now the gorgon-headed Leviathan that was the State itself. Indeed, the movements' insistence on "autonomy" by which they meant their right to organize and negotiate their demands "without vertical imposition" (Craig 1990), can only be understood in the context of the massive proliferation of these vertical controls.

Finally, the higher profile of State–people relations is a result of the organizational dynamism and the strategic discoveries of the popular movements themselves. In the city the movements began with the syndical insurgency of the early 1970s, which was marked by widespread rank-and-file militancy in many sectors both of industry and of the government bureaucracy (the FSTSE, the Union Federation of Workers in the State Sector). The "democratic tendencies" within the electrical workers' union (SUTERM) and, later, the nuclear workers' union (SUTIN) played vanguard roles, and so were crushed by military intervention, but not before they had demonstrated the rapid translation of economic demands into political demands. Over the same period in the countryside mobilization around land invasions had led to increasing coordination of regional organizations by the mid-1970s, and by the end of the decade two independent and national organizations had emerged in opposition to the National Peasant Confederation (CNC) of the dominant party. Independent syndical federations had also begun to organize in some sectors of industry, to the consternation of the old-guard leadership of the official syndicalism. In subsequent years a number of nationwide, intraunion, and popular organizations appeared on the political scene, including the "Plan de Ayala" National Coordinating Committee (CNPA), the National Coordinating Committee of the Urban Popular Movement (CONAMUP), the National Syndical Coordinating Committee (COSINA), the Authentic Labor Front (FAT), the Independent Labor Union (UOI), and, last but by no means least, the National Coordinating Committee of Workers in Education (CNTE).

This process of popular organization promoted an intense search for strategic solutions. In the case of the teachers' movement, and many others too, the key strategic choice was to take the struggle forward inside the syndical corporations of the dominant party. But reviewing the panorama of popular organization as a whole, there is no doubt that it was the recurrent effort to forge political alliances that created its strategic thrust. At the local and regional levels this was the principle that informed most of the multi-class "fronts" of the early 1970s, and in more recent time it was precisely the effort to link the peasants' and teachers' movements in Chiapas that put Manuel Hernández and fellow activists behind the bars of Cerro Hueco (see Chapter 6). At the national level, it was this same effort that led to the intrasectoral alliances such as the CNPA and CONAMUP, and to the intersectoral "anti-austerity" fronts that finally coalesced into the National Popular Assembly of Workers and Peasants (ANOCP). Without these efforts to secure the lateral coordination of hundreds of local and regional associations, it would never have been possible to mount the massive and unprecedented mobilization of a broad range of class, sectoral, and community groups in the "civic stoppages" of October 1983 and June 1984 (the first and most successful winning the support of some two million people). Without the alliance strategy, the effervescence of popular politics might never have achieved effective mobilization.

For all this organizational effort, it is worth pausing before endorsing this vision of the millenarian march of popular movements across modern Mexican history. If 1968 is indeed a watershed, then the popular movements that emerge in its wake can be seen as a rising tide of popular organization, and this is the strong image projected by Carlos Monsiváis (1987b) of "a society getting organized." But others doubt whether the movements have ever achieved an "organic consolidation" and question the real degree of continuity between them (Pérez Arce 1990). Moreover, Sergio Zermeño (1990) has offered his own provocative and apocalyptic vision of a society in radical disarray. The social disruption caused by the modernizing thrust of Mexican society was thrown into a "double disorder" as this same society careened unchecked into the deep and unforgiving crisis of the 1980s. The rapid destruction of emerging "intermediate identities" pulverizes civil society, breaking it into a thousand unconnected pieces. Tens of millions of children and teenagers without jobs, homes, or prospects drift like flotsam and jetsam in a sea of exclusion. Directly contrary to the Monsiváis image, Zermeño sees "a society disintegrating."

Zermeño is right to question the political significance of popular movements in Mexico. After all, the great majority of the population is not organized in popular movements; a capacity for popular mobilization (as the story of the teachers' movement will show) is very different from an enduring organization; and popular movements themselves may therefore be just a tiny organized part of a civil society that is crumbling under the impact of economic crisis. Even the support for the rapidly growing electoral opposition to the government may come more from the disaffected but disorganized middle classes than from popular organizations (see Chapter 11). On the other hand, the radical anomie of urban youth, which is the focus of Zermeño's recent research, should not be taken as a paradigm for an atomized civil society writ large. One must always remember that in most popular struggles at most moments in modern history it is only a small minority of any population that associates civically and only a handful that organizes politically. In the social disarray so graphically portrayed by Zermeño, militancy in a popular movement becomes an heroic act.

## Transforming popular politics

This summary analysis suggests that the relationships between popular movements and the political system in Mexico have been changing rapidly for at least twenty years. The process of change is clearly interactive, but how can this complex interaction be understood? There is no short answer to this question, which is why this book begins to provide a long one. But I think it helps to characterize the process in terms of "transformism," which describes a specific State project for neutralizing political opposition and muting political conflict. This concept directs attention immediately to the relationships between State and civil society, and especially to the dissident groups in this society, which are "transformed" by a mixture of cooptation, corruption, and concession. In this way it does not offend traditional descriptions of the Mexican political system. But having first borrowed Vincenzo Cuocco's concept, Gramsci (1971) enriched it by defining the project as "revolution from above," or the "transformation" of society itself. In doing so Gramsci captured the intrinsic contradictions of a process that depends on the continual absorption or dispersal of popular organizations at the same time that it is expanding the conditions for their emergence and growth. In its dual implication, therefore, transformism means more than the simple cooptation of potential popular opposition (which for most political systems would prove impossibly costly); it requires the construction of a specific legal and institutional terrain that is capable of containing popular demands by defining their terms of representation and, at the margin, by fixing the political boundaries of popular struggle.

Hence, the concept of transformism does not deny the vitality of civil society but recognizes and reaffirms it. The transformist project has civil society both as object and aspiration, insofar as it "transforms" real or potential opposition as well as transforming civil society itself through "revolution from above." In the Mexican case (as suggested earlier when talking of the expanding social base of popular demands) the latter process implies high rates of demographic growth, high rates of urbanization, higher literacy levels, and an exponential increase in all kinds of communication including the mass media. Although these developments create propitious conditions for the growth of popular opposition, they are not equivalent to it; and simply stating these developments is insufficient to explain popular mobilization, which is a complex result of social agency, including motivation, leadership, organization, and strategy. To study popular movements is to study the ways in which such agency finds political expression and projection, and the ways in which popular organizations find strategic room for political maneuver on the legal and institutional terrain of the political system.

The constant political goal of transformism is therefore not simply to coopt popular political opposition, but to undermine its organizations and disarm its strategies through the discursive legal and institutional means that can impose or reassert State-sanctioned terms of representation. In the Mexican case such political control has traditionally been ensured by the clientelistic relations that deepen the sectoral, regional, political, and cultural cleavages in Mexican civil society, and reinforce the divisions between its many and various political constituencies. The federal government has consistently cultivated this "compartmentalized" civil society and has sought to restrict the scope of popular movements in order to disarticulate them on a case by case basis. This could never be considered an "organic" process, but was always "rational, arbitrary and willed" (Gramsci 1971), involving specific legal and institutional initiatives designed to contain popular challenges.

The historical success of this "transformist" project is not in doubt. Of all the political systems constructed during the twentieth century, Mexico's has probably proved the most stable and durable. But while the Mexican State has been unusually successful in fixing the terms of representation available to popular actors, the rise of popular movements in the modern period has challenged its traditional controls and has turned its laws and institutions into a far more contradictory terrain for the exercise of State power. In particular, the system has proved vulnerable to the colonization of its syndical corporations, and the transformist project has proved especially susceptible to the horizontal alliances of the popular opposition. Although still embryonic, in many cases these alliances have had some success in "finessing" the many fissures of Mexico's split and splintered civil society, and the strategy has proved especially effective since the mid-1980s when it shifted into a more intense struggle for representation in the electoral arena. To the degree that popular movements succeed in reversing the equation of political control, and vindicate different terms of representation unfettered by "vertical imposition," they will have made some headway in transforming transformism.

There are signs that this may already by happening (as I argue in Chapters 10 and 11). But political science is certainly not scientific in the sense of being predictive, and the political outcome remains unsure. In particular, there is no way of knowing whether Mexico's political system will become more democratic, by whatever measure, even if the teachers' movement may be understood as a struggle for enhanced democratic control of one key piece of that system. In the meantime, the extrinsic virtue of telling the story of the movement is to reconstruct its relations with the system in all their complexity, and possibly in novel ways. Hence, the story will show how the genesis and trajectory of the movement are closely conditioned by the legal and institutional terrain linking State and civil society, and how the movement sometimes finds sufficient strategic purchase on the terrain to advance its goals and even to alter the terrain's configuration. Above all, a consistent effort is made to trace the mutual interaction of the movement's internal practices with its external linkages. In this way, the study of the movement may illuminate the popular dimension of modern Mexican politics. But remember that this small history has not ended. After fourteen years of popular struggle, this history, as always, is only just beginning.

## The analytical shape of the argument

The aim of this book is to use the story of the teachers' movement to enhance our understanding of popular mobilization in Mexico, and in general. The argument is shaped not so much by chronological narrative as by a political analysis of the movement, which is meant to make the story make sense. Thus, this analysis looks at different aspects of the movement and of its interactions with its political environment, and seeks to combine them into an integrated view of this major process of popular mobilization and its political significance.

Yet the argument still attempts to keep the actual history of the movement itself on center stage and even to deliver a little of the drama of its development and denouements.

All this seems to suppose that the movement can be identified and known without theoretical premises or pretense. But even if the argument eschews any grand display of theory in its initial stages, it does not assume that it can do without theory altogether. On the contrary, there is a clear need to "construct" the object of study and its relationship to the political system, and the intention is to do this step by step, with each analytical advance of the argument. This means that the different empirical emphases and analytical choices have to be justified, at least in terms of the argument overall, and there is a recurrent attempt to do just that.

By way of illustration, the main analytical choice was to refer much of the argument to one particular region of the country, but to do so without making it a merely regional study. Because it was the teachers of Chiapas who pioneered the movement, and who discovered its key organizational forms and political strategies, the movement in this region came to carry a special weight within the movement overall, throughout its political life. But beyond the specific empirical significance of Chiapas, the national movement was never more than regional in organization, and its capacity for mobilization was constantly bound by the operational autonomy of the regions. In short, the national movement was never more than the sum of its parts, and very often it was less. Hence, a regional perspective is a proper one to adopt on the national movement, as long as the regional case is properly located in its national context.

At the same time, there is no way to understand the real process of popular mobilization without investigating the conduct of the struggle at the grass roots; and only at the regional level can the argument aspire to a sufficiently detailed inquiry into this process. In others words, the regional focus can provide a richer empirical context, and a fuller contextualization of the complexities of organizational initiatives and strategic choices, than would be available in a national overview. At the level of the imagination, which is surely as important to the reading of social science as it is to the appreciation of art, the same complexities may be assumed to be present, if differently, in other regions; and much of the national account in later chapters is in fact illustrated by comparisons and contrasts between the movements in different regions.

Nonetheless, Chiapas certainly has its empirical specificities, and it is neither possible nor desirable to wish them away. Socially, Chiapas is a predominantly rural and peasant state, and the teachers' movement was rooted in the peasant communities, with its practices drawing on community traditions. Moreover, the original leadership of the movement finally came to favor overt political alliances with the peasantry, thus sharpening the hostility of state and federal governments. Geographically, Chiapas is a mountainous state in its central and northern areas, which are home to inaccessible Indian populations, and the

Indian teachers provided some of the most combative cadres of the movement. It is also far from Mexico City and is so far removed from the mainstream of Mexican history that traditional patterns of political power have remained remarkably intact. These patterns bore an uncanny ressemblance to the institutional controls and repression deployed against the teachers by their own union (SNTE), and thus the movement was inspired to some degree by generic traditions of struggle. Yet union officialdom was also seen as obeying an authoritarian and ultimately alien logic, which was increasingly offensive to the teachers' sense of themselves as people, and as political actors.

Such specificities are interesting in themselves, but they are only recognized and described when they serve the purposes of the analysis. Thus, much of the early part of the argument either refers to (Chapters 1, 2, and 3) or focuses on (Chapters 4, 5, and 6) the teachers' movement in Chiapas, but with the clear aim of providing the kind of detailed account that can support more general statements of national scope (Chapters 7, 8, and 9) and sustain a more global analysis of popular mobilization (Chapters 10, 11, and 12). Far from constricting the argument to a case study, the intention is to move from the particular to the general, with an accompanying shift in emphasis from empirical analysis to conceptual synthesis. And, as noted earlier, it is the particularity of the teachers' movement itself that makes the regional movement a proper point of departure.

The actual shape of the argument thus appears straightforward, as it seeks to make a virtue of this regional necessity. Part I sets the scene in general but refers the argument recurrently to the specific case of Chiapas, with Chapter 1 looking at the community context and the place of teachers in the Mexican political system, Chapter 2 examining the original economic demands and the emerging organization of the movement in its birthplace of Chiapas, and Chapter 3 analyzing the institutional context of the official teachers' union, the SNTE. Part I also considers changes in the dissident teachers themselves (which will be important to later discussions of identity) and the original motives for their mobilization, and begins to suggest ways in which the strategic choices of the movement were always conditioned by the constraints of its institutional and political context.

In Part II the argument unashamedly leaves general statement behind and turns exclusively to a detailed inquiry into the internal process of the movement in Chiapas, focusing first on its organization (Chapter 4), then on its strategic choices (Chapter 5), and finally on the factionalism that was rife within the regional movement, and its strategic and political consequences (Chapter 6). In this way the argument goes *inside* the movement at the regional level before assessing the national movement and the interaction of government policies and popular strategies at the national level.

Part III then takes up this interaction, beginning with the regional organization and trajectory of the national movement itself (Chapter 7), and continuing with the government policies and programs that influenced the movement, and the institutional controls deployed against it (Chapter 8). An investigation of the popular strategies for bypassing, combatting, or taking advantage of these controls, and a first attempt to characterize the terrain where these maneuvers take place, completes the picture of national mobilization drawn in Part III. In particular, Chapter 9 concludes with illustrations of the ways this institutional terrain can shift from one political moment to the next, thus making political outcomes yet more unpredictable.

Part IV seeks to draw lessons from the foregoing analysis. Chapter 10 generalizes the insights achieved into a broader conceptual framework for understanding the linkages between popular movements and the political system in Mexico, and Chapter 11 assesses the impact of popular movements on political change in the country. The final chapter shifts the focus from contemporary Mexican politics to contemporary popular movements and extracts some analytical lessons for their understanding: The study of the teachers' movement seems to suggest different ways of talking about the goals, the organization, the strategies, and even the identity of popular movements, and hence suggests new ways of understanding popular mobilization in Mexico, and possibly beyond. Yet the story remains the thing, and both political analysis and conceptual critique are tied as closely as possible to the teachers' movement, for what it has to say about popular mobilization in Mexico.

PART I

# Popular movement and syndical struggle

# 1

## Teachers as political actors

### The place: community and *caciquismo*

The teachers of Mexico are the natural leaders of the community. They are the intellectuals of the poor. In the countryside they work to organize peasant societies that are increasingly disperse and demoralized, and in the cities they are paid minimum wages to make schools for the dispossessed (Salinas Alvarez 1983). No matter that in recent years the teachers have come to see themselves as workers first and teachers second. Their work is distinctly cultural, serving both the material and the spiritual needs of the nation. The special nature of their work, which in Mexico is both cultural and communal, makes the teachers different from all other workers in the service sector or in state employ. The promise of the Revolution was universal education, and the legacy is a special relationship between teachers and people. In Mexico, the teachers' struggle is necessarily and instrinsically a popular struggle.

This social intimacy between teachers and people does not mean that teachers are in some way morally superior, even if the educational projects of the past may have sought to make them so. The language of Vasconcelos described a missionary of civilization, and that of Cárdenas described an apostle of socialism (Raby 1974). But equally the teachers have often sought solace for their frustrations in the demon drink or have failed to bear the harsh confines of rural life for more than two or three days a week. In modern times, the traditional role has been threatened by the increasing misery of the countryside and the material attractions of a career in the city, and every teacher is now assumed to seek city life. Some, however, argue that the teachers' movements of the 1980s have rescued many teachers from drunkeness and dissipation (Fernández Dorado 1982), and given them a new purpose. "Nothing which is proper for the people should be strange for the teacher."

If the relationship between teachers and people does not determine their moral condition, it does define their political role. The teachers have been the living links between the political system and the multiple communities of the many societies of Mexico (Simpson 1962). It is through the teachers that the Revolutionary governments of Mexico have achieved the kind of social consensus that supports stable government (Hernández 1983b). In the general terms of a sociology of modernization (Parsons 1960) the teachers can be seen as carriers of the common values that induce social cohesion. But, as we shall see, the ruling party has always striven to recruit teachers for more particular purposes of administrative and electoral control. Hence, historically, these natural leaders have acted as local *caciques* as often as they have acted as local "liberators" (some have acted as both, at different times in their lives). Still, however different their individual roles and however diverse their working conditions, all teachers are organized within the same syndical corporation of the ruling party (see Chapter 2), and all teachers are in the employ of a local state government, or, in their great majority, the federal Ministry of Education.

The image of rural communities controlled by local *caciques* closely fits the case of Chiapas, the southern state that is the original context of this story of popular struggle. Chiapas is a land of feudalism and fierce *caciquismo,* where counter-revolutionary forces fought to preserve large landholdings and suppress peasant struggles (compare Craven 1959). Even today the great majority of the population live and work in the countryside,[1] and the struggle of its 30,000 teachers[2] expresses not only their own demands but also those of the Indian and peasant communities. Chiapas is not atypical of a country where three times as many teachers serve the countryside as serve the massive population of the capital city.[3] At the same time, the political traditions of Chiapas, whether elite or popular, are isolationist, even secessionist, and accentuate the divide between Chiapas and the political and administrative center of the country (Castellanos 1961). Chiapas teachers saw the Revolutionary Vanguard, the clique that controlled the official teachers' union (see Chapter 3), as belonging to this same center, and always rose to sing the hymn to Chiapas at the close of their "democratic" congresses. Significantly, the teachers of Chiapas not only had fought local *caciques* but were also suspicious of central control.

## The moment: economic crisis and syndical decline

The 1970s in Mexico had seen a general rise in syndical struggles across the country (Pérez Arce 1990). But the rapid deepening of the crisis from the early 1980s damaged the unions, as the quickening pace of inflation led to harsh

---

1  The 1980 Census records a population of 2,100,000 in Chiapas, 66 percent of which lived in the countryside in towns of less than 2,500 inhabitants. Over 20 percent of this population is pure Indian. Moreover, 77 percent of the EAP (economically active population) of 720,457 worked in the countryside (76.9 percent in agriculture, 7.9 percent in the secondary sector, and 15.3 percent in services).

2  About 70 percent of these 30,000 teachers are "federal," or employed by the Ministry of Education, and the rest are "state," or employed by the state government. In total they represent some 4 percent of the EAP and are responsible for some 850,000 pupils.

3  In 1980 there were some 150,000 teachers working in the Federal District and about 450,000 working in the countryside.

reductions in real wages, especially among State employees. Economically and socially, it was a time of mass sackings, plant relocations, changes in work contracts, and a radical reduction in funding for health, education, and social services. Politically, the key problem for government was no longer how to include the greater part of the working class, but how to exclude it (Carr 1983). There are some exceptions to the rule, such as battles won by official unionism for workers in high-technology industries and in automobile plants; but most rank-and-file protest met with the intransigence of official syndical leaders, while independent unionism declined and its national coordinating organizations regressed to their local and regional bases. The syndical struggles of the late 1970s and early 1980s had been intense and sometimes violent, but by the end of 1983 they appeared to be exhausted. With its syndical leadership discredited, this could bring only small comfort to the government of the ruling party.

To a large extent the trajectory of the teachers' movement conforms to this general pattern. The movement began in Chiapas in 1979, and, as we will see in Chapter 3, was driven by economic pressures and economic demands. Moreover, subsequent analysis will show how the movement had reached a hiatus across the country by the end of 1983, or shortly thereafter. This hiatus is understandable in "a multitudinous sector whose behavior reflects and condenses the contradictions of the country as a whole" (Monsiváis 1981). But this sector is different from any plant or industry union, whether at the regional or national level; and both its social characteristics and its political organization and strategies make the rhythm of its struggle quite specific. To some extent this rhythm is closer to that of the "coordinated" popular movements that rose to prominence over the 1976–82 period, and in my view the new teachers' organizations express both syndical struggle and popular movement. Their concern is not only with material advance but also with citizens' rights.

## A generation of citizens

During the 1970s the number of teachers in Mexico almost doubled. The new teachers were young and restless. Some had been involved in the student movements of 1968 and 1971. Nearly all had seen one or more struggles in the teacher training schools *(normales básicas)* or had fought to defend the rural training schools *(normales rurales)*. In the latter they were taught that each teacher had a fundamental role to play in the development of the rural community, and they learned the skills that would equip them to play it. Moreover, the schools were seen as "places of struggle because it is in the school that peasant children come to understand the misery and oppression of their parents" (CNTE 1981). In addition, as students these teachers had had to fight for the meager grants that allowed them to study at all. In this way, they came to see teaching as a "political service to the people" (Palomino 1983a), and it is no surprise that the leaders of the first teachers' movement in Chiapas had first felt the stirrings of revolt in the rural schools. Manuel Hernández, the general secretary of the first "democratic" sectional committee of Chiapas, and many other leaders had graduated from the school at Mactumatzá – just outside the capital, Tuxtla Gutiérrez. And it was in the same school that the teachers held the first democratic congress to elect him, thus imbuing the occasion with a powerful symbolic content.

Not just in the countryside, but throughout the nation, student teachers were enrolled in training schools that were anticlerical and humanist, if not avowedly Marxist. Once they found work, they quickly realized that teaching had become massified into a low-wage profession with increasingly precarious working conditions. The most professionally motivated found their way to the intensive summer courses at the advanced training school in Mexico City *(Normal Superior),* where their political education continued apace. These were the students who made up the core, and occasionally the leadership, of the new movements like that in Chiapas, and they all talked of the "inconformity" or "restlessness" *(inquietud)* that preceded the movement (and of the need to keep those feelings alive). Economic pressures certainly contributed to the spread of this movement, but clearly it was also the official union's failure to take up the demands of its members that first made them restless.[4] And it was not just the inactivity of the union bosses that bothered them but also the cynical manipulation of the membership and the arbitrary actions of "that little clique" (see Chapter 3).

## Citizenship and political practice

It was new political practices, or a new political "engagement" (in the French usage), that provided the teachers with an education in citizenship. It was the strikes and the struggles of ten years that taught the teachers to recognize their allies and their enemies, and, more crucially, to recognize themselves as actors in a more encompassing piece of history. Both the grand events, like the marches, occupations, and "sit-ins" *(plantones),*[5] and the new organizations of the independent movement created compelling schools of direct democracy, where all teachers could learn of their common condition. The newspaper of the Technical Schools in Chiapas *(Escuelas Técnicas Agropecuarias,* or ETAs), which more usually struggled for a bare degree of literacy, waxed poetic in reaching to capture the excitement of this education. Before the ETAs' movement began, "the protests appeared isolated, and the struggles titanically individual." But now the struggles "had been transformed into a practical civics

4 An early publication of the Agricultural Technical Schools *(Escuelas Técnicas Agropecuarias)* in Chiapas
   quotes with evident approval the aphorism of Ricardo Flores Magón, which asserts that "human progress
   is the work of the restless" *(Regeneración* no. 240, July 8, 1916).
5 The "sit-in," or *plantón,* encouraged the sharing both of food and shelter and of stories and ideas. The
   teachers and parents of Chiapas have vivid memories of sit-ins like the one in the main square of Tuxtla
   Gutiérrez (Chiapas) during February and March 1985.

lesson, into a POLITICAL SCHOOL FOR EVERYONE" (*Chispa Sindical,* May 1978).

Citizenship, then, was not simply conferred but was achieved through an accumulation of political experience over a period of at least ten years. In a process the literature refers to as an anodyne "construction of identities" (Munck 1990), hundreds of thousands of teachers maintained a continual mobilization. Among them were the many Indian teachers from the south, who time and again walked hundreds of kilometers to take their protests to the geographical centers of political power. Their arrival in the capital was a dramatic display of the "slow but solid eruption of the habitually marginal sectors onto the national panorama" (Monsiváis 1981). In this way, the teachers made a popular movement that put people on the move and emphasized mass action in its organizations (Sección XI 1984). Mobilization and participation defined the new practices, which reclaimed civil society's capacity to civilize (Foweraker 1988). "The teacher in struggle is also teaching," chanted the marching teachers in chorus. The rhyme is lost in English, but not the message.

## The creation of political actors

Time and again the teachers of Chiapas refer to the changes taking place not only in the organization, or in the movement, but in themselves. Their experience of organization and struggle, their continual discussions, and their active involvement in taking and defending their own decisions have changed the way they see themselves. Now that they themselves decide "what is right to do and what is right to leave alone," they feel more like "people." When the movement began, said Jácobo Nazar (one of Manuel Hernández's trusted lieutenants), they talked politics as if they were still in diapers. Yes indeed, added Manuel Hernández with some irony, they were radicals then! They have grown up. Not only to a more modulated political vision but to a sense of themselves as political actors. This is made explicit. It was the old union bosses who treated them as objects. Now they are the subjects of their own political lives.

Many of the leaders of the movement in Chiapas measure their advances in these terms. Some of the most polarized debates within the Central Struggle Committee (see Chapters 5 and 6) reflected differing views of the membership's political sophistication, but it is probably in the neighboring southern states of Chiapas and Oaxaca that such mass education advanced furthest during the 1980s. Even when they lost the bitter strike of 1987, the teachers of Chiapas insisted on the political triumph of maintaining high levels of mobilization and losing all fear of "administrative repression" (compare Chapter 7).[6] In these same terms, it was by mobilizing newly political actors that the teachers' move-

---

6 One of the teachers' slogans summed it up: *"el maestro consciente, ni se rinde, ni se vende"* (the politicized teacher neither gives in nor sells out).

ments mounted their challenge to the sclerotic syndical structures of the country. But they continued to question and reject narrowly "egotistical" or "syndical" demands, in the awareness that their struggle was that of the "people" (Hernández 1985c). As Przeworski (1977) and Jessop (1980) have insisted, popular struggle is first of all a struggle to form the "people" before it is a struggle between people and officialdom.

Among the new political actors are the women who have been the majority presence on marches, in sit-ins, and at many meetings. They have come with their babies and children. They have come pregnant. They have often come against the wishes of the men, and their militancy has cost some both home and job. Despite the difficulties, many women have seized the opportunities for information and debate, and clearly enjoy their greater scope for political action. From mass participation in mobilizations they have moved into leadership roles on the delegational committees (see Chapter 4), and their presence in state assemblies has grown more numerous and more vocal. Whereas in the beginning the women rarely opened their mouths and it was the men who spoke, *now* the problem is keeping them quiet! They are proud to assert that "where the woman advances, no man dare retreat." But the women's gains can be overstated. Women make up more than half the membership, yet still provide very few of the movement's leaders.

Not only women but also many Indian teachers began to see themselves differently within the movement. This was especially the case of the so-called hispanifiers who were employed to integrate the Indian communities into mestizo culture and who were not paid but merely "compensated" for their labors (at about a third of the rate of regular teachers). Far from belonging to the union, they had never even heard of the union, and they were subjected to the worst excesses of *caciquismo*. This continued to be true in the 1970s when Indian education policy was taken over by the Ministry of Education,[7] which simply reinforced the pattern of clientelistic control in a system of "sections," each with its own coordinator. For the Indian teachers, then, the movement offered a heaven-sent opportunity to escape this system of petty despotism and multiple abuse, and the Indians of the highlands flexed their new found freedoms in successive mobilizations (see Chapter 3).

This emphasis on political actors and their sense of political rights is not a rejection of the findings of Castells (1983) and Mainwaring (1987), who agree that the great majority of popular actors are primarily concerned with resolving pressing material needs in their own lives. But material demands often entail political demands, and it is the evolution and definition of demands that unifies popular actors (Castells 1983). Thus, in Chiapas, it is clear that economic pres-

---

7 Indian education policy was first run by the Instituto Nacional Indigenista, or INI, which was established in San Cristóbal de las Casas (Chiapas) in 1951. INI was designed to provide a range of services to the Indian communities, including schools with bilingual teachers.

sure is central to political participation. Neither the university-educated professionals nor the well-heeled daughters of the local bourgeoisie will join the struggle for fear of jeopardizing their positions. Nonetheless, it is equally clear that from the beginning the teachers' struggle has to do with rights, especially their right to control their own professional lives (Street 1987d). In particular, their demands have continually focused on the criteria for job transfers and promotions (Consejo Central de Lucha del Magisterio Chiapaneco 1980b), in an effort to defend professional norms against the arbitrary impositions of the union hierarchy ("normativity" versus "verticality"). Although these demands are specific to the profession, any notion of rights as universal and equal automatically challenges general patterns of *caciquismo* and clientelistic control, which, by definition, are personal, particularistic, and arbitrary.

"I know that the teachers are the key directing union of the Revolution," said De la Madrid while still a candidate for the presidency. "The Mexican Revolution was made by transforming minds, because, in the last analysis, it is only when men think differently that societies change" (*Unomásuno*, October 28, 1981). Clearly, the candidate endorsed the view of the teachers as the living links between political system and people, but the teachers themselves only realized their specific role as political actors through beginning to challenge this system (and so understand the link). More precisely, it was in struggling to win control of their own union sections that the teachers first came to know their own political potential and to predict that their victories would give new impetus to popular movements across the country (Instituto Politécnico Nacional 1985, no. 9), as well as forge closer links between these movements and the teachers (*Chispa Sindical,* May 1, 1981). The spread of popular movements could not be divorced from the challenge to the clientelism and *caciquismo* of the political system.

## The challenge to *caciquismo* in the communities

Popular political struggle is not uniform. On the contrary, it refers to numerous conflicts led by heterogeneous and often isolated groups throughout the national territory, which fight for specific demands. But however diverse the political forces in the struggle, they are all seeking more direct control over the decisions that affect them. Popular struggle nearly always aims to assert more control over the political conditions of the social and economic life of the people. On the ground, this simple aspiration becomes enmeshed in a complicated and often fierce fight against clientelism and *caciquismo.* These ancient but still predominant forms of political control are rooted in the same soil that nurtures popular militancy. In the rural teacher training schools, the children of peasants and local *caciques* study side by side, with the latter still tied to the local *cacicazgos* as they rise to leadership roles in the teachers' union.

It is worth emphasizing (and I will pursue the point in the next section) that the fight against *caciquismo* was mainly waged inside the official union and the Ministry of Education. But sustaining any kind of challenge to the concerted power of the Ministry of Education and the official union required extensive support at the local level. For the teachers the basis of such support had to be the parents of their pupils, who were also peasants and workers; and the fulcrum of this support was the traditional role of the teacher within the community. It was usual for parents and teachers to meet every fifteen days or so, and these meetings provided an effective forum for explaining the struggle. It needed explaining because continual mobilization inevitably affected the pupils' schooling (and the parents had been imbued with the revolutionary idea of education as the key to social progress). Initially, the parents' response was cautious and noncommittal, but the teachers strove to convince them that both the teachers and the parents belonged to the "unprotected people." If the educational authorities deliberately created problems for the teachers and so damaged their reputation (as in 1980 in Chiapas), the teachers saw it as a priority task to "explain the causes of our dissidence to the parents, because it's just the same as if strangers came to tell them what to do in their *ejidos,* settlements and cooperatives" (Consejo Central de Lucha del Magisterio Chiapaneco 1980b).[8] This approach proved so successful in Chiapas that within a few years the movement was able to mobilize up to 40,000 people for major shows of strength in the capital.

The support of the parents was essential to the survival of the movement, and the teachers worked hard to achieve it. They encouraged improvements in schools and communities, they recruited the parents for courses in syndical politics, and in general they sought to educate pupils and parents alike. This meant working as many hours outside school as inside it, as well as attending endless meetings and *ejidal* assemblies. Parent support began to swell as parents and teachers together suffered the effects of government austerity policies and together bore the brunt of the "administrative repression" unleashed against the teachers (see Chapter 8). The teachers moved to capitalize on the groundswell by organizing municipal, regional, and state "parent-teacher councils" (which in some cases, as in the Costa Grande region, could draw on the experience of the municipal committees of the Ministry of Education) (see Chapter 8).[9] The results of the slow achievement of this key alliance were seen in the firm support of the parents for the sixty-five day strike of 1987, when the parents' leaders began to speak and mobilize on behalf of the teachers, and when parents themselves occupied the schools "with a salute to the democratic move-

---

8  The *ejido* is a communal or semicommunal form of landholding and farming enshrined in the revolutionary Constitution of 1917 and disseminated through subsequent agrarian reform policies. It deliberately recalled archaic patterns of land use by Mexico's ethnic populations but was really a novel way of binding peasant clienteles to the economic and political purposes of the revolutionary governments. The most intense period of *ejido* construction took place during the presidency of Lázaro Cárdenas (1934–40).

9  Where there was no democratic council of parents and teachers in the community, the support of the parents could be won through committees, mass meetings, and the *ejidal* unions.

ment." On the other hand, the aftermath of the strike sometimes left parents locked out of schools occupied by official union forces or left pupils and parents divided between "democratic" and official teachers.[10] But the enduring organizational residues such as the councils remained, and the teachers turned to recovering what had been lost of the school year, both to repay the support and to demonstrate their "commitment to the oppressed" (CNTE 1987a).

Beyond the immediate contacts with the parents, the teachers of Chiapas have been especially concerned to build alliances with the peasantry (compare Chapters 5 and 6), and it is this strategic thrust that provoked the harshest response from the authorities. As suggested above, many teachers' leaders had graduated from rural training schools like Mactumatzá, where they came to understand peasant struggles; and particular leaders such as Manuel Hernández pursued this early learning in recurrent visits to peasant communities across the state. Clearly, the alliance advanced far more in some regions than in others, and (as we saw earlier) nowhere more than in the highlands *(los altos)*. But from 1985 onward peasant organizations themselves were taking the initiative in mounting state-wide joint protests with the teachers,[11] and at moments of regional mobilization the struggle spread to include other sectors, not only in the highlands but also in Tapachula on the coast, where both peasantry and low-income urban neighborhoods answered the call of the teachers.

The Church has also come out in support of the movement in Chiapas, both in the person of the Bishop of San Cristóbal, Dom Samuel Ruiz, and through the many priests working in the "base communities"; retailers' associations have also spoken in favor, and an originally hostile press has bowed to public opinion. In this way, the teachers of Chiapas have secured a broad social base of support for their struggle. It is a particular base insofar as the movement tends to condense the contradictions of Chiapas society, but it is also general insofar as it corresponds to similar alliances in struggles against *caciquismo* across the country.[12]

10 Parents successfully occupied schools in the Costa Grande region, among them Libertad, Ejido Ignacio López Rayón, and Ejido Jésus; but in other schools of the same region, such as Ciudad Hidalgo, the official union got the upper hand. Of the 5,000 schools in Chiapas, about 50 were left with severe problems because of the political division of parents and pupils.

11 One example was the protest of July 15–18, 1985, led by about 1,000 peasants from La Costa, los Altos, Oxchúc, Jiquipilas, and Pujiltíc, who were joined by 1,500 teachers studying on intensive courses in the Advanced School. Among the peasant organizations were the Unión de Ejidos "Juan Sabines Gutiérrez" of Escuintla, the Unidad de Ordenación Forestal y Producción Agropecuaria de los Altos, the Unión de Cortadores de Cana de Pujiltíc, and the Organización Campesina Emiliano Zapata, all of which were protesting against state functionaries who had failed to respond to just demands.

12 In the neighboring state of Oaxaca, the teachers were allied locally to the Coalition of Workers, Peasants and Students of the Isthmus (COCEI), to Mixteca organizations struggling for land, and to peasant organizations throughout the state, including those within the National Peasant Confederation (CNC) and Independent Peasant Union (CCI) in the coastal region. In the Montaña de Guerrero, teachers' leaders were simultaneously peasant leaders, and in the Valle de México, teachers have played a key role in organizing marginal urban dwellers. In all three states teachers have been assassinated in the struggle against *caciquismo*.

## The challenge to *caciquismo* inside the official union

*Caciquismo* is a culturally specific network of clientelistic relations that denies popular organization the kind of authentic representation that would provide effective linkage to the political system. But as all the institutions of national political life in Mexico are permeated by such relations, the popular challenge to *caciquismo* necessarily entails institutional change. Diverse teachers' movements across the country all insisted on their own autonomy, and their organizational forms and strategic choices were conditioned by the need to defend this autonomy (see Chapters 4 and 5); but to get their demands met they had to engage with State institutions. For the teachers the frontline institution was the official union, and one of their first choices concerned *charrismo,* which was the specific expression of *caciquismo* in a corrupt union context,[13] and whether the union *charros* should be confronted or "convinced" of the cause.[14]

The teachers' National Coordinating Committee (the CNTE) sought to avoid confrontation wherever possible, precisely because the dominant struggle was one of gradualist engagement. But at the same time the political priority of most regional movements was to replace the official sectional committee with one that was democratically elected, and this inevitably led to conflict at the grass roots. In Oaxaca, during the strike of May 1980, tens of union delegations rejected the official committee and pressed successfully for a mass meeting to elect a new one, and union *caciques* in Chiapas failed in their attempt to subvert the democratic congress scheduled for March 1984. In Hidalgo, where the struggle against the *caciques* of the rural municipalities was imported directly into the union with violent and even murderous results, the movement was very clear that their struggle inside the union was an "anti-*cacique* struggle" (Consejo Central de Lucha del Magisterio Hidalguense 1981); and in Nayarit the extensive mafia inside the union was headed by the political boss, Liberato Montenegro Villa, who led powerful factions inside the state legislature and administration (Altamirano 1986).[15] Moreover, in those times and those

---

13 The term *charrismo* has its origins in the Mexico of Miguel Alemán and in the struggles of the railroad workers, who were fighting for a democratic Executive Committee for their union (Montes 1975). The President prevailed and imposed his own leader, Díaz de León, who used to dress himself up as a cowboy, with riding chaps and a big sombrero, and went by his nickname of "The Cowboy," or "El Charro." Hence the use of the term *charro* for a leader who may no longer wear his big hat but who puts himself at the bosses' bidding in return for political favors or advancement.

14 During the struggles within the public sector union federation (FSTSE) in Chiapas (related in Chapter 2), the teachers successfully drew supposedly *charro* leaders into dialogue on union issues such as health services and housing, and capitalized on these leaders' political ambitions by convincing them that a combative union federation would advance their own political careers. In fact, the leaders ended up "compromised" by the cause.

15 "The struggle against Liberato is a struggle against *caciquismo,* corruption, and *charrismo.*" Liberato's control was so complete that even the opposition movement that finally emerged in 1979 called itself the Democratic Vanguard, thus mimicking the name of the dominant clique in the union, the Revolutionary Vanguard, and refusing to risk a complete break with the *cacique.* It came to call itself the Recov-

regions where the Ministry of Education bolstered the union bosses, the teachers' movements also battled to oust the Ministry's delegates, as they did repeatedly in Chiapas. In all cases *caciquismo* was a problem for the teachers precisely because it denied them authentic representation and thus prevented any effective link to the political system overall.

Despite the pervasive operation of *caciquismo* within the official union, the teachers' movement stayed inside it. The movement came to measure its political and institutional advance by the conquest of sectional executive committees or, where this proved impossible, by whatever means of institutional participation the teachers could create and maintain. As the union was itself one of the central syndical corporations of the ruling party, there is good reason to focus in the first instance on the "corporative arena" provided by the union, with the aim of "operationalizing" the relationship between the teachers' movement and the political system writ large. And the reason does not reflect the narrow conviction that popular movements are themselves "corporative," insofar as they defend or extend sectoral interests (Ramírez Saiz 1987), so much as the broader perception that popular struggles, and even very partial and limited popular victories, can contribute to reshaping political institutions.

As outlined in the Introduction, this study of the teachers' movement aspires not only to investigate its internal organization but also to characterize its strategic choices, and there is no way to do this without focusing on the laws and institutions that provide their historical frame. The official union occupied the high ground of the legal and institutional terrain linking movement and political system, and thus provided the institutional context for the struggle. In other words, whereas the teachers had traditionally been the living links between the political system and the people in the creation of social consensus, the teachers' movement sought to reverse this relationship and register political dissent by securing institutional links with the same system. In itself, this could never resolve the central contradiction of popular practice: The State's complex clientelistic control of civil society has traditionally succeeded in dispersing and disarticulating popular organizations that are not of its own making,[16] and in any case State laws and institutions shaped and conditioned the development of popular organization and strategy.[17] But in challenging *caciquismo* the teachers'

---

ery Movement and succeeded in mobilizing nearly all the teachers of Nayarit, but it failed to take the battle to the enemy and seemed to forget that Liberato and his henchman Gerónimo Jimenez were men of the system. As the movement was controlled from within by Liberato, none of its demands ever implied a definitive break with the Revolutionary Vanguard. Indeed, its first document, which outlined its program, was addressed to the "Authentic Vanguardists."

16  Kowarick (1985) suggests that in general "state bureaucracies give rise to conflicts and demands which are structured in such a way as to dilute and segment . . . multiple groups in their actions to conquer wider socio-economic and political space."

17  As Mainwaring (1987) argues, popular movements are not simply shaped by elite values and state institutions, but these institutions "set parameters that define most popular political behavior," by shaping the "way different interests are organized and articulated, and consequently the way different sectors

movement was seeking representation on its own terms and was fighting to define the form of its insertion into the political system.

## Conclusion: the duality and ambivalence of popular struggle

The teachers' movement is rooted in popular communities but framed and conditioned by the institutional context of the official union (the National Union of Workers in Education or SNTE). It must already be clear, therefore, that it is a movement that is simultaneously syndical and popular. This initial empirical finding helps resolve the problem of linking specific struggles in civil society to a "general interest," which has often been posed in terms of the relationship between class and popular (or popular-democratic) forces (Jessop 1980). Possible theoretical approaches to the problem have ranged from the complete class reductionism of the Second International to an extreme "jacobinism" that sees the "people" as the only political alternative to existing systems of domination (Laclau 1977). Mao Ze-dong (1965) chose the middle road by insisting on the "necessary duality of all social forces," which are either predominantly class or popular forces, depending on the conjuncture. I am convinced of the wisdom of this remarkably Confucian response to a rather arcane debate, and this account of the teachers' movement will highlight the demands that emerge in the course of the struggle (rather than socially defined "interests"), as well as the conjunctural influences on the trajectory of the movement itself.

Conjunctures are always difficult to define, but it is possible to discern changes in the availability and configuration of channels of representation and forms of control as the political system reorganizes internally to deal with economic crisis or popular political demands. But just as popular movements are often ambivalent in their simultaneous insistence on autonomy and representation, so government policies are often ambivalent in promoting popular participation as a way of subsidizing the crisis and avoiding social conflicts, while simultaneously striving to restrain popular organizations and constrain the real popular impact on decision making (Arau Chavarría 1987). Contemporarily this ambivalence is inscribed in the combination of neoliberal economic policies with diverse attempts at social "concertation." All these points I take up in the final chapters.

It is noticeable that some accounts try to deal with the ambivalence of popular political practices in a rather formal fashion. Thus, Evers (1985) seeks to avoid the issue altogether by suggesting that popular movements create "small scale counter culture" but have nothing to do with politics per se, whereas Zermeño (1987a) suggests a formal division between popular organizations that

perceive their interests and the way to pursue them." A more sophisticated discussion of the question of "form determination" is found in Jessop (1982), and there is an applied analysis in Foweraker (1989b, Chapter 13).

risk cooptation through participation and those with a "restricted identity" that try to keep a safe distance from the political system. But these formal responses tend to misconstrue the nature of popular political struggle and in doing so avoid the most interesting aspect of its analysis. In my view, whether popular movements flourish or are finally coopted, repressed, or ignored does not depend on some life-or-death struggle with a Leviathan they can choose to fight or flee. The reality is both less dramatic and more complicated. Popular movements have to organize and advance on a specific legal and institutional terrain, which they cannot choose, but which in no small measure is itself the political legacy of past popular struggles. The terrain is strategic and presents a shifting pattern of constraints and opportunities. Popular movements cannot choose not to be there because there is nowhere else. They can only choose to struggle to change conditions that are not of their own choosing. For the teachers those conditions were condensed in the corrupt control of the official union over their working lives.

2

# The original impetus

The 1970s had seen a rapid expansion of the educational system in Mexico, with a subsequent increase in job mobility, especially from countryside to town. But with the onset of economic and fiscal crisis, career structures were frozen and wages were rapidly eroded by inflation. The 325,000 primary school teachers were worst affected, but those in secondary education were not much better off. Hence, it was economic demands for a fair wage, a moving wage scale (to be adjusted against inflation), and greater job security that provoked the first protest action by the teachers. This took place in the Agricultural Technical Schools (ETAs) of Chiapas in 1978 (*Chispa Sindical*, March 1978).

For many workers the economic pressures of the mid-1970s had been temporarily relieved by the oil-led boom of the late 1970s. But in Chiapas, especially in the north of the state, the teachers were far from feeling any relief. In this corner of the country they were suffering dramatic price inflation unleashed by oil exploration and hydroelectric construction. In effect, the heavy investment programs of the federal oil company (PEMEX) and the federal electricity commission (CFE) raised the local cost of living some 300 percent during the two years prior to September 1979. As the teachers tell it, everything was "at gringo prices" *(a precio de gringo)*, and these inflationary pressures led them to focus their campaign on the unfreezing of the so-called cost-of-living bonuses *(sobresueldos)*, which in Chiapas had remained unchanged since 1956 and were far inferior to those paid in other states such as Chihuahua and Baja California. In the teachers' view, changing conditions demanded a revision of the bonus.

This was not the only motive for teachers in the south to take up the struggle first. If conditions were bad for all teachers, they were much worse for the Indian "hispanifiers." In the highlands of Chiapas they suffered from starvation wages and fierce *cacique* control, and had been restless and angry since the mid-1970s. In Oaxaca, the 400 hispanifiers were paid much less than primary school teachers and had already begun to build a primitive solidarity. Almost half of the teachers of the Montaña de Guerrero were similarly hispanifiers who complained that "the wage simply does not meet the most elemental needs of we who work here" (*Excelsior*, October 30, 1980). And if poor wages were not bad enough, it was worse when they were not paid at all. Wages for some 2,000

32

teachers in Oaxaca had not been paid for more than two and sometimes three years, and wages were paid irregularly and late throughout the south.[1]

As suggested in the last chapter, the 1970s had also been a period of major syndical struggles, many of which took the form of syndical movements within the official unions of the ruling party. These movements challenged the *charrismo* of the railroad and oil unions, while the "democratic tendency" of the electricians' union (SUTERM) came to serve as the standard bearer of these struggles across the country. At the same time, the National Popular Action Front (FNAP), which was itself spawned by the "democratic tendency" in May of 1976, inaugurated an era of national popular alliances, not least of them the National Coordinating Committee of Workers in Education (CNTE). So the teachers' movement emerged within a highly mobilized civil society, where the terrain of industrial relations in particular had been turned into a battlefield. But by the time the teachers began to organize, the major syndical and popular movements of the decade had been defeated, including the electricians' democratic tendency and the FNAP, and popular movements everywhere were in retreat. However, the immediate syndical precedent for the teachers of Chiapas was not the series of national defeats but the spectacular regional success of the Agricultural Technical Schools, which had taught the basic lession that any movement worth the name had to mobilize. Hence, it was the immediate combination of economic pressure and political context that catalyzed the teachers' movement in the north of Chiapas.

## The struggle of the Agricultural Technical Schools (ETAs)

The ETAs were part of Echeverría's plan for reforming education in the countryside and were set up to create the resources that might solve the crisis in Mexican agriculture. But they themselves lacked resources, and their rapid expansion after 1974 led to the usual problems of late payment or nonpayment of wages and acute job insecurity. Poor working conditions were aggravated by the isolation of the new teachers, which made contact with the official union precarious and frustrating. In the absence of institutional support, they began to seek each other out to discuss wages, jobs, and the usual question of corruption, and by 1977 the ETAs of Chiapas had organized a syndical "current" that was separate from the SNTE's sectional committee. Within the increasingly complex educational sector a new and highly volatile group had emerged, which for the first time would successfully combine radical action with effective coordination.

---

1 Given these conditions there is a special poignancy in the Chiapas movement's early plea for solidarity with the literacy campaign in Revolutionary Nicaragua, which advises that "*Compañero*, you too can join the campaign by sending your individual contribution of a pencil and a lined writing block, letter-size" (*Chispa Sindical*, April 1980).

Informal meetings in the schools taught the teachers that they had common problems. They drew up a list of demands that were first voiced at a meeting of the delegational assembly of San Pedro Buenavista (Delegación D-II-10, Villa Corso, Chiapas) on September 25, 1977. The meeting was emotional, and there were many calls for the SNTE's sectional committee to attend to their problems. The delegational committee, in the meantime, sent commissions to schools on the coast and throughout the state to canvass their support for the committee's demands, and to call for a demonstration in Tuxtla Gutiérrez, the capital, on the following October 7. To their surprise some 800 people turned up from the ETAs, but there was "no sign even of the dust raised by the sectional committee" (*Chispa Sindical,* September 1978). Encouraged by this show of support, the new group began to make its demands known both to the Minister of Education and to the Director General of the ETAs, and with no response to the deadline agreed at the rally, it also resolved to back these demands by work stoppages. This prompted the authorities to set up a Syndical Commission (with representatives from the Director General of the ETAs, from the National Committee of the SNTE, and from the key delegations in Chiapas) to study their demands, but the Resolution of the Director General, which was publicized during February of the following year, fell far short of a solution to the multiple problems of late payment, low wages, unjust transfers, and bureaucratic inertia *(tortuguismo burocrático).* At a meeting in the headquarters of the official union in Tuxtla, the ETAs then decided to go on strike.

The same meeting took the historic step of naming its representatives to the Central Struggle Committee (*Consejo Central de Lucha,* or CCL), which would run the strike. All schools would be directly represented on the Committee by electing three or four militants from each union delegation. At the same time the CCL sent special commissions (they were not yet called "brigades") to seek support from schools across the state. In this way the movement maintained direct links with the base and sought widespread support, in order to build a horizontal organization to contest the vertical and centralized control of the SNTE and Ministry of Education. Despite the support of many school directors, the leaders were nervous about the reaction of the SNTE's sectional committee. Setting up an alternative organization to challenge the notoriously ruthless Revolutionary Vanguard (the political clique that controlled the union) was no easy step. But it was the essential step for a successful strike, and one that created the organizational prototype for all subsequent teachers' struggles in Chiapas and across the country. From small acorns great oak trees grow.

In March the CCL published an open letter to protest the ambiguous and unsatisfactory replies received from the authorities, and to repeat the call for a strike on April 3. The strike was launched to back their basic demands for the payment of late wages and a guaranteed twelve-hour pay floor, and the CCL sent out commissions to disseminate their demands to ETAs throughout the country. Despite the narrowly economic nature of these demands, the local press alleged that the delegations were being manipulated by "Marxist ideologues" (*La República en Chiapas,* April 1978); but in their April 11 meeting with the general secretary of the sectional committee, Jorge Paniagua Zenteño, the ETAs' leaders replied that they demanded nothing more than had already been agreed by Jorge Andrade Ibarra, general secretary of the SNTE, and Fernando Solana, Minister of Education. Just two days later Zenteño and his committee published a letter asserting that all demands had been met, but the CCL stayed out until it was quite sure that all back pay would be made up. The strike was lifted on April 19. It had lasted seventeen days. The movement's demands had been won.

During the strike the CCL had been in permanent assembly. Right after the strike some school directors tried to dismantle the organization, and some of its leaders were coopted by the SNTE. But the attempts at repression and cooptation only served to confirm the need for the CCL, which continued intact and continued to press for the fulfillment of the ETAs' demands. In October it led a march of more than 800 teachers to the Palace of the Governor to repeat its call for the payment of late wages and to insist on the reinstatement of ETAs' leaders who had been sacked. Finally, about 80 percent of its demands were indeed met, and the victory further reinforced the ETAs' autonomous organization. Furthermore, the victory advertised the CCL as an effective form of organization, which had obliged the SNTE at both sectional and national levels to take up the ETAs' demands; teachers throughout the state, especially in the primary schools, began to resist the SNTE's political control. By the beginning of 1979 the teachers of Chiapas had ousted several of their delegational committees and were demanding more information and more participation. It was a time of "oxygenation," one teacher told me, when the teachers began "to breathe differently." For its part the ETAs' movement was actively seeking alliances with other sectors, especially the federal and state primary schools (*Chispa Sindical,* June 1979). In this way, the ETAs' movement of 1978 was a catalyst for the takeoff of the teachers' movement across Chiapas in 1979, just as its CCL provided the organizational blueprint for this and subsequent struggles.[2] In both senses the CCL of the ETAs was the political pioneer of the teachers' movements.

This was true at both state and national level, for the ETAs' movement was important not only in Chiapas but across the country, especially in Coahuila and Durango (in the region of La Laguna). Everywhere the demands reflected common concerns over late pay, poor working conditions, job insecurity, and corrupt union control. At a national meeting of ETAs' directors in Morelos (March 1978) the Chiapas representatives "were surprised to see the general

---

2 The organization of the CCL of the ETAs prefigures exactly that of the CCL of the teachers' movement in Chiapas. In both cases the CCL was divided into three major commissions, namely, Organization, Finance, and Propaganda, which were then split again into their respective subcommissions.

support for our movement throughout the Republic"; and following this meeting the ETAs of Durango, Chihauhau, and Tabasco held twenty-four hour strikes in solidarity with Chiapas, while those of Michoacán and Durango sent messages of support. Just a year later the ETAs set up a National Struggle Committee (*Chispa Sindical,* May 1979)[3] that first drew up a long list of common demands[4] before meeting again to decide strategy, especially the work stoppages that would culminate in a seventy-two hour strike beginning on September 17, 1979. By June sixteen states were represented on the National Struggle Committee, which now led a national movement of some 25,000 teachers in around 1,000 schools. This national organization clearly heralded the historic arrival of the National Coordinating Committee of Workers in Education, which was set up in December of the same year, while (as we see later) its first national strike closely coincided with the first state-wide strike of the federal teachers of Chiapas, which began just two days earlier.

## The rise of the teachers' movement

With the prices of basic goods doubling every six months, the teachers of the north of Chiapas were living in desperate times. What they were going to do about it became the only topic of conversation after soccer matches, in the bar, or during break. In October of 1978 the teachers of delegation D-I-23 in Estación Juárez decided on joint action. They called a regional meeting of twelve neighboring delegations that was held on November 30 in Yajalón, where they agreed to take their demands to the sectional committee. They then drew up the now famous "Declaration of Yajalón," which was only remarkable for its moderation. The main demand was for an increase in the cost-of-living bonus, which had remained frozen for the past twenty-three years.

Time passed. This spontaneous display of disquiet by hungry primary school teachers seemed to dissipate on the wind. But word of the Declaration reached other delegations, which made their sympathy known to the SNTE's sectional committee, which was already under pressure from the ETAs' movement. So secretary-general Paniagua met with the Yajalón delegations on April 15 in the following year at Estación Juárez, and sent a telegram in their support to the

---

3 But the same edition of *Chispa Sindical* records a drop in the rhythm of the struggle in Chiapas, which it says is owing to the failure to "sustain publication of the Informative Organ and political leadership represented by CHISPA SINDICAL." It then makes solemn reference to the Leninist dictum that "a movement without a press is a movement defeated." In fact, *Chispa Sindical* brought out twenty-five editions over the early years of the struggle, which is a remarkable achievement in precarious circumstances and provides a proper measure of the movement's sense of its own historical importance.

4 These demands still focused on late payment. Some 40 percent of the ETAs' teachers nationwide were not on fixed contract, and largely the same 40 percent were owed wages from several months or several years back. In some states the teachers were actually paid by "tiendas de raya," i.e., by scrip not money, which was then exchanged for goods in controlled stores. This indentured labor system was clearly open to abuse by the *charros* of the SNTE and their apparatchiks in the Ministry of Education.

National Committee of the SNTE. This demagogic demarche was to prove his undoing because it was Paniagua's failure to fulfill his promises that finally pushed the teachers to strike. They agreed to strike on May 16, but delayed the strike in order to satisfy all the legal requirements of the sectional committee and of the Conciliation and Negotiation Board (*Junta de Conciliación y Arbitraje*). Nonetheless, despite the long gestation, when the strike began on May 23 it did so with just 108 teachers from delegation D-I-23. Within a week, however, there were eight delegations and 1,100 teachers on strike, and after another few days twenty-two delegations and 2,000 teachers were out. By the end of the strike forty-two delegations were solid, and "for the first time in more than forty years, red and black flags fluttered over the schools." But note that it was both economic distress and the SNTE's failure to respond that "in a country full of oil, put the teachers on the boil."[5]

## The success of natural leadership networks

The teachers who first called for action had no official platform. They were natural leaders who had become increasingly restless. Once on strike they sent out messengers in what were now called "brigades" to spread the word to other regions of the state. Sometimes teachers came from elsewhere to find out what was going on. The message moved with speed precisely because it was immediately understood. At the same time, the teachers dismissed delegates who refused them information or who tried to suffocate the movement, and in this way illegal delegations emerged with no ties to the SNTE's sectional committee but with increasing contact with each other. In other words, the spontaneous rejection of the *charros* spawned what came to be the "struggle committees," which soon set up a Central Struggle Committee to coordinate action and run the strike (though this committee had yet to find a name). In these early days, the key leaders came either from the north itself, like Amadeo Espinosa, or from the south, like Manuel Hernández, or from the ETAs' movement, like Octavio López and Víctor Sánchez Bautista. The "center" was almost the last region to organize. The ETAs' cadres formed the backbone of the brigades.

It was different in the highlands where no brigades arrived to tell them what was happening. Teachers there first learned of the struggle from newspapers and radio. But once they knew that the union officials were against it, that was enough for them. They sent teachers to Tuxtla to learn more, and then the word was spread by "internal brigades" of teachers who had done their training in Mactumatzá. The hispanifiers came out 100 percent in support of the action, even if many Indian teachers had first to overcome their fear of the coordinators and supervisors before they were convinced to join. In the end every community of the region elected representatives to the incipient Central Struggle Commit-

---

5 This was one of the striking teachers' slogans: "*país petrolero, maestro sin dinero.*"

tee, and the bilingual teachers proved to be one of the most combative sectors within the state. On the committee they joined the leaders who had already been blooded in the ETAs' struggle of 1977 and 1978, and by primary school leaders who were challenging *charrismo* for the first time. Thus, by the summer and fall of 1979 the teachers' movement in Chiapas had a range of leadership cadres, who were recognized by the mass membership and who had assumed the task of solving its problems.[6]

## The failures of the official leadership

The movement of May 1979 was driven by economic demands, and the SNTE was not at first a target. Although the sectional committee had first seemed to support the demands, it had then called a May meeting of all delegational secretaries to stop the strike. The effort failed because of the fourteen who resisted the pressure and responded to their memberships' demands, and once the strike was launched many more delegations were taken over by natural leaders from within the membership. The struggle thus turned against the SNTE and in favor of a bigger bonus, but only because the official union had withdrawn its initial support. With twenty-two delegations already out the sectional committee was forced to reconsider its position; it promised an extraordinary state assembly of delegational representatives for June 4 to resolve the demands. Apparently the committee planned to use its continuing majority at the state level to channel the struggle into the bureaucratic structure of the SNTE, where it might be left to wither and die during the summer vacation. But the assembly turned on the official leadership and refused to endorse the committee's "solution." More delegations joined the strike, bringing the total to forty-two, and on the day following the assembly they formed the Central Strike Committee *(Comité Central de Huelga)*. Far from managing to contain the movement at the local level, the committee's maneuver left it facing a more formidable foe that threatened state-wide insurrection.

As the situation went from bad to worse for the sectional committee, it was forced to recognize the Central Strike Committee if it was to negotiate an end to the strike. Furthermore, on the direct and personal initiative of the representative from the National Executive Committee of the SNTE, Antonio Jaimes Aguilar, the committee then gave formal notice of a strike by federal teachers on September 15, should their central demand for a 100 percent increase in the bonus not be met by that date. Aguilar had endorsed the move only to stop the strike. He could not return to his masters in Mexico City having failed his instructions. For its part the SNTE never took the notice seriously, even ignor-

6 The leadership would also include more seasoned leaders from outside the region who arrived with defined political projects. One such was Rafael Arellanes, who used his street theater group to popularize his ideas. See Chapters 5 and 6.

ing its legal requirements. It simply awaited the September date when the President of the Republic would announce the teachers' annual wage increase and so placate their restlessness. In fact, the lack of any mention of the bonus in the President's speech only impelled yet more teachers to join a movement that had been catalyzed at each critical moment by the bureaucratic and dismissive attitude of their official leaders.

## Strike organization

The President's speech provoked disillusion and anger in equal measure, and the teachers now called regional meetings to prepare for the strike, while some 5,000 teachers showed their resolve by marching through Tuxtla. As foreseen the strike was launched on September 16 by a permanent assembly of delegates from the regions, who elected a Central Struggle Committee (CCL) to direct it. The experience of the ETAs' strike organization was evident in the close contact the delegates kept with the membership, with all major decisions being taken in open session of the assembly. Under the leadership of the Central Committee the delegates then set up local struggle committees, which either replaced the official delegational committees or acted despite them. Under instructions from the sectional committee, the official leaders fought a rearguard action to stop the strike by splitting the movement, but the CCL forbade that these officials attend delegational meetings and vetted all agreements at the delegational level. At the same time the CCL ran an intense program of brigades to counter the propaganda campaign of the Revolutionary Vanguard (see Chapter 3) and drew more and more delegations into the permanent assembly to keep the strike solid. For the same motives, the CCL stuck to the single demand for an increased bonus because this is what had unified the movement in the first place.

The results were impressive. By September 20, 115 delegations and 10,500 teachers were on strike, with 1,935 schools closed down. An average of eighty-five delegations were attending the weekly assemblies of the CCL, and the teachers of the highlands, who had had no idea of what a strike was before they began one, swore solidarity "whatever the consequences." By September 25, 152 delegations, or all but 3 percent of the teachers, were out, and 2,096 schools were closed down; and when thirty-nine of the forty state delegations joined the federal teachers in rejecting the authority of their own sectional committee (Section XV) and set up their own State Watch Committee (*Consejo Estatal de Guardia*), the strike was pretty well 100 percent solid throughout the state. Moreover, twenty-three delegational committees had been dissolved and replaced by struggle committees, while pressure was maintained by a series of demonstrations, the first of 8,000 on September 8, the second of 15,000 on September 22, and a final mass march of 40,000 teachers and parents through the streets of Tuxtla on October 2. The marches took on real weight once the public sector unions (FSTSE) had thrown their unconditional support behind the movement on September 22. In the meantime the Revolutionary Vanguard had sent hundreds of strikebreakers from Mexico City, but the teachers mounted guard over the schools to lock them out, and any local officials seen to collaborate were immediately ousted by the "democratic guillotine."

Besides mobilizing, the teachers sought to negotiate by sending a commission to the capital to see Andrade Ibarra, the secretary-general of SNTE. At first Ibarra had rejected the movement as being the work of a cabal *(grupúsculo)*, but the teachers chose the Revolutionary Vanguard's sacred day of September 22 (see Chapter 3) to mount their first mass demonstration and so disabuse him of this idea. By the beginning of October, Andrade Ibarra was ready to send representatives from the SNTE's National Committee and the Ministry of Education to negotiate an agreement (Consejo Central de Huelga del Magisterio Chiapeneco 1979a, October 2). The SNTE first put a "special increase" of 1,500 pesos on the table, which effectively offered almost 25 percent on top of the 13.5 percent announced by the President in his speech (while the government of Chiapas promised its state teachers whatever was won by the federal teachers). The union officials within the sectional committee argued that the offer was a good beginning, which allowed the movement to continue pressing for wage increases "by legal means"; but the striking teachers were worried that this special package could be withdrawn at any time and that after tax it did not look quite so special. On the other hand, despite the large demonstration of October 2, it was becoming more difficult to maintain mobilization and so conduct an effective strike. In the end the teachers settled for the 1,500 pesos free of tax and the payment of all wages lost during the strike. Moreover, while they did not win their main demand, they did win a joint commission of the CCL, the SNTE, and the Ministry of Education (with equal representation from the two sides) to guarantee the proper payment of the special increase and to promote an increased bonus. Perhaps most important of all, the agreement signed by the CCL's negotiating commission and Andrade Ibarra on October 10 offered de facto recognition of the CCL as the real representative of the Chiapas teachers, and this recognition was reinforced by the promise of a sectional congress to legalize this situation. With the wage increase in hand, and significant syndical advances in prospect, the CCL lifted the strike on October 13 after 27 days of mobilization.


## Economic demands and the national movement

The teachers' strike in Chiapas spurred quick responses among teachers in Tabasco, Oaxaca, Sinaloa, and Guerrero, all of whom struck or marched in solidarity with Chiapas. A little later teachers in the Montaña of Guerrero and in La Laguna also struck to press their own wage and bonus demands. And when the official leadership in Oaxaca mobilized the teachers to oust the Ministry of Education's delegate in May 1980, the local struggle committee seized the moment to advance their own wage demands, which were also taken up by teachers in Michoacán, Puebla, Morelos, the Valle de México, and Hidalgo during these months. In the meantime, the December 17–19, 1979, meeting in Tuxtla Gutiérrez of representatives from the new movements in Chiapas, Tabasco, Guerrero, Morelos, the Valle de México, and elsewhere had founded the National Coordinating Committee of Workers in Education (CNTE), on the shared assumption that the different regional movements all expressed a common struggle.

This assumption found concrete expression in the agenda of demands agreed by the CNTE, which included a 30 percent emergency wage rise from the beginning of 1980, increases in the cost-of-living bonuses, and the immediate payment of late wages. But, in retrospect, not all the leaders were convinced of the virtue of concentrating on wage demands. Given the union monopoly, they could not negotiate these demands directly, and even the mass mobilizations that finally freed the cost-of-living bonus for Chiapas in January 1981 saw it rise by only 5 percent. Indeed, it was precisely the difficulty of winning higher wages that led the Chiapas teachers to focus on alliances within the public sector union confederation (FSTSE) that might improve the social wage. Others disagreed and defended the success of these demands. As early as 1980 the teachers surpassed the wage ceiling imposed by government and advanced the routine September deadline for awarding wage rises to federal employees; many improvements in the social wage (from insurance to social service and tax reform) claimed by the National Committee of the SNTE were in fact won by the teachers' movements (CNTE 1982). Moreover, by April 1983 cost-of-living bonuses were revised to a 40 percent minimum and 100 percent maximum across the country. However, it is the nature of wage demands that they are never won once-and-for-all, and by February of 1985 the Chiapas teachers were pursuing another Program of Economic Demands, which again focused on an increase in the bonus and its equal application across the state.

## The aftermath of the strike and the struggle for the Congress

During the strike the teachers had dismissed many official union leaders for ignoring agreements and setting the parents against them, and had replaced them with militants who supported the CCL. In this sense the strike strengthened the movement. On the other hand, many teachers were exhausted by the constant mobilization and wanted nothing to do with a political struggle for the control of the union. Therefore, it was easy for the Ministry of Education delegate in Chiapas to begin a witch-hunt of strike leaders. The response was spontaneous and did not even await the approval of the CCL. Teachers took over the Ministry building in late October and did not vacate it until the delegate had been dismissed. At almost the same time the National Executive

Committee of the SNTE dismissed Zenteño Paniagua and his committee, which had been completely discredited, and installed a new "official" leadership. The CCL decided to recognize the new committee, *pro tem,* while still demanding a sectional congress where the Chiapas teachers could finally elect a democratic committee. This was the regional context of the national meeting where the movement's National Coordinating Committee was established.

In January 1980 some 15,000 teachers marched to protest the delay in releasing the 1,500 pesos and called again for a democratic congress; a manifesto of the CCL in mid-March alleged that the special increase had still only been paid spottily or not at all, while no negotiated agreement on a congress was forthcoming. On the contrary, at the beginning of March the SNTE had imposed yet another sectional committee headed by the aptly named Ramón Arias Custodio. Hence, by May 1 the congress had become the main demand for the 12,000 teachers who marched and chanted that day *("QUEREMOS CONGRESO")* and for those who later occupied the SNTE's regional headquarters to back it. Not that the other demands had disappeared. On June 9 Chiapas contributed a contingent of 5,000 to a national demonstration of 70,000 in Mexico City in support of increased bonuses and a 30 percent wage rise. But the rejection of the SNTE's committee and the demand for a democratic congress marks a clear transition from a mainly economic struggle to a broadly political one.

Internally, although the initial impetus for the movement had come from the north, the struggle against the SNTE's committee was now led from the region of the Coast in the south. This was the region that organized the protests of spring 1980 and was most active in resisting the committee's attempts to divide the movement. "The sectional committee is not even visited BY THE FLIES," said the teachers (*Chispa Sindical,* May 1, 1980). But when by October of that year there was still no satisfactory response the teachers decided on a march to Mexico City, to be followed by an "encampment" *(plantón).* Oaxaca had already pursued this tactic and had won a majority of the positions on the committee to prepare an equivalent congress. Chiapas then followed their example with similar success: Even though they did not have a clear majority on the Mixed Executive Commission, they were confident that it could not deny the will of the membership. They were proved right at the Congress of March 1981, where the democratic teachers won 135 delegates against the 11 controlled by the Revolutionary Vanguard, and so were able to elect the first democratic sectional committee in the country.

## The syndical core of popular struggle

The background to the teachers' struggle was not only economic crisis but a project of educational expansion in conditions of economic austerity and ineffective administration. Neither the Ministry of Education nor the Ministry of

Planning and Budget *(Programación y Presupuesto)* had the resources to integrate the 96,000 extra teachers taken on in 1978 and 1979, and this led to the late payments that often triggered the wage and bonus demands. But as official union leaders at the local level refused to take up these demands, it was the Revolutionary Vanguard that seemed responsible for the declining wages. Hence, the teachers' movements were always explained by their own militants as emanating from their "most immediate needs" *(demandas más sentidas),* and it was in seeking to meet those needs that the movements "forged unity, organization and conciousness" (Hernández Gómez 1985). All the major meetings of the Chiapas movement at the state level emphasized the primacy of these needs and demands, and hence the primacy of syndical struggle.

It was clear that the movement focused on strictly syndical demands to secure the support of the membership and the cohesion of the movement itself. Without achieving this basic ability to get some satisfaction of these "most immediate needs," the leaders would be discredited and the movement would decline. But the problem for the teachers was not only the "boss," whether the Ministry of Education or the state government, but also the corrupt control or *charrismo* of their own union; thus, the syndical struggle to get demands met necessarily came to entail a political struggle for control of the union. Yet this struggle too had to be seen to address the real needs of the movement and hence came to focus on gaining control of the sectional executive committees, thus enhancing the capacity for winning visible concessions.

Syndical demands focused on the regular payment of wages and wage increases, on the provision of services, especially health and housing, and, last but not least, on the respect for professional rights. Gaining control of the sectional executive committee was no guarantee that such demands would be satisfied, but in the case of Chiapas it certainly helped. Even though the partisan left criticized the Chiapas movement for being reformist or even *neocharro* (Arellanes Caballero, Constantino, and Peralta Esteva 1985), its syndical record for the years 1982 to 1985 included 16,000 loans, 5,000 job transfers, 2,000 promotions, and 8,000 tenured jobs. Moreover, it had successfully contested the authoritarian control of numerous supervisors and directors, as well as ousting several Ministry of Education apparatchiks for ineptitude and corruption. The Ministry had been encouraged to make up late wages, and after 1981, the new committee won Ministry compliance in setting up locally based payment procedures. In all, it was "a practical demonstration that the correct strategy is to win control of the union executive, as the best way of winning the most basic demands of the workers" (Sección XI 1984).

In the real growth of the movement, the move from syndical to political demands was often contingent on a particularly aggressive, arbitrary, or inept act of the authorities. In Morelos it was the negligent medical care and subsequent death of a teacher that spurred the move, which in any case lost the movement the support of many parents and many of its own members. But even where the move was deliberate, as in Chiapas, it still exposed the leadership to the charge that it was neglecting economic needs for its own political goals (*Chispa Sindical,* October 1986). Yet the struggle had taught the strategic lesson that an insistence on the professional rights of tenure, transfer, and promotion was the most direct and defensible route from syndical to political demands. This was the syndical business of immediate needs, but it was also a challenge to corruption and a defense of the principle of equal rights. For this reason the movement in Chiapas came to concentrate its long battle in the arena of professional rights,[7] where both the Ministry of Education and the Revolutionary Vanguard bitterly resisted the least concession.

7 At the center of the arena was the Joint Promotion Commission *(Comisión Mixta de Cambios),* where the movement continually fought for effective participation.

# 3

# The institutional terrain

The teachers' movement emerged within the National Union of Workers in Education, or SNTE, which stood as the centerpiece of the legal and institutional terrain linking the teachers with the Mexican State. As one of the major syndical corporations of the ruling party, the SNTE contained the legal and institutional constraints and incentives that most closely conditioned the syndical and political practices of the movement. As the original site of the movement, the SNTE inevitably influenced its organization, as well as shaping its main strategic choices. If the teachers' movement represented a process of political organization within civil society, then the SNTE can be seen as a proxy for government control of this society; the official leadership of the union looked on its mass membership in much the same way as State officialdom looked on the "people." The teachers' movement was therefore a popular movement that chose to struggle inside a major institution of the State.

The SNTE was created during the first years of intense construction of the modern Mexican State, and it soon became a mainstay of the institutional carapace of the political system. In 1938 the revolutionary government set up a syndical organization for its own employees, the Union Federation of Workers in the State Sector (the FSTSE), which was separate from the industrial and commercial sectors within the Confederation of Mexican Workers (the CTM) (Sirvent 1973, 1985).[1] It took a little longer to cajole the four existing teachers' unions into the one organization of the SNTE, but this finally took place at the end of 1943. The formation of the FSTSE had been a concession that aimed to secure firm support for the government, with the FSTSE's leadership guaranteed a privileged place within the federal bureaucracy; similarly, the creation of the SNTE was designed to eliminate the opposition of the teachers' unions and to secure this sector for the government, as part of a more general reorganization of the popular sectors within the National Confederation of Popular

---

1 This it did by the Estatuto de los Trabajadores al Servicio de los Poderes de la Unión (1938), most of which was incorporated into Clause "B" of Article 123 of the Constitution in 1959. This clause regulates the organization of workers in the FSTSE, who are forbidden from belonging to working-class or peasant unions. Contemporarily the FSTSE contains sixty-three different unions.

Organizations, or CNOP, which was founded in the same year. Dissident factions continued to trouble the new union until the end of the 1940s, when government control was consolidated under the leadership of Jésus Robles Martínez, who finally succeeded in silencing the union's left wing.[2] In this way the SNTE became the most powerful union within the FSTSE, a central organization of the CNOP, and the institutional core of the ruling party's popular sector.[3] It was common practice for members of the National Executive Committee of the SNTE to sit on the National Executive Committee of the ruling party.

## The official union and the contemporary political system

By 1983 the SNTE had some 850,000 members, fully 10 percent of all unionized workers in the country, whether in the private or public sectors. These members, over half of whom were women, were distributed between fifty-five different sections (or locales), with a federal section in every state, a "state" section in some states, and five "unified" sections in which some teachers were employed by the federal government and others by the state government.[4] Each section was in turn divided into delegations, which organized a "school zone" that, depending on local circumstance, might comprise four or five or more schools. Union careers began with election to the delegational committees, which in turn elected the sectional committees, comprising a general secretary and about twenty members. These elections were carefully controlled by the SNTE's National Executive Committee, which alone could convene sectional congresses, or even full meetings of delegational committees. Hence, neither the sections nor the delegations had any autonomy, still less the right to strike, and every decision had to be referred to the National Committee, which sat squarely at the apex of a pyramidal system of political control that was buttressed by a mass of statutes more bulky than the constitutional provisions of the Mexican State itself. Until 1979 even the statutes defined the SNTE as a "vertical" organization.

As suggested in the Introduction, the SNTE has played a special role within Mexico's political system. It is by far the largest union in the country, and, more importantly, it is present throughout the national territory, which made it the perfect vehicle for mobilizing, monitoring, and controlling the vote, especially

---

2  In 1946 the 3rd Article of the Constitution had been changed to require not a socialist education but a democratic and nationalist one.

3  The SNTE joined the Labor Congress (CT) in 1966. Originally this was an umbrella organization for all unions affiliated with the ruling party, but in the 1970s it came to include "independent" unions as well.

4  In addition there was also a federal section in La Laguna, which is a well-defined region but not a state, and four in the Federal District. In its struggle with the teachers' movement the National Executive Committee was sometimes able to sow discord between federal and state sections (as occurred between Sections VII and XL at the beginning of the movement in Chiapas).

in the countryside. For these reasons the SNTE became integral to the current operations of the government and essential to electoral campaigning and voting; its strategic role and "specific gravity" gave it a political influence that did not depend directly on its relations with particular sectors of the federal bureaucracy and allowed it to extract concessions from the government, especially at election time. Nonetheless, its political priority has been the constant liaison with the many federal deputies, the hundreds of municipal presidents and local deputies, and the thousands of Ministry of Education employees who are the loyal retainers of the SNTE.

The SNTE is also big business, and finance is one key to the political control of the organization. Dues are deducted at the rate of 1 percent of wages, and this vast inflow of funds remains entirely at the disposition of the Finance Secretary of the National Committee, who distributes it as the Committee decides. No more than 5 to 10 percent is disbursed directly for financing the administration of the sections, the rest remaining with the Committee. In addition, the SNTE runs a huge business empire, including hotels, restaurants, factories (for school supplies), travel agencies, and a publishing house. Even individual sections are involved in commercial enterprise. The SNTE is bigger and controls more resources than any federal ministry, and yet the Ministry of Education pays all its telephone bills and also pays the wages of about 1,000 SNTE "commissioners," who carry out the political and economic business of the National Committee.

## The contested political control of the union

The teachers' movement of the 1980s was not the first to challenge the political control of the union. As long ago as the late 1950s the 80,000 teachers of Section IX in Mexico City had fought not only for higher wages but also for union democracy (Loyo Brambila 1979). This protracted struggle long outlasted the famous railroad workers' strike of the same years, as well as engendering the Revolutionary Teachers' Movement (MRM), which was to remain a significant force among the teachers for some twenty-five years. The struggle was notable for the unprecedented length of its strikes and for the ferocity of the government response, which finally succeeded in crushing the movement and incarcerating its leaders. Nonetheless, the tasks of securing mass support and guarding against cooptation seemed to leave some organizational residues that later surfaced in the "struggle committees" and "vigilance committees" of the 1980s, and at least some of the leadership cadres continued to fight for control of the Advanced School of Mexico City *(Escuela Normal Superior)* in the brave belief that "rights are not requested, they are seized" (Fernández Dorado nd).

During the student movement of 1968 the teachers were active again in the "school assemblies" and "struggle committee," and participated on the

National Strike Council, which provided an authentic blueprint for the CNTE (National Coordinating Committee of Workers in Education) of 1979. But despite the historical salience of 1968, it is difficult to argue that the struggles of the 1950s found a stepping-stone in 1968 to connect them to the movement of the 1980s. The organizational continuities are not there.[5] Yet these historical struggles are important in at least two senses. In the first place they created a generic tradition of struggle and acted as a powerful myth that provided *figurae* for what followed.[6] In the second place they did have a perceptible impact on government, particularly on the administration of Luis Echeverría (1970–6), and on the pattern of political control within the SNTE itself. Both these assertions are borne out by the continuing contest for control of the Advanced School in Mexico City, which also, and exceptionally, did have direct links to the movement of the 1980s.

Through its intensive summer courses the Advanced School reached thousands of teachers from across the country, and many of the teachers' leaders of the 1980s saw it as the cradle of their movement. The struggle within the Advanced School culminated in the students repudiating official control and setting up their own commissions, and finally a Coordinating Commission, to run their own courses,[7] and by 1976 the students had forced through an educational reform, which disseminated new training methods and study programs. All of these developments had a perceptible medium-term impact on the emergence of the teachers' movement. Their immediate impact on the union, and especially Section IX in Mexico City was less positive, insofar as the mobilization of 1972 revealed the relative weakness of the democratic currents within the union, contributed to the political divisions that exposed the old leadership to Jonguitud's coup (see the next section), and opened the way for the Revolutionary Vanguard's ascent to power.

As we shall see, the struggle in the Advanced School had clearly convinced

---

5 The MRM continued, but as a tiny "vanguard" that in no way resembled the mass organization of the 1950s (and that signally failed in its leadership of the teachers' movement in Section VIII of Chihuahua). Its leader, Othón Salazar, also survived the years and was present at the first upsurge of the movement in the Montaña de Guerrero in 1979.

6 The march of 80,000 teachers, parents, and workers from the occupation of the Ministry of Education to the Advanced School in 1958 foreshadowed the dramatic arrival in the capital of the mass contingents of teachers from the south in June of 1980. The Ministry's refusal to recognize the democratically elected Executive Committee of the Section IX, and the expulsions, sackings, and arrests that followed look like an historical dress rehearsal for similar struggles and responses in Oaxaca, Hidalgo, Morelos, and the Valle de México in the 1980s; and the army's attacks on the teachers on August 4 and 9, 1959, resonate with the assassinations of tens of teachers in more recent years.

7 The August 4 Movement, which had split from the MRM in 1963 on the strategic issue of staying to fight within the SNTE or forming an independent union, used the struggles of these years to recruit cadres for a new organization, the National Independent Teachers' Front (FMIN), which would play an important role in the movement of the 1980s, even if its strategic line of "no contact with the SNTE" would soon have to be abandoned.

the Echeverría administration of the need for firmer control of the SNTE, just as radical mobilization had persuaded Echeverría, as Minister of the Interior in the late 1960s, to close fourteen of the twenty-nine rural training schools *(normales rurales)* on the grounds that they were "subversive."[8] The rest of the schools were put under close military control, which further politicized the future generation of teachers' leaders, most of whom (including the leaders on the future National Coordinating Committee) "came from the rural training schools" (Equipo Pueblo 1984b). This politicization certainly occurred in Chiapas, where the harsh regime imposed within their own training school in Mactumatzá provoked the future leaders to fight to regain their freedoms. The disputes inside the school spilled over into popular struggles in the capital of Tuxtla Gutiérrez and across the state. By 1974 the students had helped organize strikes and protests among construction workers, peasants, and urban squatters,[9] with the predictable result that over 20 percent of the students were expelled; many more left "of their own accord." In effect, the rhythm of this local experiment in popular organization closely followed the trajectory of Echeverría's new populism at the national level, which began with calls for popular participation and with support for popular education but ended with renewed repression.

## The rise of the Revolutionary Vanguard

Because the revolutionary principle of "no re-election" applied at every level within the SNTE, continuity of control was provided by the political cliques that have commanded the organization. Jésus Robles Martínez was the *eminence grise* from 1949 to 1972, but as soon as he could no longer be counted on to maintain "vertical" discipline, he was ousted by Carlos Jonguitud Barrios. Jonguitud had made his career within Section IX of the SNTE, the strategic center of the union.[10] When the National Committee changed hands in 1971,

---

8 Echeverría was right. The core of the guerrilla combatants for the September 23 and Union of the People movements came from these schools, which during and after 1968 had taken the lead in setting up "struggle committees" and searching for links with peasant organizations. The guerrilla movement was defeated by the strategic effectiveness of the military's scorched-earth offensive, not for lack of an extensive social base. In a little-known chapter of modern Mexican history all suspect guerrilla supporters were thrown into concentration camps, and their crops and home were razed.

9 Some 5,000 workers were concentrated in the capital of Tuxtla Gutiérrez because of the huge hydroelectric projects under construction in the region, and the students led them to a solid state-wide strike. At the same time, in December 1974, students working with the peasant groups from Venustiano Carranza occupied the main square of the capital just as the President of the Republic was about to arrive. It looked like popular insurrection, and the response of the state was predictable. The leader of the Carranza peasants, Bartolomé Martínez Villatoro, was assassinated, the peasant organizations were repressed, and the construction workers were forced back to work.

10 Jonguitud had joined the Executive Committee of Section IX in the late 1950s as its Secretary of Development and Cooperation, once the majority MRM committee had been crushed by arrests and impris-

Jonguitud became president of the National Vigilance Committee (responsible for union discipline), and early in the following year he captured the leadership of Section IX itself. From this position of strength he launched an internal coup that successfully seized power. The figurehead was one Eloy Benavides Salinas, but Jonguitud was the new boss.

The coup took place on September 22, 1972, and was backed by the SNTE's National Council on September 26 and ratified by the Federal Conciliation and Arbitration Board on September 29. In rapid succession the new National Committee was then received by the Minister of Education, the president of the ruling party, and President Echeverría himself, all before the month of October was out. Meanwhile, nearly every sectional committee in the country had rallied to support the "22 September Movement," which was formally endorsed by the National Congress in the following year. At its meeting of August 1973 the Congress also agreed to create a National Unified Front (*Frente Nacional Unificador*), which was to spawn Jonguitud's own creature of political control, the Revolutionary Vanguard. By the time Jonguitud became secretary-general of the National Committee in January 1974, sectional and delegational leaders throughout the country had been recruited into the Vanguard, which could then count on mass support among the middle-levels cadres in the regions (supervisors and principals) as well as unconditional support from the ruling party in the center. The Vanguard appeared to provide a faithful reflection of Echeverría's populist attempts to modernize Mexican unions and easily mimicked his nationalist and "third world" discourse. The surge in government spending on education meant increased patronage for the regional cadres, simultaneously assuring their support and creating conditions for consensus within the membership at large.

The Vanguard set out to take over the SNTE, lock, stock, and barrel, and acted as if it were the union and not merely a political faction within it. Central to this project was the National Committee of the Vanguard, composed of key secretaries of the National Committee and National Council of the union, as well as the more important sectional leaders. This committee was chaired by Jonguitud himself, who thus concentrated all final powers of patronage and decision making in his own person. Moreover, by creating a range of new tasks and new commissions attached to the national and sectional committees, he enlarged the leadership cadres of the union by "democratizing corruption" (Espinosa 1982), thus extending vertical lines of clientelistic control. These lines

onment. Indeed, he was one of the *pistoleros* who had fought the democratic movement at that time. Prior to the coup he also sat on the National Executive Committee of the ruling party as its Secretary of Organization. Since his period as secretary-general of the SNTE, he has been Secretary of Social Action of the ruling party, president of the FSTSE, president of the Labor Congress, director of the Institute of Social Security and Services for State Employees (ISSSTE), a federal senator, and governor of San Luis Potosí.

wove a network of prebendary positions embracing directors, inspectors, and supervisors, who themselves dispensed favors in the form of jobs, transfers, promotions, loans, and houses (not to mention bonuses and "sick leave"). As what was given could also be denied or taken away, this massive *cacicazgo* operated through a sui generis combination of repression and consensus.

The union had always played a central part in the training and career patterns of teachers, and had intervened directly in the assignment of jobs and promotions. In particular, the union controlled promotions to the positions of school director and district supervisor, and seniority counted for nothing without union support. As both directors and supervisors owed their positions to their union bosses, they could be counted on to dispense favors to those loyal to the Revolutionary Vanguard and to sanction dissidents. Even where dissidents were in the majority, the director or supervisor was able to build a strong faction of teachers and parents through this system of "massified corruption." Moreover, the control over the schools led to a parallel control of the delegational committees, with supervisors and directors drawing up their own exclusive slates for the "elections"; this led in turn to a control over the composition of the sectional committee. So clientelistic control over the union at the grass roots was consolidated in its executive committees, until nearly every director, supervisor, and sectional secretary-general had been bought by the Vanguard.

By way of illustration, transfers and promotions were handled by a Joint National Promotion Commission, which was staffed by two union representatives, two Ministry of Education representatives, and one arbitrator – from the union. The Vanguard worked through the Commission to ensure the loyalty of the key cadres of directors and supervisors. The teachers at the grass roots, on the other hand, soon became aware that training, seniority, and professional skills could not compete with servility, bribery, and personal connections; many women teachers even suffered sexual pressures (Consejo Central de Lucha del Magisterio Chiapaneco 1980b). Far from defending the teachers, said Amadeo Espinosa, the union came to operate as a corrupt "employment agency," which consistently undermined their professional rights. But individually there was little that the teachers could do. Whatever their "representative" said was Holy Writ, and anyone who denied it was branded as a traitor. In this way the Revolutionary Vanguard was successful in securing greater benefits than the previous ruling clique, but it was ruthless in the patrimonial use of these benefits to control the membership and maintain itself in power.[11]

---

11 By extension, Jonguitud was most ruthless and corrupt of all in maintaining himself in power at the peak of the organization. After he had served his three years as secretary-general, he filled the position with a loyal henchman, José Luis Andrade Ibarra, who had proved himself as the executioner of the democratic tendency in the state of Chihuahua. Andrade Ibarra was followed in 1980 by Ramón Martínez Martín, who had occupied the post of Secretary of Finance on the National Executive Committee from 1977–80, but who was also Jonguitud's private secretary and son-in-law.

## *Charrismo* and political control

The syndical rule of the Revolutionary Vanguard exemplifies the particular form of political control called *charrismo*. Within the union itself it depends on the comprehensive hold the Vanguard has over the economic and professional lives of the teachers, and its ability to advance its own adherents into the key administrative and political posts; for this reason *charrismo* has been defined as the "expression of the subjection of the masses by their own means of struggle, the union" (Fernández Dorado 1982). Union business is corrupted by the sale of jobs, the chicanery of sectional leaders, and the careerism that uses the union as a political springboard. At the same time, the Vanguard diverts union funds to maintain a massive apparatus of chauffeurs, waiters, bodyguards, and simple lackeys – not to mention the so-called aviators, who draw teachers' wages without ever entering a classroom and who lend their dubious services to the "union" as spies, agents provocateurs, and even assassins. This vast criminal network centers its operations in the SNTE's headquarters in the capital, which is the very "cathedral of corruption" (Hernández 1982b). Although corruption characterizes the modus operandi of this *"charro* unioneering" (FMIN 1981), *charrismo* is finally defined by its insertion into the political system overall.

*Charrismo* certainly describes a semisecret system of shady deals and betrayals, but it is clearly driven by the political careerism of union representatives and officials. A place on a delegational committee may be the first step in a career that might include delegate to a sectional congress, union apparatchik at sectional level, secretary to the sectional leadership, salaried factotum for a local or federal deputy (or for an official of the ruling party), or administrator of some peasant or Indian organization. From there the aspiring *charro* may rise to the sectional committee, or to a modest post on the National Committee, and then into the next stage of a national career in the union, the ruling party, or the Labor Congress. At the same time, sectional leaders may seek preferment as local or federal deputies for the popular sector of the ruling party, or as municipal president; they can continue their advance at the regional level with the support of the National Committee or of the state government. It is not at all unusual for the successful *charro* to hold a number of such posts simultaneously, thereby increasing his influence and his income.[12]

What is career for the individual is connection for the institution, and through the process of *charrismo* the Revolutionary Vanguard has inserted itself into the federal bureaucracy. It has captured many posts within the ruling party's "popular" (CNOP) and peasant (CNC) sectors, at both local and

---

12  An excellent example was the secretary-general of Section 29 in Tabasco, Ruben Magaña Mendoza, who was rarely to be found on the sectional committee because he was also a "reserve" federal deputy, a local deputy elect for Xalpa, the PRI's mayor of Tabasco, the secretary of the Electoral Commission of Tabasco, a full-time secondary school teacher (in principle putting in his forty-two hours a week), a state teacher, and Secretary of Literacy and Professional Problems of the SNTE.

national level, and it holds so many posts within the Ministry of Education that the Ministry's administration is effectively fused with the Vanguard's *charrismo* in some instances. At the same time, the Vanguard has spent massive sums on the political campaigns of federal deputies, not to mention the fortune it invested in winning the governorship of San Luis Potosí for its "lifetime leader" Jonguitud. Within the union itself the Vanguard's power base rested squarely on Sections IX, X, and XI in Mexico City.[13] These sections continued to receive the most political favors, especially Section IX, which provided core support for Jonguitud and the Vanguard leadership ensconced in the National Committee. Through close monitoring and control of its political networks, this Committee maintained a jealous monopoly of all contact and communication with the federal bureaucracy.

## Institutional terrain and economic demands

During the 1970s some groups and regions within the SNTE continued to mobilize to contest the political control of the union, but it became increasingly hard to break the tightening grip of the Revolutionary Vanguard. The teachers of the TV-secondaries *(telesecundarias)* became notorious for their anarchic tactics and revolutionary rhetoric, but their combination of direct democracy and direct action had little impact on the official operations of the union.[14] A very combative movement led by the MRM and ARS (Revolutionary Syndical Alliance) in Chihuahua's Section VIII finally failed to consolidate the alliance and succumbed to the machinations of the Vanguard (Luna Jurado 1977). Meanwhile, in Chiapas itself a mobilization of the "united delegations" in the early 1970s merely reflected disenchantment with the corrupt leadership of the Robledo clique and was easily dispersed,[15] whereas the protest by supervisors and

13 Section IX comprises all primary and nursery teachers; Section X encompasses all post-primary teachers both in secondary schools and in the Instituto Politécnico Nacional, the Universidad Pedagógica, the Instituto Nacional de Antropología e Historia, and all teacher training schools; and Section XI represents all the manual, technical, and administrative workers of the schools and other educational establishments of the capital.

14 The TV-secondaries were designed by the Echeverría government to extend secondary education to the poorer regions of the country through the use of television, and the teachers of the National Commission of TV-Secondary Teachers (CNMCT) faced working conditions entirely different from those of teachers elsewhere. Their direct links with the communities they served, and the hopeless lack of equipment to serve them, motivated the constant mobilization of the 10,000 teachers in the sector. The CNMCT inaugurated the tactic of occupying the Ministry of Education in Mexico City (which had last been seen in 1958). Despite its limited numbers, the CNMCT's strongest regional bases were strategically concentrated in the Federal District, or relatively nearby in Puebla and Toluca. A meeting in Mexico City in 1978, which was convened by the TV-Secondaries, the National Independent Teachers' Front (FMIN), and the Independent and Democratic Syndical Tendency (COSID), served to set up a "support committee" for the TV-Secondaries' struggle.

15 The thirty or forty dissidents involved in this protest lacked a clear political line, and some of its leaders were coopted. Nonetheless, the seeds of strategic thinking had been sown, especially in conversation with

directors of Tuxtla Gutiérrez in early 1979 was, on the contrary, provoked by the arrival of a high-minded Ministry of Education delegate who sought to suppress the corrupt privileges of official union leaders (Corriente Revolucionaria 1979).

The Revolutionary Vanguard appeared increasingly confident in its control of the union during this decade, and the exercise of its particular brand of *charrismo* seemed secure. But its rule was compromised by the rapid increase in union membership at a time of fiscal crisis and financial stringency within the political system overall. Restrictions on the social services available through the welfare network for federal employees (ISSSTE), for instance, plainly impaired the Vanguard's capacity for cultivating its political clienteles (Equipo Pueblo 1986a), and as working conditions deteriorated and real wages began to fall the teachers soon discovered that they had no effective channels for voicing their economic demands. Given these developments, the rise of the teachers' movements might be explained by the combination of economic pressures with a specific institutional context characterized by *charro* extortion and the lack of effective representation: It was the Vanguard that provoked demands for more sectional or regional autonomy by its autocratic attitude to the union's fifty-five sections and 15,000 delegations.

But such an explanation would be incomplete without a proper emphasis on the regional question. The syndical sections of states like Chiapas had grown in numbers and strength, and were seeking a corresponding share of resources. Yet the Revolutionary Vanguard continued to favor its own power bases in the center and north of the country, leading to a marked disparity of resources between these regions and those of the south of the country, where working conditions and wages were clearly inferior. This made wage demands central to the initial impetus of the teachers' movements. Moreover, the large number of Indian teachers in the southern states of Chiapas, Oaxaca, Guerrero, and Hidalgo suffered political disdain as well as social misery, and their presence lent a certain desperate energy to the first movements to emerge.

The question of regional variation is also important to the gradual construction of the Revolutionary Vanguard's system of union control, which entailed a differential insertion of the union apparatus into regionally specific *cacicazgos* and political alliances. In effect, this was not one union, but many different unions; or it was one union with different political forms, which responded differently, and more or less successfully, to the new demands. Most critical was the Vanguard's cooptation and control of the intermediate cadres of supervisors and directors. Where this control was relatively weak, as in Chiapas and Oaxaca, the teachers' movements could make rapid progress because the Rev-

one of the MRM militants from Mexico City, Ramiro Reyes Esparsa; and some of the leaders of the protest like Octavio López and José Domingo Guillén would have an important role to play in later struggles.

olutionary Vanguard had never reached the mass of the members. In Chiapas the syndical leadership had become entirely bureaucratized by the end of the 1970s and had lost effective control of the organization by default; in Oaxaca the Vanguard had attempted to implement its system of cadre control, but this had taken root only in restricted areas like Tuxtepéc.[16] Where the Vanguard's controls worked well, as in Morelos and the Valle de México, it could count on 40 percent or more of the membership to resist the movement, and for a long time this proved sufficient. In Hidalgo, which is different again, even though the Vanguard lacked effective cadre control, the pervasive presence of local *caciquismo* put up violent resistance to the teachers' advance.

The regional and institutional variations made all the difference to the relative success of different sectional struggles. But despite the regional challenges (and possibly *because* they were regional) the Vanguard displayed an impressive resilience in resisting the restless mobilization of almost a third of the union's membership (see Part III). A few fissures appeared in the Vanguard's organization, and nearly every region saw some minor inter-*charro* disputes. Some groups wanted negotiation with opposition movements; others, especially in Hidalgo, Guerrero, and the Valle de México, called for harsher measures. But the Vanguard repeatedly appealed for unity and used congress platforms to exalt its leaders and vilify its opponents. The triumvirate of Jonguitud, Andrade Ibarra, and Martínez Martín were compared to Mexico's national heroes, Hidalgo, Juárez, and Morelos (Congress of Section IX 1981), whereas the dissidents were "failures and deformed beings who betray us because they never had their parents' love" (XII National Congress, Chetumál, January 1980). In the end the Vanguard successfully avoided any serious split by "happy and authoritarian recourse to antidemocratic methods" (*Excelsior*, January 29, 1980), and especially by methods of indirect election to ensure central control of its own congresses. In consequence the majority opposition in several states had no democratic channel for presenting their views or influencing executive decisions (*Excelsior*, January 28, 1980; Consejo Central de Huelga del Magisterio Chiapaneco 1979).

## Institutional terrain and political rights

The pervasive patterns of *charro* control and the systematic denial of union and professional rights by the Revolutionary Vanguard made the achievement of these rights a political priority for the dissident teachers. The first strike in Chiapas was launched for exclusively economic motives (see Chapter 2) and pursued no others, but within a few months the movement was accusing the sectional

---

16 The struggle in Oaxaca was described as "a confrontation between the exercises of democracy by 38,000 workers and the interests of a band of gangsters" (Section XXII 1986), so that here and in Chiapas the Vanguard could win only a handful of delegates to the multitudinous sectional congresses.

executive committee of "stamping on our rights." Economic pressures had first given rise to the movement, but its continuing impetus was created by specific political demands that were to shape the later trajectory of the struggle. This progression from economic or social demands to the vindication of political rights is a further expression of the simultaneously syndical and popular nature of the teachers' movement, and is one of the keys to understanding popular mobilization in Mexico overall.

With the rise of the movement in Chiapas and the conquest of its sectional committee, the questions of rights then became central to its political agenda. New jobs and promotions were granted according to seniority, welfare loans were divided fairly between different delegations, criteria for the distribution of housing were decided collectively, and the teachers themselves were encouraged to "professionalize" their performance and their relations with the parents. In all cases the teachers began to participate in the decisions affecting their own professional and social lives, and with participation came changing attitudes. In other words, the teachers themselves had to be convinced of their own rights regarding jobs and housing, and the only way to achieve this was by debate in open forum. "Now it is different," one teacher told me, "if I don't get a transfer I know it's because there's a colleague who has priority, and I have to respect that."

With this new sense of their rights the teachers won a new confidence in handling union issues and showed a greater readiness to take responsibility for their own professional lives. Possibly the most dramatic changes occurred in the female[17] and Indian[18] teachers. The women were now familiar with their rights and were competent at managing union procedures. This they demonstrated beyond any doubt by their reform of the sensitive sector of "special education," where they imposed proper respect for professional criteria despite opposition from the official SNTE. The result, they declared with pride, was that their work was now done with "a different mentality." This change in attitude was also evident in the highlands, where formerly submissive Indian teachers had begun to confront their supervisors and "coordinators," and had even expelled

---

17  One of the most isolated groups had been the female teachers in the nursery schools. These women were kept ignorant not only of the union but also of their rights as employees of the Ministry of Education. Their supervisors controlled every aspect of their job and demanded complete obedience. Even where the women had heard of the movement, they were at first prevented from joining by the threats of the supervisors. On the other hand, it was too often the case that favoritism, connections, and corruption decided privileged job locations in the city, and even jobs in "special education" for the backward and handicapped.

18  The Indian teachers not only did not enjoy their professional rights but also suffered multiple abuse at the hands of the regional *caciques* or "coordinators" who sold jobs, robbed wages, and sexually assaulted female teachers. They had only occasional access to the kind of rudimentary medical care that killed more often than it cured. Needless to add, they were absolutely forbidden from forming their own union delegation. Even so, their working conditions were similar to those of all teachers in far-flung rural communities, and the discrimination they suffered was exceptional only in degree.

those who did not endorse the movement. At that the *charros* changed their tune too and began to offer promotions and higher wages, but it was too late for such cynical concessions.

It was in the months following the first "democratic" congress of the SNTE in Chiapas, and the election of the first "democratic" sectional executive committee, that the Indians of the highlands first put their new-found strength to the test. This test was the long winter struggle in 1981–2 for better medical services led by the union delegations of the Regional Coordinator of the Chiapas Highlands (CRACH). With their patience exhausted after three months of evasive replies to their petitions they occupied the clinic and medical store, and supported the occupation by a mass encampment (or *plantón*). This action galvanized other public sector unions throughout the state to come out in solidarity, and the teachers won the day. The local administrators were retired or fired, a new clinic for the highlands was promised, and in the meantime, the facilities and personnel of clinics throughout the state were upgraded. Thus, by winning a victory in the battle for their rights, the Indian teachers lent new impetus to the movement throughout the state. In the years to come this struggle was always remembered as marking a special moment in the trajectory of the movement.[19]

For the most part, however, union work was nothing so heroic. On the contrary, it was a constant round of discussion, preparation, and organization — renewing delegational committees; mounting solidarity actions and demonstrations; holding education meetings, strategy meetings, and meetings to agree on professional criteria and procedures; planning intensive courses; preparing state-level assemblies of delegational committees; and preparing for sectional and national congresses. And all this was in addition to general negotiations and to the staple of all union work everywhere, individual case work. But despite the enormous and usually unpaid effort put into union business by the militants of the movement, they were sometimes themselves accused of violating the teachers' rights by dismissing teachers on the simple supposition that they were *charro* or by insisting on union militancy as a prerequisite for jobs and promotions. The militants replied that there could be no professional rights without professional participation, and, in any event, it was always the membership who decided whether sanctions should apply. No longer were the teachers' professional lives decided by favoritism, bribery, and blackmail. "Now no-one owed anything to anybody, because it was only rights which mattered."

19 After the successful struggle for the democratic congress of March 1985, the Indian teachers joined the victory march: "the Indian teachers chanted slogans in Spanish with some difficulty, because even though they rhymed in their native language, they were some way from doing so in Spanish. It didn't matter. People applauded and smiled at them with gratitude" (Hernández 1985b).

# Inside the movement in Chiapas

4

# Leadership and grass roots

The struggle against the political control and corruption of *charrismo* was simultaneously a struggle for democratic principles and for mass participation in the syndical arena. Moreover, as the struggle itself could advance only through mobilization, such participation was never passive; on the contrary, it was always actively expressed through marches and meetings, campaigns and strikes (Trevino Carrillo 1984). This was seen as a virtue of the movement. It was right in principle that the teachers should achieve more power over their own lives, and this could only begin with respect for "the majority decisions taken by the base." It was also right in practice because this was how the teachers themselves might progress politically, and it was often asserted (sometimes demagogically) that the real changes occurred first in the base and that "many of the ideas which have guided the movement are in fact ideas of the base" (*Chispa Sindical*, March 1978).

Once the teachers felt the power of a mobilized membership, they exulted in it. "The supervisors who were accustomed to kick the teachers around have had to think again and change their attitude when facing an organized base which insists on respect for its rights" (Consejo Central de Lucha del Magisterio Chiapaneco 1981). And the teachers knew that this "Unity, Organization and Consciousness" (Consejo Central de Lucha del Magisterio Chiapaneco 1980b) was critical in sustaining their gains. Whatever problems of discipline this base might create (such as the spontaneous occupation of the Ministry of Education building in Tuxtla in October 1979), this was seen as a small price to pay for the political and ideological advantage of a movement with no chiefs or *caciques*. In this respect, all the teachers were "Indians." Such a view was perhaps inevitable in a movement committed to combatting *charrismo* in all its manifestations, but the role of the base in "determining the direction, character and objectives of the movement" also served the further strategic purpose of "avoiding betrayal and dishonest maneuvers" (*La Puya*, September 1979). It had traditionally been all too easy for the federal government to suppress popular movements by coopting, or even eliminating, their leaders and leading cadres. The basist democracy and circulating leadership of the teachers' movement made it more resilient, if not entirely immune to such tactics.

## Basism in practice

Mass participation began in the local assemblies that prepared for the first strike, and it was these assemblies that elected delegates to the Central Strike Committee. In this way the mass of the teachers soon created a parallel structure to the official union, and this structure represented the real force of the movement. Most of the assemblies were at delegational level, and where the officials of the delegational committee either did not support or actively obstructed the movement they were dismissed. In this and much else the Central Strike Committee of these early days (also called the Coordinating Committee of General Representatives) followed every line and particular of the practice of the CCL of the ETAs' movement, even to the point of asserting that its principle of organization was "democratic centralism" (*La Puya*, September 1979). As long as this alternative organization went unrecognized by the SNTE it was illegal, but insofar as it struggled to solve the memberships' problems it achieved a "legality in practice" that made it representative. Just fifteen days into the first strike it was observed that the teachers "had created a structure of struggle that had been so lacking in their union" (*Cuarto Poder*, September 30, 1979).

At the beginning of October 1979 it was agreed that the Central Strike Committee be changed to a Central Struggle Committee (CCL), which would be permanent and meet at least every fifteen days, and which would be made up of those delegational secretary generals "elected by the base" (Consejo Central de Huelga del Magisterio Chiapaneco *Actas*, October 2, 1979). In effect, the teachers had consciously sought a form of organization that could break the "official verticality" of the SNTE and provoke a sea change in the dominant relations of control within the union, and, like the General Commission for Wage Rises of the railroad workers in 1958 and the National Strike Committee of the student movement in 1968, they actively promoted mass participation. The first step was the creation of "regional coordinating committees" *(coordinadoras regionales)*. These committees brought together representatives of the schools and then split them into working groups for gathering information and preparing proposals, which were then taken to the delegational assembly, and so to the state assembly. With the shift from purely economic to broadly political demands the regional committees changed to "struggle committees," the better to equip them for political work. But the starting point for whatever was intrinsically democratic about the movement remained in the school assembly where representatives to the regional or struggle committee were elected, which then took their concerns to the CCL. Equally, the school representatives had to seek the authority of their membership for any decisions contemplated by the CCL, which ensured a high degree of accountability and left little margin for manipulation. In this respect at least the movement resembled, and perhaps drew on, the Indian tradition of the communal assembly.

The main point about the organization of the movement, then, is that it was different in *form* from that of the union. This was because its committee structure operated on the principle that only the teachers themselves could direct the movement, which was effective only insofar as it grew out of their mass assemblies. Nonetheless, the elaborate mechanisms of representation from school to delegational struggle committee to state assembly were designed to create a central political command that was the CCL. The state assembly was composed of two delegates from every delegational struggle committee and so had a valid popular base. Moreover, these delegates were accompanied by members of the vigilance committees *(comités de vigilancia)* to make sure they remained accountable. But at the end of the day the most democratic decisions have to be executed, and this was the domain of the CCL. However strong the struggle committees in the regions, they finally had to defer to the CCL. Furthermore, in its executive role the CCL was divided into committees for press, propaganda, finance, brigades, and political work, which were staffed by its most active militants; and when the assembly was not in session the organization was run by a Coordinating or Centralizing Committee of the main leaders, who took most of the operational decisions and often drew up the programs of action that would be debated by the base. Thus, even if the power of decision lay with the base, it was at the very least concentrated in the CCL.[1]

In this connection it is clear that the democratic content of the movement necessarily depended on how well its democratic mechanisms worked in practice. In May 1980, after several months of struggle, the priority tasks were still stated as strengthening the struggle committees and intensifying the brigades to schools not yet committed to the movement. During 1980 the movement had begun to create "regional coordinating committees" that (very differently from the early committees of the same name) were intended to counteract the centralizing tendencies of the CCL. Unlike the struggle committees, which had more to do with political action and political alliances with the parents, the new "regional committees" were concerned mainly with union matters. There were thirteen such committees, each containing between ten and forty delegations, which were designed to get problems solved within the region and thus decentralize the work of the CCL; they were consolidated once the teachers had won control of the sectional committee in March 1981. Eventually, each committee came to organize the work of different "councils of representatives," so creating two representative "tracks" within the movement. The first linked the school to the council of representatives to the regional coordinating committee to the state assembly; the second linked the school to the struggle committee (dele-

---

1 Even then, the democratic defense of the CCL is that it was assembly based, and indeed the assembly met every Saturday from October 2, 1979, until September 1982, so that "the maximum organ of political leadership of the teachers which can affirm or deny any agreement is the State Assembly of Syndical Representatives, that is, what the National Executive Committee is for the SNTE, the Assembly is for us."

gational committee) to the CCL. In this way the formal opportunities for participation were further amplified, but real participation probably varied considerably from place to place and moment to moment.

It was natural that the movement should advance faster in some places than others, but if it was to survive it had to have a solid regional base, and for that reason the teachers "developed the grass-roots brigade to strengthen the unity and permanent democratization of the organization" (Sección VII 1982b). The brigade took teachers from one community to another carrying word of the struggle, and so was at the same time tactic, organization, and metaphor for the movement itself. In this sense the brigade was integral to the movement from the beginning. At every assembly of the Central Strike Committee of 1979 there was a priority report from the brigade committee on the activity in different areas of the state: the kindergarten in Pueblo Nuevo had pulled down its flags and started to work; Tapachula was falling behind in the struggle; the municipal presidents of the highlands had sent telegrams to the President of the Republic in support of the movement; the struggle committee of San Cristóbal had taken on lawyers to advise it, "under strict control of the Central Committee"; the supervisors of Villaflores had declared their support for the struggle; comrade Chacón of Arriaga had complained of being accused as an informer; the secretary apologized for forgetting to bring the minutes, but he had been busy with the brigades. Clearly, the political terrain at the grass roots was very varied, with the alliance with the parents wavering in some areas and more schools entering the struggle in others. But overall the impression is one of a political effervescence of activity and organization, with marches and meetings, reports and debates, which could serve both to recruit new members and to politicize them through argument and analysis.[2]

The brigades were so good for the movement that there could never be enough of them. In fact, the main business of the state assembly of the Central Strike Committee of October 4, 1979, envisioned a reform of the committees, especially the brigade committee; only a few militants would remain on the Central Committee, while the great majority would join the brigades and so "raise the spirits of the comrades in struggle." The assembly agreed to maintain a skeletal staff to take care of press and radio, accounts, vigilance, external relations, political planning, and archives, and resolved to send "ALL THE REST TO THE BRIGADES." This was but one measure of the importance of the brigades, which, in the often lamented absence of a regular news sheet, were seen as essential to the consolidation of the movement.

---

2 One interesting variant on the standard brigade was the political theater that toured the state in the early days of the struggle under the direction of Rafael Arellanes, a militant of Línea Popular (see Chapter 6). The theater ridiculed *charrismo* and educated the teachers to the virtues of the movement. As the brigade committee reported in the state assembly of the Central Strike Committee on September 8, 1979: "one of the main tasks has been the theater tour of several delegations, such as Acalá, Carranza, Villa Corzo, Villaflores, Jiquipilas, Cintalapa and Tuxtla . . . the theater plays a most important part in our struggle."

## The making of the movement's leaders

At the beginning of the movement most of the teachers' leaders were about twenty-five years old, and some were as young as twenty-one or twenty-two. The really old ones were approaching thirty. Nowhere was the movement hampered by a lack of leadership cadres. Many potential leaders were lying latent in rural communities with a history of clandestine struggle against *caciquismo*, and they then emerged through the movement itself, having won the confidence of their comrades by their commitment to the collective struggle. The early ETAs movement in Chiapas insisted that the strike leaders must be fighters of "proven honesty" (*Chispa Sindical,* May 1978), and the Central Strike Committee of the main movement was led by regional leaders who had "risen from the very struggle itself" (*La Puya,* September 2, 1979). This native and popular leadership was evident everywhere, although it was most characteristic of the movements in Chiapas and Oaxaca, with their broad base of support and extensive leadership cadres.

But not all the leaders were the natural offspring of the movement itself, nor were they all native to the region. Many more were teachers who already knew each other from their schooling in the rural training schools or in the Advanced School of Mexico City, and had maintained contact through informal networks that only needed activating. These leaders had already had first- or secondhand experience of the students' movement or had learned their political lessons in other popular struggles. Indeed, in the opinion of the early leadership of the Chiapas movement itself, "the great majority of the leaders of the movement have had other experiences of struggle (student, popular, peasant, teacher, party, etc.) before coming to the teachers' movement, and so they all bring with them whatever they have learned" (Hernández Gómez et al. 1985).[3] In some cases they may also have brought a sense of themselves as "a vanguard for the rest of the workers" (*Chispa Sindical,* May 1978), and they may have held clear political objectives that they kept to themselves, either for fear of State reprisals or for fear of being misunderstood by a politically uneducated membership.[4]

3 A typical case is that of Teodoro Palomino, who has been a leading figure in the movement, first in the Valle de México and then at the national level. He was born to a large family of peasant origin in Colima, where his father worked as a postal employee and his mother as a rural teacher. With eight brothers besides himself to feed, he had to work as well as study, and then he decided to train as a teacher. In 1968 he left teacher training school in Jalisco for the Advanced School in Mexico City and arrived just a month before the massacre of Tlatelolco. He immediately joined the movement, and he has no doubt that it changed his life. Many leaders from the Advanced School went on to leadership positions in the movement, and some 80 percent of secondary school teachers in Mexico had attended the School's intensive courses.

4 The idea of a membership that is uneducated and can therefore be manipulated surfaces in the factional disputes within the movement (see Chapter 6). The ETAs' leaders accused militants of Línea Proletaria of having too much influence among the less politicized teachers, "despite their black record among the telephone workers, metal-workers of Monclova and peasants of Chiapas."

"Vanguardism" was evidently alien to the spirit of a movement that had the Revolutionary Vanguard as its principal enemy. But most popular struggles depend initially on "self-elected" leaders to promote some form of organization, and the teachers' movement was no exception. Without such leaders the Central Struggle Committee could not have become the modular form of organization for the movements of many different regions, but, equally, the success of these initiatives could never be guaranteed. Where sufficient support was lacking for a full-fledged central committee, the new leaders set up "campaign committees" to promote one (the cases of Tabasco and La Laguna among others); but this failed to mobilize the membership of Section IX of Mexico City (Valdez Vega 1986), and the incipient leadership in Morelos was exhausted by similar efforts. Equally, where the new leaders failed to found an alternative organization at the base (the cases of Michoacán and Nayarit), the movement was easily dismantled and defeated (Altamirano 1986). Thus, the vanguardism of the new leaders, if such it was, was effective in building organization only if they "recognized that permanent consultation with the membership is indispensable for any kind of sustained action" (Consejo Central de Lucha del Magisterio Hidalguense 1981).

The ambiguities of "self-elected" leaders seeking democratic credentials were most evident in Oaxaca, where mechanisms of basist democracy initially failed to supplant the official delegational committees, and the two coexisted uneasily in the Permanent Assembly of Delegational Secretaries. This parallelism reflected a clear division in the original leadership of the movement between young and radical leaders from the base, who sought a Central Struggle Committee as in Chiapas, and an older generation of delegational secretaries, who were used to working within the SNTE's bureaucracy. As the movement grew, so did the strains between the militants of the struggle committees (called coordinating committees), many of them ex-student leaders on the left, and the more cautious members of the delegational committees, who wished to keep the struggle within legal limits.[5]

---

5  These tensions were only resolved through the process of struggle itself. The coordinating committees had organized long and hard for the strike of May 1980, and in the second week of the strike the Permanent Assembly had voted to dismiss the sectional committee and set up its own executive committee, composed of representatives from the seven regional delegations of the state. This move both united the leadership and sparked an enormous upsurge of militancy, which first brought 20,000 teachers onto the streets of Oaxaca City on May 15, and then took 25,000 teachers to Mexico City at the beginning of June. The political impact of this unprecedented mobilization won Oaxaca a wage increase and a mixed executive committee to prepare for the congress that would ensure democratic representation for the first time; the extent of the victory tended to dissolve the tensions between leadership and base, and opened the way to further reform of the regional union structure.

## The changing shape of the movement: the congress of March 1981

The teachers of Chiapas had to take their struggle to Mexico City, where they "encamped" early in November 1980, before the SNTE agreed to their congress. Even then, the SNTE insisted on seven delegates to the Central Struggle Committee's six on the "mixed" commission that would oversee the arrangements, in an effort to retain the strategic initiative.[6] In the delegational assemblies that elected representatives to the congress, the SNTE's delegates and agents provocateurs from the Revolutionary Vanguard attempted to manipulate the meetings, either to disqualify the election or pack the slate with their own candidates; but the struggle committees held "pre-assemblies" where the real voting took place and so were able to outmaneuver the Vanguard. As the teachers were only too aware, they were in fact imitating Vanguard tactics in national congresses of the SNTE, and so were simply "taking a card from the *charro* pack." Moreover, although only 240 delegates were elected to the congress, each delegate was accompanied by two more militants to counter attempts at cooptation, and these militants swelled the number of teachers crowded into the "pre-congress." In three intense days of twenty hour debates that preceded the congress proper, the Revolutionary Vanguard secured only 12 delegates against 192 for the "democratic teachers," thus ensuring the election of the slate so arduously agreed during the "pre-congress."[7]

It was an historic victory and was the first time a sectional committee of the SNTE was elected against the wishes of its National Executive Committee. The victory came after more than eighteen months of mobilization and tactical inno-

6 The National Executive Committe of the SNTE argued that the union's statutes made it impossible to do differently (even though they had already done differently in Oaxaca). The Central Struggle Committee's delegates to the commission were Manuel Hernández, Amadeo Espinosa, Sergio Nijenda, Felipe Arrastro, Jésus Ordoñez, and Víctor Sánchez Bautista. The last named never attended the commission because of the political conflicts that were already beginning to emerge within the movement (see Chapter 6).

7 The slate was Manuel Hernández Gómez as Secretary-General, Sergio Nijenda Capito as Secretary of Organization, Amadeo Espinosa Ramos as Secretary of Primary School Conflicts, Naím Ferreira Gómez as Secretary of Post-Primary School Conflicts, Excel Díaz Palacios as Secretary of Finance, Atalia Serrano López as Secretary of Social Action, René López as Secretary of Social Security, Manolito Padilla Bollanos as Secretary of Loans, Ricardo Aguilar Gordillo as Secretary of External Relations, Mariano López Díaz as Secretary of Professional Issues, Librado Santiago Constantino as Secretary of Events, Felipe Arrastro López as Secretary of Housing, Julio Peralta Estevan as Secretary of Ideological Orientation, and Rafael Arellanes Caballero as Personal Secretary. Seven of these new leaders (six men and one woman) were graduates of the rural training schools, and two were representatives of the Indian teachers of the highlands. The latter had insisted in the March 1981 congress that they be allocated two posts on the committe, no matter which, to secure their professional integration into the union. They were awarded Social Security and Professional Issues.

vation. The turning point came with the mixed commission, where the leaders on the Central Struggle Committee cleverly conceded the majority, knowing they could still control the process at the grass roots, while insisting on the stipulation that the congress be held within ninety days. As a result they now had control of the sectional committee and so could begin to address union issues, which now became primary. In effect, with the achievement of legal representation it was the delegational assemblies, the regional coordinating committees, and, of course, the state assembly that formed the backbone of the new organization, while the Central Struggle Committee itself fell into disuse. Militants from the base still maintained "vigilance" over their delegates, but the extralegal organizations themselves seemed less necessary. On the other hand, it was only after the victory of March 1981 that the Chiapas movement could act as the nucleus of the CNTE, and so promote an effective but extralegal political organization at the national level (see Chapter 7).[8]

At first sight, the leadership of the first "democratic" sectional committee seemed to have captured the real needs and aspirations of the membership. The focus was on the practical problems of the workplace and the community, and under the direction of Manuel Hernández the committee secured the *capacidad de gestión* to get conditions improved and problems solved. Just as this leadership had compromised to win the congress, so it compromised to solve problems, and it was especially careful to avoid major disputes with loyalists of the Revolutionary Vanguard. In doing so the leadership always said it was simply defending the demands of the membership, which had total autonomy in defining the political strategy of the movement, but others suggested that this softly-softly approach was crafted to suit more particular and even personal objectives (Salinas Alvarez and Imaz Gispert 1984). The details of these factional debates will be subject to close scrutiny in Chapter 6. Here it is sufficient to note that the debates often reflected organizational ambiguities, especially those inscribed in the continuing but subterranean relationship between the Central Struggle Committee and the sectional committee.

Control of the sectional committee implied an organizational transition from extralegal to legal forms of struggle. Before March 1981 the Central Struggle Committee had called meetings, conducted negotiations, run the brigades, and directed the movement overall. In effect, it had become an alternative sectional committee, backed up by struggle committees throughout the state. After March 1981 the Central Struggle Committee was subsumed within the new sectional committee, which could now defend the same demands by legal means. But confusion remained between a Central Struggle Committee that was never formally disbanded and a sectional committee that took on some but

---

8  Although the CNTE had been constituted by the December 1979 meeting in Tuxtla Gutiérrez (Chiapas), it was only after the Chiapas victory that it began to fulfill its promise as a real coordinating committee of teachers' movements across the country.

not all of the Struggle Committee's tasks. The "vigilance committees" went on meeting, but this led to problems of dual leadership at the delegational level; and as local activists were gradually neglected, the movement began to lose impetus at the grass roots.

Although the sectional committee was now the executive of the movement, the representative role of the Central Struggle Committee continued in the state assembly, which still represented the mass membership and which, in parliamentary fashion, could propose programs of action that were then approved, modified, or rejected by the base. But the assembly was also designed to play the part of a Struggle Committee in political campaigns, and its coordinating committees were not so much administrative branches of the movement as platforms for systematizing and presenting demands and strategies. Moreover, at moments of intense mobilization (work stoppage, strike, encampment, congress) the assembly would meet in permanent session to coordinate the struggle and advise the sectional committee. In this way, the Central Struggle Committee was not so much abolished as given new form in the assembly, which not only reflected all political opinions but also decided the political direction of the movement. Hence, it might appear that the assembly had resolved the problems of operationalizing the new phase of the struggle by a successful blend of basist democracy with central direction.

But it was not to be. The state assembly was to decide the political direction of the movement, but it proved an entirely inappropriate forum for such a task and the division of executive responsibility between the extralegal assembly and the sectional committee remained unclear. Hence, the movement's axiom of "ideological struggle and political unity" (see Chapter 5) finally went unrealized because the organizational basis for this unity was lacking. On the contrary, as the movement advanced, the institutional form of the assembly seemed to encourage internal political disputes. And it was not only political convictions that were in contention. With the victory of March 1981 and the move from "opposition" to "situation," the movement came to command real resources, which clearly exacerbated the fight for political and often personal power. Thus the story of successful union organization is also a story of increasing factionalism (see Chapter 6), and the movement began to lose the cohesion it required to face the Revolutionary Vanguard.

## The shift from unity to division: the congress of March 1984

If some of the criticisms of the original leadership of the movement were to be believed, the state assembly had become a mere appendage of the sectional committee and therefore was subject to a kind of bureaucratic control resembling *charrismo* (*Chispa Sindical*, February 1984). If this "basist" critique were true, the congress of March 1984 was an opportunity to change the style of leadership; but even were it not, the massive increase in the size of the congress to over a thousand delegates in all (five from each delegation) had now made it much more difficult to manipulate. At the same time the sectional committee itself was reformed and amplified until it contained some sixty political posts, which were divided among four major commissions (politics, labor relations, social services, and finance) and their various subcommissions. The reform sought to make the sectional committee more responsive to the membership, but it also made it broader and more accountable, with all of its officers subject to recall, and consequently more difficult to dominate politically.

These changes in the character of the congress made it almost unmanageable. The debate in the "pre-congress" lasted twenty-eight hours without interruption, and the election itself took a further twelve. Before anything else the 800 or so delegates had to decide whether to implement the SNTE's principle of "no-reelection" or to accept all candidates. The two-to-one vote for an open field only served to sharpen the competition between rival groups that maneuvered to secure their position in a complex process of political alliance and realignment. The result was a plural sectional committee, with twenty secretaries, where no single political group could command a majority or establish effective control. And to the degree that the sectional committee's political colors became more confused, it became less capable of directing the movement. Indeed, with the rival groups finely balanced the committee itself became increasingly unstable, not least because the tensions between them caused several members to resign. But the root of the problem was not so much the competition between different political tendencies, which is endemic to every popular movement, as the organizational ambiguity of the sectional committee, which combined, or failed to combine, executive and "representative" roles in a way that made it neither beast nor fowl.

Once the disputes within the sectional committee reached the membership, they changed the political content of the movement. No longer the simple expression of the social and economic needs of the teachers, it was now increasingly defined by internal confrontation and intrigue. Ironically, although this change led to a loss of confidence in the leadership, it had been caused in part by the organizations constructed to guarantee the operation of basist democracy. It was in the name of such democracy that some tendencies had affirmed the state assembly's preeminence and insisted that the composition of the new sectional committee should faithfully reflect the balance of forces within the assembly (*Chispa Sindical*, March 1984). But the assembly was quite unsuited for an executive role, and the more plural composition of the sectional committee only led it to pull apart. Broadly speaking, it became clear that even though basism was attractive in principle, it was difficult to implement in practice. It became doubtful too whether democratic consultation was always effective: Possibly it was too easy to silence dissident voices with the charge of *charro* or simply to allege that the base was too backward to hold coherent political views. As a consequence, many teachers were disappointed by the changes and shocked by the bitterness of the disputes. The original innocence was lost, but they went on learning the only way possible, by experience and practice. And with the learning came the confidence to choose their own way forward.

## The base defines its own direction

The leadership of the movement became increasingly fragmented and ineffective during the last months of 1984. The details of the disputes will be examined in subsequent chapters, but the growing disarray was clearly demonstrated on the day when two separate groups of teachers with distinct agendas arrived simultaneously at the governor's palace. In such circumstances it proved impossible for the movement to coordinate its struggles, which became increasingly local and isolated, and hence more easily suppressed. In the meantime, the secretary-general of the recently elected sectional committee (José Domingo Guillén) was pressing the different tendencies to present clear platforms and plans of action so that the members themselves might then decide the direction of the movement.

In effect, it was the membership within the delegational assemblies that decided on the strike of 1985. While the leadership remained preoccupied with its own internal divisions, the teachers at the grass roots continued to suffer from poor pay, late payment of wages, and the general offensive of the SNTE's José Luis Andrade Ibarra, who was intent on building a bridgehead for a *charro* counterattack. During the strike, the memberships of the two Chiapas sections, VII and XL, worked in solidarity, but their leaderships remained out of step. Disputes in the state assembly of Section VII meant that logistic decisions could only be taken by continual consultation with the membership, leaving the movement with no executive control over the conduct of the struggle. As a consequence the leadership was also incapable of agreeing on joint political action with the National Coordinating Committee and was severely criticized for confining the struggle to purely local, union, sectional, and even sectarian issues (Corriente Democrática Magisterial 1985). But the membership stayed solid, and when the Ministry of Education offered fat bribes to teachers who would break ranks, only two or three hundred throughout the state took the bait.

Following the strike the factional divisions only got worse, so that by October of 1985 the movement had regressed into uneven and uncoordinated local struggles. The state government and the Ministry of Education seized this opportunity to launch their assault, with the intention of finishing the movement once and for all. But the teachers at the grass roots mobilized in their own defense, with the firm support of the peasant communities and parents. Their leaders could not help them, and the different political tendencies within the leadership had anyway been rejected. In the "pre-assembly" of October 1985, which met to prepare the section's report to the National Executive Committee of the SNTE, the delegates insisted that the first priority was to repair the damage to the sectional committee; they then took the exceptional step of forbidding any committee member to speak during the debate. By this time an increasingly combative base had clearly overtaken the leadership in their appreciation of the urgent need for political unity.[9]

## The search for political unity and the strike of 1987

The teachers had to find a way to reform their leadership. In October 1986, some 15,000 teachers gathered to denounce the government's repression, and in the speeches there was considerable unity on the question of unity. An even larger meeting at the end of November demanded freedom for the prisoners of Cerro Hueco (see footnote 9) and a democratic congress. The authorities promised concessions, but they did so in bad faith. The sectional congress scheduled for March 1986 was long overdue; the Ministry of Education's delegate, Filiberto Guzmán, had conspired with the Vanguard's special envoy, José Luis Andrade Ibarra,[10] to step up the pressure by provoking conflicts throughout the union; and the Ministry, Vanguard, and state government together were preparing for a final confrontation. The teachers for their part were demoralized and desperate. Wages were not being paid and jobs were on the line. So the strike call for February 19 was a last throw of the dice. They could go down, or they could go down fighting.[11] Their internal disputes were put aside long enough for strike commissions to form, but they did not foresee a long strike. One way or the other, it would all be over within fifteen days.

In the event, nearly all the teachers supported the strike, which continued for many weeks, but their support began to waver with the approach of the Easter vacation. The Assembly, which had been in permanent session during the strike, was split once again; and the strike vote anyway became entangled with the election of a new sectional committee, which in turn entailed a further vote on the principle of "no-reelection." This time the principle was upheld in a clear rebuff to the leadership, while the vote to continue the strike reflected

9 During the offensive of the state government Manuel Hernández and his lieutenants had been thrown into the prison of Cerro Hueco (Tuxtla Gutiérrez) alongside some of the peasant movement's leaders. Mass protests followed, but even this shock seemed insufficient to persuade the leadership to resolve its differences (see Chapter 6).

10 José Luis Andrade Ibarra was the ex-secretary-general of the National Executive Committee of the SNTE. His credentials for the job included his dismantling and repression of the democratic teachers' movement in Chihuahua in the mid-1970s, and he was sent to Chiapas in the early 1980s to repeat the performance. The Chiapas teachers had mobilized to oust him some three years previously, but although he had been "dismissed" he had never actually left and had continued to plot the defeat of their movement.

11 While this judgment (which I heard from many teachers) may seem slightly melodramatic, this has often been the only choice left to popular movements once the Mexican government has become determined to defeat them. Examples include the democratic tendencies of the SUTERM and the SUTIN, and the movement within the Advanced School of Mexico City.

the combativeness of the base. But this was pure bravura, for by now there was no avoiding the imposition of a sectional committee controlled by the Vanguard. The long-expected *coup de grâce* came on March 9, 1987, when the National Executive Committee of the SNTE finally dismissed the democratic sectional committee.[12]

On April 21, 1987, the teachers of Chiapas accepted the so-called Equal Executive Commission *(Comisión Ejecutiva Paritaria)* as the lesser of two evils. To reject it was to discard the option of recuperating legal control through a future congress. The commission was headed by a Vanguard delegate, which gave the Vanguard a permanent majority;[13] with one exception, the teachers elected to the "democratic half" of the commission were all untried, which was a further reflection of the strategic failures that followed the divisions. The combativeness of the base, which was evident throughout the strike, could find no expression in a leadership lacking in political vision. Some leaders were singled out for special opprobrium, but all the leaders seemed equally guilty of forgetting the grand aims of the movement. Indeed, many teachers refused to recognize the new commission, rejecting *charros* and democrats alike, which was a sure sign of the widening gulf between the teachers and their leaders. It was not that a more radical base wanted to pursue the struggle whereas its more moderate leaders sought negotiation. The underlying reason for the growing gap was the membership's continuing concern with union issues when the leadership had become so embroiled in political debate that it negotiated badly and cheaply. The irony of this political debacle was that the original political motive for the movement lay precisely in the separation between grass-roots members and *charro* leaders within the SNTE itself.

The length of the strike of 1987 had exhausted all the movement's militants economically and emotionally. But more dangerous was the confusion caused at the grass roots of the movement by the political divisions in the leadership. The ideological debates, even the political competition, could be interpreted as positive for the political education of the movement (see Chapter 6), but only so long as they did not destroy its political unity or the broad base of its support. For most teachers the political differences between their leaders were still irrelevant to their immediate concerns. After the debacle many more "basist" leaders turned away from the internal disputes within the political apparatus of the movement and returned to grass-roots political organization and education, in the recognition that most teachers were more motivated by immediate syndical gains than by longer-term political goals. But the choice was not quite this sim-

---

12 This decision was pushed through a special meeting by the "maximum leader" Carlos Jonguitud Barrios himself, with the fervent support of former secretary-general José Luis Andrade Ibarra and future secretary-general Elba Esther Gordillo Morales.

13 It was left to the Ministry of Education to make a small conciliatory gesture by dismissing Filiberto Gamboa Guzmán, an ambitious opportunist who aspired to be governor of Chiapas. He had enjoyed the unconditional support of the governor at the time, Absalón Castellanos, but he appears to have received his marching orders directly from the Minister of the Interior, Barlett Díaz.

ple (and never had been). Without legal representation on the sectional committee it was likely that the struggle would regress to separate sectors and local-
ities, where it could more easily be contained and repressed. At the very least,
therefore, the continuing struggle for the control of the committee was a necessary evil. The priority task in late spring of 1987 in Chiapas was to revive the
struggle committees in the delegations and reconstruct the Central Struggle
Committee.

5

# Strategic choices

The teachers' movement of Chiapas not only pioneered new forms of organization but also crafted unusual political strategies (Reyes 1980). The leaders of the ETAs movement (see Chapter 2) insisted that its success was a result of its "method of mobilization," which was "the only correct method of struggle" (*Chispa Sindical*, October 1983). Above all, there was "no trusting the famous DIALOGUE, which only serves to slow movements down," and they lamented that the first Central Strike Committee of June 1979 had "opted for negotiation" (*Chispa Sindical*, June 1979). But in retrospect, it is clear that the teachers were correct to resist the siren calls of the "ultraleft" and so avoid an "all or nothing" confrontation. Instead they mobilized the base while simultaneously carrying on negotiations, in a combination that the Línea Proletaria tendency graphically described as "war in Vietnam, negotiations in Paris" (Arellanes Caballero, Constantino, and Peralta Esteva 1985). Without mobilization there would be no negotiation,[1] but exclusive use of this "method" would invite defeat. By combining the two, the teachers could pursue an overall strategy of "partial advances" and tactical retreats.[2]

Many of the teachers' leaders came from the radical rural training schools and had later joined in the violent struggles of the Advanced School in Mexico City. Some of them had taken part in the guerrilla wars of the early 1970s. If the movements had arisen two or three years earlier, they might never have sought negotiation and the movement itself might never have prospered. But they had learned from their failures and now favored a more flexible approach, which the Chiapas delegation defended in the National Conference of the CNTE in September 1980. Rather than seek immediate syndical control through a national strike, or tie the movement to the political goals of a national political party, the Chiapas movement recommended gradual and regional

---

1 Without mobilization, one teacher explained, the *charros* simply say "Fine, they've stopped making a fuss, there's no problem, so damn negotiation, we don't have to give them a thing"(*"Bueno ya dejaron de patalear y ya no hay bronca, ni madres de negociación, no les damos nada"*).

2 Or as the teachers' marching chant has it, *"Ya venimos, ya nos vamos, pero pronto regresamos"* (Now we're here and soon we're gone, but we're sure to be back soon").

75

advance through a combination of mobilization and negotiation with federal authorities.

Negotiation might entail seeking at least temporary alliances with what the teachers called "the apparatus," and this could not go uncontested because of the "hundreds of syndical representatives who in conversation with the authorities or the *charros* had come to betray the movements" (CNTE 1982). All negotiations therefore had to be mandated by the base in order to avoid individual approaches that "might distort the principles of the movement" (Sección XXII 1985). It was the fear of such distortion that fueled the criticisms of the leadership's relations with the state government in the early days of the movement in Chiapas. It was correct to take advantage of openings created by institutional divisions within "the apparatus," so long as this remained a mere tactic and so long as the approach to government apparatchiks did not come to define the interests or constrain the strategic range of the movement. The internal democratic mechanisms of the movement made it unlikely that the membership could be manipulated into any kind of agreement without consultation, but there was a risk that the *strategic* potential of mobilization might be sacrificed to mere *tactical* advantage.

In any popular movement it is difficult to disentagle the strategic debates from the political rivalries that are both their cause and consequence. In Chiapas the initial debate polarized between the Trotskyists, who had been blooded in the early mobilization of the ETAs movement, and the more moderate militants of Línea Proletaria, who controlled the first sectional committee (see Chapter 6).[3] But at the bottom of their differences lay a basic strategic divide. The Trotskyists suspected negotiation to be collaboration; they saw Línea Proletaria as negotiating behind the backs of the base, and even participating in the Labor Congress, which was "the headquarters of *charrismo*." Línea Proletaria, on the other hand, openly sought alliances with the Labor Congress, the public sector unions (FSTSE), and even the peasant sector of the ruling party (CNC), because these were the places where working people were organized. The political point of combining mobilization with negotiation was to resolve such differences. But it was hard to get the balance right, and the issue was clearly cross-cut by the question of leadership accountability (see Chapter 4).[4]

At the same time strategy must be sensitive to the prevailing political situation, which was originally quite favorable to the movement. The Chiapas politics of the time was punctuated by the persistent rivalry between the cliques of

3  The Trotskyists claimed that Línea Proletaria's conciliatory stance had led the movement into stagnation; Línea Proletaria replied that the Trotskyists' strident calls for basist democracy would provoke needless confrontations.

4  At one point the secretary-general of the first democratic sectional committee, Manuel Hernández, split temporarily from Línea Proletaria to try to recover his democratic credentials and demonstrate his belief that in matters of strategy, and especially in relations with the government, it was the base that must decide.

Governor Salomón Blanco and Federal Deputy Juan Sabines Gutiérrez, and Sabines came to replace Blanco as a reward for his success in promoting an agreement between the SNTE and the striking teachers. Sabines himself belonged to the political group of Edgar Robledo Santiago, a native of Chiapas who had been secretary-general of the SNTE in the 1960s[5] and who was now Sabines's minister of education. In short, Robledo was a loyalist of the SNTE leadership that had been ousted by Jonguitud's Revolutionary Vanguard, and in any case Governor Sabines did not welcome interference from other governors, least of all the governor of San Luis Potosí, Jonguitud Barrios. As a result the state government actually encouraged the movement among the federal teachers (assuring its own state teachers that it would match whatever gains the federal teachers won) and guaranteed their right to peaceful protest (*El Heraldo*, January 19, 1980).

In these circumstances it made perfect sense for the movement's leadership to cultivate good relations with the state government. Moreover, the political opening at the state level was reinforced at the federal level, where Minister of the Interior Olivares Santana also belonged to the Robledo group. Hence, the embryonic movement found ample space to grow, and even when the state government's attitudes began to harden,[6] it continued to give succor to the teachers, or, more precisely, to the leadership of Línea Proletaria. And there was the rub, for this left the Trotskyist leaders of the ETAs on the outside, where they liked it less and less. In this way the same circumstances that favored the movement also catalyzed the political disputes within it, which (as I will show in Chapter 6) then took on their own impetus.[7]

## The decision to struggle inside the SNTE

It was a long-running debate, almost as old as the teachers' struggle itself: whether to fight *charrismo* from inside the SNTE or form an independent union and fight in the open. It split the Revolutionary Teacher's Movement (MRM)

---

5 Edgar Robledo Santiago was born in 1917 in Motozintla, Chiapas. After his stint as secretary-general of the SNTE he went on to become secretary-general of the FSTSE, taking up this post in March 1968, the same month that Carlos Jonguitud Barrios became Secretary of Labor and Conflicts of the National Executive Committee of the SNTE.

6 The state government turned against the Emiliano Zapata Peasant Organization (OCEZ) in Venustiano Carranza, the Emiliano Zapata Committee for Popular Struggle (CLPEZ) on the coast, the Revolutionary Peasant Alliance (ACR), and the Indepentend Union of Agricultural Workers and Peasants (CIOAC) in Simojovel.

7 Again in 1985, in a replay of the original disputes, Manuel Hernández of Línea Proletaria was criticized for his connections with Eduardo Robledo Rincón, the nephew of Robledo Santiago and candidate for federal deputy, and was accused of diverting the movement to support the candidacy and so advance the covert objectives of Línea Proletaria. The accusation lacks plausibility and probably reflects the kind of paranoia so often prevalent in popular organizations that are only too aware of the permanent dangers of cooptation and manipulation.

in 1963 (see Chapter 3), it influenced the course of the battle for control of the Advanced School of Mexico City, and it was still a potential source of discord when the teachers' movement began. In fact, the teachers had very little choice. Clause B of Article 123 of the Mexican Constitution, which governs the association of federal employees, makes it very clear that only one union may exist in each government sector and that, in the event of competition, the majority union will receive legal recognition. In their different ways all the minority struggles of the 1960s and 1970s were conditioned by this constraint. Thus, however radical the rhetoric in the Advanced School or among the ETAs, the teachers still fought to combat *charrismo* from the inside: The ETAs' leaders were successful in converting SNTE officials to their demands without any attempt at parallel unionism, just as delegational pressure on the sectional committee during the first strike of 1979 led to an unprecedented official strike call, which also bore the imprimatur of the National Executive Committee of the SNTE (see Chapter 2). In sum, the teachers discovered their own forms of organization without contemplating parallel unionism.

Nonetheless, the very success of these *sui generis* forms of organization posed an acute strategic problem. The Central Struggle Committee of the teachers' movement of 1979 had won a measure of *de facto* official recognition. But if its increasing strength quite obliterated the sectional committee, there was a real danger that the National Executive Committee might simply dismiss it, thus cutting off Chiapas from the national union. It was to prevent such an outcome that the state assembly voted to send a commission to Mexico City for an interview with the National Committee.[8] On the following day (the Revolutionary Vanguard's "birthday" of September 22) the teachers declared that "in no way did the movement threaten the unity of the union" and called on the SNTE's José Luis Andrade Ibarra to support the movement, and not "the incapacity of the sectional leader Jorge Paniagua Zenteño." In this way the movement renounced parallelism and was careful to avoid any public denial of the statutory status of the sectional committee (Consejo Central de Huelga del Magisterio Chiapaneco *Actas*, October 2, 1979).

But in the founding meeting of the CNTE in December 1979, some organizations continued to press for independent unionism. Faced with an invidious choice between legal but dependent and independent but illegal unionism, the Central Struggle Committee of Chiapas chose neither, or perhaps both, in opting to continue inside the SNTE by combining legal and extralegal struggle. The meeting finally accepted the pragmatic argument that independent unionism had repeatedly proved vulnerable to State strategies, and the Struggle Committee mixed pragmatism and principle in explaining the choice to its own

---

8 The commission asked the two MRM members on the National Executive Committee (Ivan García Solis and César Nuñez Ramos) to try to arrange the interview.

members: They comprised only a tiny minority of the national membership, and to leave the SNTE would therefore be political suicide; their "mini-union" would inevitably be absorbed by the SNTE's "maxi-union," and it would anyway be a narrowly sectarian move that sought to secure their own interests while forgetting the "great mass of workers controlled by the Vanguard." Hence, "the democratic path implies striving to rescue our union" (*La Puya*, February 1980).

The teachers' leaders drew piecemeal on their own experiences in the rural training schools and on their sometimes imperfect sense of the popular struggles of the 1970s. They knew that the many self-styled radical organizations had a rather rarified notion of political struggle and lacked real support at the grass roots,[9] so their response was above all practical. Because they needed the union to get their demands met, their main strategy was to work to control it from the base up, using all its assemblies and committees, and deploying all available forms of mobilization (III Foro de la CNTE, Mexico DF, April 1981). Even the ETAs' leaders concurred in making control of the sectional committee a priority objective (*Chispa Sindical*, May 1980). But the resistance of the Vanguard meant that institutional advance would only come through continual mobilization, and the ensuing frustration provoked some regional movements to convoke mass congresses and elect committees, despite the lack of official recognition (see Chapter 7).[10]

It was in this way that economic demands served as a springboard for a political struggle that focused on the capture of the sectional committee as the most effective means of getting these demands met (and as the first step in achieving a more democratic union that would also defend professional rights). And the Central Struggle Committee of Chiapas also advocated a national strategy for the progressive conquest of sectional committees (II Foro de la CNTE, February 16–17, 1980). Economic demands were acceptable: They did not inspire automatic hostility in the SNTE or the Ministry of Education, nor did they frighten teachers who still balked at the idea of political struggle.[11] Hence, there was a

---

9 As the leaders imprisoned in Cerro Hueco put it: "Our opinion is that the problem of the left in Mexico is basically an organizational problem. What use are parties with very populist or radical names (*nombres muy chingones*), like Revolutionary Movement of who knows what, if, at the end of the day, their platforms do not respond to the reality which the workers are living?"

10 In Hidalgo the first mass congress elected one such committee in December 1980, which the SNTE refused to recognize in the agreement of February 1981. Instead, an extra five posts on the sectional committee were offered to delegates from the congress. This gave the movement a foothold on the sectional committee, which was a "partial advance," but the agreement was mainly accepted in order to stop the repression and so preserve the movement.

11 The main demand of the first phase was for a 100 percent increase in the bonus, but henceforth the movement imitated the practice of the Revolutionary Vanguard by never specifying wage claims but always demanding "a substantial increase." In this way the movement was less likely to be demoralized by obvious defeats, and economic demands could continue as a channel to political goals. Nonetheless,

broad consensus among the leadership that the translation of economic
demands into political demands was the best way forward. But political
advance within the union cóuld only be a negotiated outcome, and the consensus broke once the movement had to pay the costs of this strategy. For in return
for official permission to hold its first democratic congress the Central Struggle
Committee of Chiapas (on the Mixed Commission) had to make public its
pledge to "honor the legal status of the National Executive Committee of the
SNTE and its secretary-general Ramón Martínez Martín, and support it in all
its actions in benefit of our members." Some groups, especially the Trotskyists
of the ETAs, damned this pledge as a "betrayal of the base" (*Chispa Sindical*,
April 1981), but, in retrospect, it seems clear that the movement gained more
from the fact of its first democratic committee than it lost from a tactical and
testimonial concession.[12]

## Combining legal and extralegal struggle on separate fronts

This combination was inscribed in the very origins of the movement of Chiapas,
where the teachers always tried to persuade their official representatives to take
up their demands, before bypassing or dismissing them if they proved recalcitrant. Similarly, the struggle committees were sometimes composed of militants
from the base alongside the legal secretary-general of the delegational committee. But "walking with both feet" was not always this easy. The imposition of
a Mixed Commission by the SNTE at the end of 1979 presented the teachers
with a complex choice. By accepting the Commission they could work for a
democratic congress from the inside, as well as dealing with many of their members' syndical demands; but compliance would automatically postpone the congress, legitimate a nondemocratic committee, demobilize the membership, and
hand the strategic initiative to the National Executive Committee. In the event,
they joined the Commission to show their commitment to legal channels, and
because the conquest of the sectional committee took strategic priority over
mobilization around national demands. Hence, they avoided confrontation

some teachers remained critical of a strategy that inevitably led to a political struggle for control of the
union: "this is a power question, these are different motives, this is political ambition, you are already
into another game, these aren't the demands which gave birth to the movement, which are mainly
economic."

12  The leadership of the CNTE became increasingly aware, moreover, of the dangers implicit in the primacy
of political over syndical struggle, and especially the dangers of "playing the State's game." It recommended that the conduct of the political struggle always depart from unifying demands at the base
(Asamblea Nacional, Teotihuacán, February 14–15, 1982). On the other hand, where economic
demands were temporarily assuaged by tactical wage concessions, then it was political demands that could
maintain the movement's impetus. In Morelos in 1980 the teachers wondered, "well we've got our wage
rise, and now what?" The answer was the occupation of the SNTE headquarters in June in support of
their political demands for a democratic congress.

with the *charros* and simply used the Commission to confirm their political leadership; by combining extralegal "pre-assemblies" with the legal assemblies convened by the delegates from the National Committee they achieved their democratic committee.[13]

The failure of the strike of 1987 and the renewed imposition of a sectional committee by the Vanguard led some teachers to doubt the substance of the strategy. The Trotskyists charged that the real combination was one of legalism and spontaneity. The movement had been defeated at the negotiating table, so there was little point in struggling for a democratic committee within an organization under *charro* control. But 1987 was not the first time that an executive committee had been dismissed and a new one imposed,[14] and the overall strategy anyway envisaged a long process of partial advances and occasional retreats, where nothing was ever lost or won definitively. "Power was always in play" (Arellanes Caballero, Constantino, and Peralta Esteva 1985).

The variable fortunes of this struggle were conditioned by the laws and institutions that composed its "political terrain," which was the metaphor used by the teachers themselves. Although this terrain was certainly constructed by the State, the teachers did not see this State as monolithic, but, on the contrary, sought strategic opportunities offered by openings within and contradictions between State institutions. The objective was to focus the struggle in specific places and on specific institutions, so as not to invite an overwhelming attack. In particular, the teachers knew their three main antagonists to be the *charrismo* of the SNTE, the Ministry of Education, and (depending on the conjuncture) the repressive apparatuses of state or federal governments; and it was strategically important to keep them separate in the struggle because the balance of forces never favored simultaneous confrontation with all three. For this reason the teachers even restrained their language to avoid provoking general hostility in their potential enemies: They were not against the governor or government, they simply sought a solution to this or that particular problem; they knew the need for "national security," which they expressed in their concern for education; and they always invoked Zapata, not Castro. Above all, they rigorously eschewed the tired incantations of the political left and avoided all reference to "the repressive bourgeois State," "the corrupt government," "the authoritarian regime," or "the decadent capitalist system."[15]

---

13 By doing so the Chiapas teachers blazed a trail for teachers nationwide (see Chapter 7). The National Assembly of the CNTE of January 16–17, 1982, in Acapulco set the formal objective of a statutory transformation of the SNTE, which meant legalizing the results of each stage of the struggle (Salinas Avlarez and Imaz Gispert 1984).

14 Nonetheless, whereas in 1980 a congress had finally been promised within ninety days, in 1987 it was only promised for "when the conditions are right."

15 In this connection an early meeting of the Central Strike Committee in Chiapas recommended that no mention be made of the Tlatelolco massacre during the march on October 2, 1979 (this being the day of its anniversary).

Right from the beginning the teachers were largely successful in separating their "fronts of struggle." When the teachers of Chiapas occupied the head-quarters of the Ministry of Education late in 1979 to protest its "administrative repression," they were careful to avoid confrontation with the Revolutionary Vanguard at the same time; the teachers of the highlands, on the other hand, always sent commissions to support the struggle against the Vanguard and never actually abandoned their schools, thus denying the Ministry any motive to intervene. Later on, as during the strike of 1985, the teachers adopted a policy of modular negotiation, whereby they sought more effective services from the public sector confederation (FSTSE), took their wage demands to the state government (without ignoring other appropriate institutions), and tried to resolve their professional problems with the Ministry of Education and other departments of the state and federal governments. The immediate point of deploying this range of negotiating tactics was to prevent any attack by the Revolutionary Vanguard, which was the movement's main adversary at the time. The overall success of this strategy in the initial years meant that the movement's survival was never threatened, which left ample margin for the rival factions within the movement to pursue their own political goals (see Chapter 6); but when in 1987 the fronts were not kept separate, the movement was in immediate danger.

Before this occurred the movement had tried to systematize its strategic objectives, which were reorganized around five main axes during the division of the sectional committee into different commissions in March 1984 (see Chapter 4). Broadly speaking, it was decided to struggle, first, for the economic demands of the teachers, including social services; second, for their professional rights; third, for more participation in education itself by encouraging more interaction between teachers and parents, and emphasizing community work; fourth, for programs that might respond better to the real educational needs of the people; and finally, for deeper union democracy within the state and across the country through the CNTE. Simple as these objectives may seem, they raised heated debate over the political and social role of the teacher. On the one hand, professional rights could be attained only through political qualification (which meant political work in school and delegational assemblies) (see Chapter 3); on the other, the deeper commitment to the community was integral to the local level alliance strategy, and hence to the overall trajectory of the movement, for it was the local alliances that provoked the harshest response from the government.

## The strategy of local alliances

The strategy of alliances with other sectors within the state was debated in open state assembly. It was once more a question of whether the teachers' struggle was narrowly syndical or more broadly political. And this was not simply a matter of strategic principle but one of strategic necessity. Once it became obvious that the State was squeezing the political margin of maneuver the movement had enjoyed in the first years, it was clear that principled autonomy within the corporative boundaries of the State had to give way to a search for alliances that might alter the balance of forces in the movement's favor. But stating a strategic need for alliances was not the same as achieving them, and the Assembly also debated the operational options for linking up with the "people," especially the peasants of Chiapas. However, there was little point in abstract inquiries into what was politically correct when the real process was advancing piecemeal at the grass roots. And since the struggle of Mactumatzá (see Chapter 3) there was no doubt in the strategic value of a cautious and differentiated approach to alliances, which might escape or diffuse repression by the State. Thus, the strategy sought to build links at the local level while postponing any attempt at broader organization, and these links were seen to foster the long-term political learning that might make such organization more possible.

The key to the teachers' links with local society was the parents, and the great majority of the parents lived in peasant communities (see Chapter 1). The parents had lent solid support to the teachers' movement during its different mobilizations, but now they began to ask for support in return, and to this extent the alliance process was demand led. On the teachers' side it was also pushed by Manuel Hernández's group of "populists," whose activism had put them in contact with about three-quarters of the communities of the state.[16] Hence, by the beginning of 1985 the teachers were organizing extensively at the grass roots, but among the many initiatives, three particular struggles stand out. The Indian communities of the highlands mobilized to defend their forest patrimony from speculatory logging and succeeded in (sometimes literally) stopping the trucks; the coffee workers organized to demand better prices than were paid by either the speculators *(coyotes)* or the corrupt state government, and appealed to the teachers to join their protests and advise on new marketing mechanisms;[17] and finally the maize growers of the Fraylesca region refused the low "guarantee prices" for their product in a series of protests that led to violent confrontations with the government, and to the imprisonment of Manuel Hernández and the "populist" leaders.

The maize growers of La Fraylesca were under increasing pressure to pay back a loan from the local rural credit bank, but at the prices on offer from the government marketing agency (CONASUPO) they could not come close. Pro-

---

16 For this reason they were also called the *talacheros* or "hard grafters," who worked all hours of all days of the week among the farthest-flung communities. These were the real grass-root activists.

17 Thousands of teachers and peasants gathered in the capital to protest the speculatory price manipulation of the government's "financial consultant," Jorge Martínez Rosillo, but were violently dispersed on the orders of Governor Absalón Castellanos. The teachers then advised withdrawal from the government scheme, and the coffee growers succeeded in setting up their own marketing arrangements despite police repression, arrests, and the refusal of further government credit.

tests had already erupted in several other states, and in Chiapas the low prices
were aggravated by late payment and the arrogant attitude of CONASUPO
staff. The teachers were already working with peasant movements in neighboring areas, but they had hesitated before entering La Fraylesca, where the pro-
ducers were organized by the ruling party's National Peasant Confederation
(CNC) in the person of Germán Jimenez, a *cacique* of the old school. Jimenez,
however, now needed the kind of backing that might bolster a failing political
career, and Manuel Hernández was eager to join forces with one of the major
peasant organizations in the state. The spectacular results of this rather unholy
alliance included a mass protest, which cut the Panamerican Highway, and the
arrest of Jimenez and Hernández, who, with several other "populist" leaders,
were to spend more than two years behind bars.[18]

Like most other popular movements of the time, the teachers' movement
was highly suspicious of all political parties on the grounds that their platforms
and agendas were likely to distort the goals of the movement. The National
Coordinating Committee (CNTE) repeatedly pronounced against affiliation
with political parties and against any part in electoral politics, the movement in
neighboring Oaxaca resisted any vitiating alliance with political parties so
fiercely that in its early years it had even rejected formal links with the CNTE,
and in Chiapas a majority of teachers had refused to join the national "civic
stoppages" *(paros cívicos nacionales)* of the early 1980s because of the participation of political parties. Little wonder, then, that the "populists" were criticized for forging an alliance with a creature of the ruling party. But Manuel
Hernández, speaking from behind the bars of Cerro Hueco, was clear that the
Fraylesca alliance had served the strategic objectives of the movement without
threatening its autonomy. It was not local level alliances, even with the peasant
sector of the ruling party, that endangered the movement, but rather the internal disputes to which they unjustly gave rise.

## Ideological struggle and political unity

It will become increasingly clear (in Chapter 6) that the question of strategic
choice cannot be divorced from the competition between different political tendencies within the movement. The crystallization of this competition began
once the Línea Proletaria group had won control of the first democratic com-

---

18  Ten thousand peasants and teachers marched on Tuxtla and took over the stores. The governor sent in
    the police to reimpose control, but they were met by serried lines of women and children. By now new
    prices had been agreed in Mexico City, but when the governor swore "not a penny more" the teachers
    and peasants cut the Panamerican Highway. At one moment a group of seven or eight thousand pro-
    testers faced a large force of armed and mounted police. Accepting the government's guarantees, the
    protesters withdrew, leaving behind a commission to negotiate an agreement; but as soon as the dem-
    onstration had dispersed the twenty-nine leaders who had remained behind were arrested. Some were
    released the next day, but not Jimenez and Hernández.

mittee in March 1981, and it corresponded to the strategic divide between a purely syndical struggle and a broader project of political alliances. Even then, the strategic issues were never pristine: An emphasis on welfare services to the community and subsidies for school materials could create the conditions for subsequent, more radical political initiatives. But it was not so much the strategic debate as the incipient political divisions that precipitated the central strategy of "ideological struggle in political unity," which sanctioned all internal disputes as long as they were disciplined by majority decision. In this respect the struggle also had an "internal front" of organization and identity where an effective unity had to be constructed. In this interpretation unity was built on common economic and professional demands, and was consolidated by internal democratic procedures. But by the time of the congress of 1984 it was clear to everyone that this central strategy was itself designed to make these procedures operational.

The strategic need for political unity applied *a fortiori* to the National Coordinating Committee itself, which (as I will argue in Chapter 7) never managed to forge a properly national organization; and the complicated relationship between regional autonomy and national struggle was the context of the strategic choice taken to secure the first democratic committee in Chiapas. According to the criticisms of the Trotskyists, the Línea Proletaria group insulated the movement in Chiapas from the struggles in other states and won control of the sectional committee at the price of abandoning the national project; it had been impossible to correct this strategic mistake because of the "centralist deviation" that had divided the movement (*Chispa Sindical*, February 1981). What was required in its place was "ideological plurality but unity of action," and this call for unity against the Vanguard while continuing the ideological contest was repeated prior to the congress of 1984. However, as the dispute between Línea Proletaria and the Trotskyists turned ever more bitter, the political position of the latter became increasingly bland. "The solution cannot be black or white. We have to seek precise targets and be ready to negotiate . . . making the congress of 1987 a priority" (*Chispa Sindical*, October 1986). In other words, not only did the Trotskyists come to accept the central strategy of "ideological struggle in political unity," but they moved progressively closer to the original position of Línea Proletaria. And whereas the adoption of "political unity" may have served their own tactical purposes, the calls for negotiation and the priority given to the struggle for syndical control reflect real strategic shifts. In effect, the strategic orientation of different political tendencies within the movement could change, or even cross over in different conjunctures, which were themselves defined in some degree by the strategic choices of the movement overall.

The movement itself stated the strategic importance of advancing by stages, each of which had its own specific objectives. In this respect, each strategic choice condensed the political unity achieved by majority decision in successive "decisive moments" (CNTE 1980). But it was clearly incorrect to suppose that the strategies were defined beforehand. On the contrary, the movement discovered its strategies in the process of struggle itself, including "the confrontations with forces opposed to our demands, as well as the internal debates at the grass roots and in the Central Struggle Committee" (Hernández Gómez et al. 1985). In this sense the ideological struggle led not so much to political unity, which could never be complete, as to strategic choice; and the strategic choices contributed to define the conjuncture, along with the institutional and legal context, the government policies and programs, and the initiatives and responses of other actors in Mexican civil society (see Chapters 8 and 9). In this sense, a political conjuncture is the result of an encounter between specific, and often contending, political practices.

At the beginning of the teachers' movement in Chiapas, the conjuncture was almost completely undefined, but its character was progressively shaped by the accumulation of tactical and strategic choices. Over these first months the militants of the movement had to decide whether to confine their call for an increased bonus to the oil region of the north or extend it to the whole state and so mobilize greater numbers, whether to continue the initial strike once their official leaders had backed the strike call for September or lift it and regroup, whether to press further demands in the fall or stick to the one demand that spurred the mobilization, whether to form an independent union or struggle within the SNTE, whether or not to respond to the leaders of political parties and tendencies, whether to seek negotiation while mobilizing or wait to be approached, whether to lift the strike even though the main demand had not been won, and whether to retreat from the occupation of the Ministry of Education's headquarters when threatened with eviction. Although the examples could be multiplied for these months, it is clear that such choices influenced the course and conduct of the struggle, which was punctuated by the first stoppage, the first strike, and the occupation of the Ministry; the rhythm of later events like the arrival of the Mixed Commission, the march to Mexico City, the encampment, the retreat to the Advanced School, and so on, was marked by subsequent choices in similar fashion.

A political conjuncture can only emerge over time, and the strategic choices that contribute to shape it may also define different stages of struggle. It was the predominance of economic demands that defined the first phase from the moment of takeoff in 1978 to May of 1980, when the occupation of the sectional headquarters in Tuxtla Gutiérrez signaled the shift to the second phase of political struggle for democratic control of the sectional committee. Once in charge of the committee, the movement became intensely involved in a period of syndical struggle for professional rights and the equitable distribution of syndical and social services, which itself gave way to the stage of "ideological struggle and political unity" at the pre-congress and congress of 1984. At this moment, however, the heightened competition between better organized political tendencies in the movement entailed more extensive strategic debates, which impelled a shift from purely economic and syndical preoccupations to broader political concerns.

When a marked strategic shift of this kind coincides with major changes in the political environment, it may signal the transition to a new political conjuncture. There are new constraints and new political horizons. The name of the game has changed. From the point of view of the movement itself Political Unity could only resolve Ideological Struggle by constructing a political project for the defense of democratic gains and the search for political alliances, and this internal motivation was conditioned and reinforced by the need to resist the renewed destructive resolve of the Revolutionary Vanguard. In short, the political differences could only be settled on a new strategic terrain, and the movement took a new strategic direction to contain the contending political forces within it.

6

# Factional strife

In the years before the rise of the teachers' movement, tens of political groups were engaged in grass-roots agitation and organization throughout Mexico. Rather than composing a coherent opposition, these groups wove a tangled web of political projects that ranged from the pragmatic to the utopian. Whereas the radical opposition of earlier years had been largely confined to the Mexican Communist Party (PCM),[1] the 1968 student movement had spawned a plethora of competing political tendencies, which included Maoists, Trotskyists, left Christians, and "Cubans" (see Introduction). Among these, just two groups were to have a decisive influence on the teachers' movement in Chiapas: the Trotskyists, who formed the hard core of the Revolutionary Workers' Party (PRT), and the Política Popular, which had rejected left-wing party politics in favor of Maoist tactics of direct mass mobilization. By the usual process of fission and fusion on the radical left, Política Popular finally appeared in Chiapas as Línea Proletaria.[2]

Both the Trotskyists and Línea Proletaria arrived in Chiapas in 1974. The Trotskyists found their foothold in the Agricultural Technical Schools (ETAs) and played a key role in the ETAs movement of 1977 and 1978. Línea Proletaria had sent Heraclio Blanco, one of its militants from La Laguna, to "teach the teachers the theory," as well as to begin to organize among the peasant groups that were later to form the Union of Unions, one of the most successful

1 The Mexican Communist Party had always had a strong presence among Mexico's teachers, and in the 1960s some 30 percent of its members were still teachers. But as its affiliated organization the MRM, or Revolutionary Teachers' Movement, became increasingly isolated from the mass membership after the mobilizations of the late 1950s (see Chapter 3), it lost any significant influence within this sector.

2 Política Popular was first led by Arturo Whaley and Adolfo Uribe (and found one of its first political footholds in Altos Hornos, where the managing director was Adolfo Uribe's father). Some of its militants had stayed in Mexico City after 1968 to work in the National University (UNAM) and the Polytechnic, while others had joined brigades that promoted popular movements among the peasants of La Laguna, Nayarit, and Oaxaca, and among the slum dwellers of Monterrey. Later the organization split between Whaley's Línea de Masas, which worked largely with the new urban movements, and Línea Proletaria, which had most success among the telephone workers (under the leadership of Hernández Suárez) and the teachers. Línea Proletaria finally extended the scope of its operations from Sonora in the north to Chiapas in the south, but its organization and influence had peaked by 1978.

88

peasant organizations in the region (Harvey 1990a). The seeds of division were already discernible in Blanco's insistence on the differences between Línea Proletaria's position and the "extremism" of the Trotskyists. But the Trotskyists were not at all keen to avow their identity at this time, and Línea Proletaria's presence was everywhere precarious, with its militants attaching piecemeal to separate struggles as "each monkey found its own branch" (*"cada chango en su mecate"*). In retrospect, it was probably fortunate that these political tendencies failed to achieve greater influence among the teachers of Chiapas for most of the 1970s: The movement in Chihuahua had been destroyed by factional infighting over the same period.[3]

By the time the teachers' movement did take off in 1979, Línea Proletaria's national leaders had dissolved their organization, advising its militants to go their own political ways. Hence, the connections between Línea Proletaria and the incipient movement were made by personal contacts between individual militants and natural leaders. Manuel Hernández was already in touch with Rafael Arellanes, one of Línea Proletaria's activists in the region. Even the first strike of May 1979 seemed to reflect some of Línea Proletaria's tactics, and the strike itself introduced Línea Proletaria to young leaders from the north like Amadeo Espinosa. Amadeo and Manuel were already known to each other, and to many others in turn, and in this way Línea Proletaria entered the movement not so much as an organization but as a strategic approach, which favored an assembly-based syndicalism free of party interference.[4] Nonetheless, the label stuck to a group of leaders who came to be identified with Línea Proletaria's strategic style, if nothing else. As the movement grew the government responded to these leaders as strategically adept activists, but as it divided they were criticized for their collaborationist attitudes.

The criticisms came from the Trotskyists, who initially defended ultraleft views of the revolutionary but utopian variety, arguing that the teachers' problems could only be resolved by "the destruction of the capitalist State" (*Chispa Sindical*, September 1978). As early as June 1979, with the official union leadership already committed to a September strike, the Trotskyists wanted to purge the Central Struggle Committee of "those leaders who have agreements with the authorities," which apparently meant anyone who was "opposed to mobilization" (*Chispa Sindical*, June 1979). And they tried to prolong the

---

3 The movement in Chihuahua was split between the rival organizations of the MRM and the ARS (Revolutionary Syndical Alliance), which fought each other for control of the sectional committee. The ninth congress of the section elected 36 MRM members and 35 ARS members to the committee, which only served to sharpen the internal struggle and spread it to the base. The Revolutionary Vanguard took advantage of the situation to reimpose its own rule, which it did once the ARS had made the fatal mistake of inviting the federal government, in the form of the Arbitration Board (*Junta de Conciliación y Arbitraje*), to deny the committee legal recognition (Luna Jurado 1977).

4 Línea Proletaria's leaders alleged that their motive for dissolving the organization was precisely that it had begun to imitate political party practices rather than acting as a mass organization.

strike in October, against the wishes of the state assembly, which voted to accept the Ministry of Education's and the SNTE's offer and so protect the fledgling movement. Clearly, the Trotskyists wanted more confrontation and less negotiation than Línea Proletaria's leaders, but it was the latter's success in consolidating their hold on the movement, and not strategic differences, that provoked most animus. Hence, even when the Trotskyists later moderated their political stance[5] and adopted positions resembling those of Línea Proletaria (see Chapter 5), the hostility between the two groups was hardly attenuated.

In this connection it appears that the causes of internal struggle changed through time. The ideological seeds of factional strife were embedded in the teachers' movement from its beginning, and they grew into strategic differences that first divided these two main groups and then multiplied as more political divisions emerged within the movement. The divisions that occurred along strategic lines were accompanied by political infighting that defined strategy to some degree (see Chapter 5). In the early days the movement welcomed the "struggle of ideas" as a way of clarifying the strategic issues and saw it as the "motor of struggle at every level" (Consejo Central de Lucha del Magisterio Chiapaneco 1981); this optimism was maintained for some years by Línea Proletaria, which characterized the contradictions as "part of the struggle" so long as they did not degenerate into personal conflicts or factional disputes (Arellanes Caballero, Constantino, and Peralta Esteva 1985). In short, it was strategically positive for the diverse groups to respond both to each other and to their political environment because "ideological struggle in political unity" sharpened strategic choices. But this assumed that the divisions were ultimately doctrinal, whereas they clearly came to express a political struggle for the control of the movement itself. This internal struggle, which had never been entirely absent, became more apparent with the gradual formation of opposing political factions.

From the Línea Proletaria viewpoint the Trotskyists in the PRT wanted confrontation with the federal government rather than a real solution to the teachers' problems. But despite their left-wing rhetoric the Trotskyists also sought electoral success, which meant capturing the movement for their own sectarian objectives. Their leaders were therefore not so much militants of the movement as agents of the party, who failed to put the movement first. To the left of the Trotskyists were the so-called ultras; their influence was confined to some small student and peasant groups, but they tended to mistake their own inflated language for their real strength. Their "left infantilism" imagined a rising rhythm of frontal conflict with an oppressive and monolithic State apparatus. Very dif-

---

5 As the Trotskyists became more moderate, other groups moved to occupy the space on the far left, including the 27 April Teachers' Organization (which found its inspiration in the teachings of Rosa Luxemburg), the Democratic Syndical Tendency (COSDE), and the Union of Workers in Education (UTE). These were tiny but noisy groups, whose main strength was in their propaganda.

ferent were the "opportunists" associated with Ricardo Aguilar, who occupied no particular place on the political spectrum but continually changed tack to suit the circumstances of their one goal, which was to gain political advantage.

In its turn Línea Proletaria was accused of collaboration by the Trotskyists and the ultras, who rejected negotiations or alliances that "sold out" or "handed over" the movement. In particular, the alliance with the peasants of La Fraylesca (see Chapter 5) had linked the movement to a sectoral organization of the ruling party. This was bad enough, but because the peasants' leader, Germán Jimenez, was a political enemy of the state government, the movement was also drawn into the internal disputes of the ruling party's apparatus, which was worse. Whatever the virtues of the alliance strategy overall, Línea Proletaria was opportunistic in pursuing only those alliances that strengthened its own position within the movement. Línea Proletaria's leaders replied that the alliance had been sought by the peasants and that it anyway strenghtened the whole movement. It was all very well to debate the alliance in theory, but what made it possible in the first place was the work of "populist" leaders like Manuel Hernández, Jácobo Nazar, and Jésus Constantino, who had spent the days and nights of the preceding years traveling to the communities and making grass-roots contacts. In short, Línea Proletaria's leaders did not so much deny their political ambitions as suggest that they had "paid their dues."[6]

It is clear from this example that at the heart of the criticisms of Línea Proletaria's leaders lay the suspicion that they were trying to achieve a permanent hold over the movement and that their strategic initiatives were therefore self-serving. But the point to emphasize is that every political tendency tried either to lead the movement or to influence its leadership, and local observers were immediately aware that divergences within the movement stemmed from "this search for posts on the sectional committee, and the power to continue leading the teachers" (*La República en Chiapas*, February 12, 1980). But if competition between the tendencies was inevitable, even desirable, in a democratic movement, it was sometimes carried on in an undemocratic and underhand fashion, and so exposed the movement to the machinations of the *charros*. In other words, the efforts to disqualify internal opposition by labeling it sectarian

---

6 Línea Proletaria and the populists were also criticized for imposing their own candidates in the municipal elections in Oxchuc and Villa Canaltitlán. In general, the Trotskyists were on softer ground than other groups in joining the common condemnation of party connections, but in these cases they alleged that Línea Proletaria was guilty of supporting the electoral manipulation of the ruling party. Línea Proletaria conceded the point in the case of Oxchuc. The great majority of Indian communities in the municipality had joined the teachers' movement in ousting the Revolutionary Vanguard, and a mass assembly had then elected a "populist" teacher as president of the municipal council. But the movement could not prevent his subsequent cooptation by the ruling party (PRI), which then defended him against popular demands for his dismissal. In Canaltitlán, on the other hand, the "populists" had forged a tactical alliance with the municipal authorities against the prevailing *cacique*, but the Trotskyists had not recognized, or not wanted to recognize, the political purpose of the alliance.

or opportunistic only served the purposes of the Revolutionary Vanguard and
the federal government, which sought every opportunity to sow discord and so
disperse the movement. It was generally supposed that many of the mutual
accusations, and not least those of betrayal, were in fact made by *agents provocateurs* in the pay of the government or the SNTE.

## The development of factional divisions

In its first phase the teachers' movement in Chiapas was led by Línea Proletaria
and its leader Manuel Hernández, and it was Línea Proletaria strategy that provided the principle of unity. Right from the first strike Línea Proletaria was
identified by its moderation when it argued for accepting the SNTE offer and
therefore against the Trotskyist insistence on forcing the issue further; this disagreement defined the tenor of subsequent differences between the two tendencies. Immediately before the democratic congress of March 1981, the Trotskyists finally launched an open attack on the "incorrect, tendentious,
collaborationist, opportunist, confusionist and *neocharro*" positions of Línea
Proletaria and, moreover, began naming names.[7] What had most infuriated the
Trotskyists was the compliant attitude toward the representatives of the
SNTE's National Committee adopted by Línea Proletaria during the prepa-
rations for the congress, and what most concerned them was the expectation
that with the achievement of democratic committees at the delegational and
sectional level the struggle committees would disappear (*Chispa Sindical*, February 1981).[8]

The Trotskyists could not deny that the rapid advance of the movement in
this first phase had been achieved by Línea Proletaria's moderation, but they
were resentful of the initial reverence for the Hernández leadership. Hence, they
criticized him and his lieutenants for pursuing the unionism that best suited
them and for securing support through the kind of favoritism and clientelism
that were characteristic of *charrismo*. In short, they began to deveolop a "basist"
critique of the leadership, finally alleging that the state assembly had become a
mere appendage of the newly elected sectional committee, thus distorting the
original principles of the movement. The scene was set in the pre-congress of
March 6, 1981, which was marred by the bitter squabbles that would dog the
movement in the years to come.[9] The Trotskyists were quite consistent in calling

7  The prime culprits in their view were Rafael Arellanes, Neín Farrera, Jésus López Constantino, and Amadeo Espinosa.

8  The Trotskyists were especially keen to defend the Central Struggle Committee and insisted that its future
must be decided by the membership. But they admitted that the Línea Proletaria line had been backed
by a majority of the state assembly of January 17, 1981.

9  The Trotskyists objected to both procedure and content of the pre-congress. Línea Proletaria's Sergio
Nijenda presided over the meeting. The Central Struggle Committee's report unjustly diminished the
ETAs' campaign of economic demands and falsely claimed the honors for winning them. Línea Proletaria

the first democratic sectional committee in the SNTE's history "a partial triumph; or rather the triumph of Línea Proletaria over the grass roots of the Chiapas teachers" (*Chispa Sindical*, April 1981).

Línea Proletaria replied that, on the contrary, it was the Trotskyists who had not understood the common obligation to "abide by the decisions of the base," the logic of their rhetoric leading them into "attempts to divide the movement" (Arellanes Caballero, Constantino, and Peralta Esteva 1985). Thus, the Trotskyists had refused to join the rest of the Chiapas teachers in supporting the Oaxacan encampment in Mexico City; they had threatened the sectional congress by an ill-timed encampment of their own in the regional capital; they had attempted to split the movement in the pre-congress; and once the committee was won, they had rejected the majority decision to refrain from forcing a specific wage demand on the National Committee of the SNTE (and so consolidate the movement's political gains at the grass roots).

The fact was the Línea Proletaria and its maximum leader Manuel Hernández had secured the majority support within the movement that was to underpin stable leadership for at least two years, and many suggest that it was Hernández's charisma that did the most to contain the Trotskyists, who were now largely excluded from decision making and reduced to the role of not-so-loyal opposition. But the Trotskyists still had four delegates on the committee, including Octavio López and Víctor Sánchez Bautista, and they still spoke for a substantial minority of teachers who were receptive to the charge that Línea Proletaria was compromising, and possibly collaborating, too much. Moreover, as their members tended to be more politicized than the majority, they had an edge in the delegational committees, where their cadres could make their influence felt. Thus, it is surprising that they did not mount a more coherent challenge to Línea Proletaria's organizational predominance. The Trotskyists explained this by the constant attacks against them, their leaders being ousted from the committee by a campaign of calumny. Línea Proletaria replied that it was the Trotskyists who had besmirched the committee in a scurrilous broadsheet and who had mounted mass protests against the committee during the assembly of October 1982: Indeed, their preferred tactic was now being used against their rivals in the movement (*Chispa Sindical*, February 1984).

The factionalism within the movement continued to be expressed and in

leaders on the Committee, on the other hand, defended their record and rejected allegations that they fought for anybody other than the mass of Chiapas teachers. The bitterness of the debate continued in the congress itself, where, once again, the Trotskyists complained of the opprobrium heaped publicly upon them and accused Línea Proletaria of "centralist deviation" in sacrificing the demand for a 100 percent increase in the bonus. No matter that Línea Proletaria's leaders defended this sacrifice as a symbolic and tactical concession required if the SNTE's National Committee were to ratify the congress, they were still condemned as "the Judases of the teachers' movement . . . who want to hand us over like cheap goods to our former bosses." The Trotskyists vowed "no quarter in the war against opportunism disguised as democracy" (*Chispa Sindical*, March 1981).

some sense contained by the rivalry bertween these two groups until about June 1983, but by the following September it was clear that the movement had begun to pull apart under the strain of this intense political competition. The Trotskyists had been in loose alliance with sundry groups on the left like the MRM, but the second congress of the ETAs in June had recognized that there were ideological and political differences within the Trotskyist camp (which were again blamed on Línea Proletaria's provocations). At the same time, Línea Proletaria was suffering from internal tensions, with Manuel Hernández openly objecting to the "false division of labor between those who think and others who act" (and pointing up the contrast between the *talacheros,* or hard-grafters, who were working at the grass roots, and the *parfumados,* or "sweet-smellers," who sat behind their desks all day). In fact, Hernández had simply decided to assert his authority over Línea Proletaria's theoretician, Rafael Arellanes, but the squib (a pamphlet called "New Times") precipitated a real split inside the committee, which was no longer "just one but two or more committees" (Sección VII, Coordinadora Regional de la Costa 1983). The impending congress of March 1984 had also galvanized Ricardo Aguilar's own ambition to be secretary-general and hastened his separation from Línea Proletaria. Consequently, the sectional committee was now divided into three groups: the rump of Línea Proletaria led by Rafael Arellanes, the "populists" of Manuel Hernández, and the scornfully named "opportunists" of Ricardo Aguilar, the Secretary for External Regulations. As a result it was to prove impossible for Manuel Hernández to control the succession, and he eventually had to settle for a compromise candidate as the new secretary-general.

In the run-up to the congress Manuel Hernández went on negotiating with the state government, Ricardo Aguilar looked for political allies in Mexico City, the Trotskyists built a new platform around a demand to double the wage, and the Revolutionary Vanguard mounted a major campaign within the delegational assemblies. Inside the congress itself Línea Proletaria and the "populists" managed to mend their fences in an attempt to shut out the Trotskyists, but they fell out again over the choice of secretary-general; the Trotskyists found an uncertain ally in Ricardo Aguilar and a critical one in Hernán Villatoro, the most "basist" of all the leading activists, and so were in a position to influence but not determine the outcome of the voting. Because many of the delegates either remained unaffiliated or came from minor cadre-based organizations, it is no surprise that an increasingly divided movement elected a very diverse sectional committee, which included all the main factions as well as some independents.

It was probably still true at this time that the great majority of the membership was a long way from being Trotskyist or "populist" or even entirely convinced by Línea Proletaria, and so it might appear that some consensus was possible under the new collective leadership of secretary-general José Domingo Guillén. But José Domingo clearly lacked the moral authority of Manuel Her-

·nández and anyway found no effective way to appeal for political unity. On the contrary, he soon had to shore up his own position by allying with the Trotskyists, Ricardo Aguilar, and others in a new Democratic Bloc,[10] which could muster a slim majority of about thirty-six votes against the thirty-four of Línea Proletaria and the "populists," who had joined forces again within a few months of the congress.[11] Hence, by the beginning of 1985 the committee was comprehensively divided between two opposing camps, which were themselves unstable: The new secretary-general disagreed with the position of his allies the Trotskyists and distrusted the ambitions of his ally Aguilar, and Línea Proletaria, which in principle could count on more internal discipline, now had to contend with the individual initiatives of Manuel Hernández.

Hernández continued to sit on the new committee. Possibly he expected to act as its *eminence grise* and to bend the new leadership to his own political purposes. Or perhaps he was simply constrained by the debts and deals accumulated during his time as secretary-general. In any event he balked at majority discipline and bypassed the committee in seeking to maintain his personal contacts with the state government and Ministry of Education. The easy access he enjoyed to these authorities split the committee into separate de facto negotiating commissions (see Chapter 4), thus undermining the movement's, and finally his own, credibility. Indeed, insofar as Hernández's activities smacked of collaboration, pure and simple, they damaged his "hegemonic" strategy of gradual and negotiated advance, and contributed to an increasing strategic incoherence in the movement overall.[12]

In any case, the central strategy of simultaneous mobilization and negotiation had been stunted by the continual conflicts between the two camps in both the state and the delegational assemblies, which caused confusion among the membership and a loss of confidence in the leadership. At the same time, in the later months of 1984, the Revolutionary Vanguard had launched a "repressive avalanche against the movement" (invited by Hernández's advertisement of its divisions, according to the Trotskyists), but the movement could not agree on

10 Immediately before the congress the Trotskyist PRT was joined by other left parties, such as the Unified Socialist Party of Mexico (PSUM), and by the increasingly active "ultras," such as the Union of Workers in Education (UTE) and the People's Revolutionary Movement (MRP), to form the Democratic Teachers' Tendency (CODEMA). These are the groups that entered the relatively stable alliance of the Democratic Bloc in the months after the congress.

11 In the folklore of the movement, the reconciliation came after Línea Proletaria footed the bill for the medical treatment Hernández needed in Mexico City, and it was only the newly consolidated Línea Proletaria that persuaded the Trotskyists to join the Democratic Bloc.

12 The signs were plain to see. In a meeting of November 1984 the Trotskyists approved the principle of a very unlikely alliance with the National Committee of the SNTE to preempt intervention by the Ministry of the Interior, and in January 1985 a bona fide offer from the state government to take up the movement's demands with the Ministry of Education was rejected because the deeply divided committee could not agree on its response. But these signs were only the prelude to the confusion surrounding the subsequent strike call.

its response. In the assembly of January 1985 Línea Proletaria called for an indefinite strike to defend the movement's very existence, but the Democratic Bloc disagreed. It was not convinced that the differences between the Revolutionary Vanguard and the federal government (see Chapters 8 and 9) were so profound as to guarantee a favorable outcome. In this way the permanent state assembly was turned into a battleground, with the Línea accusing the Trotskyists of trying to subvert the movement (and postpone the strike until they could use it for their own electoral purposes) and the Trotskyists retorting that "it was suicide to strike now." The strike vote was finally won with a mere 53 percent majority, which looked like the worst possible result. But a mass demonstration in the state capital, followed by a meeting of the negotiating commission with the President of the Republic, encouraged overwhelming solidarity once the strike began on February 25, and the adherence of the public sector unions, peasant organizations, and Section XL of the SNTE (the state teachers) augured well for winning their demands.

Although the base now firmly refused to retreat, the leadership still found no clear way forward. It was not that the two main camps disagreed on the need for negotiation but that they agreed on little else. Línea Proletaria rejected the Trotskyist line of direct negotiations with the National Committee of the SNTE as too risky, while the Trotskyists saw the Línea Proletaria's approach to the state government as further evidence of collaboration. The state assembly had voted priority to the state-level negotiating commission composed of Línea Proletaria militants, but the counterpoint to the main debate was a recurring suspicion that Manuel Hernández was pursuing his own negotiations without even consulting the assembly.[13] However, when Hernández was confronted by his accusers in the heated assembly of February 10, he replied robustly that any individual negotiations were in his role as mediator of many peasant struggles throughout the state; he was rewarded by a standing ovation. But this did not resolve the confrontation between Línea Proletaria and the Trotskyists because at the heart of the matter was the factional struggle for negotiating space, or what the movement called a *capacidad de gestión*. As they were both only too aware, the group that could get real results from the strike and the ensuing negotiations could win both mass support and political control of the movement.

The state assembly of February 10 had finally finessed the question by resolving to engage on all fronts but emphasize the government of the local state. The assembly then elected negotiating commissions, which were clearly dominated

---

13  It was known that Hernández, Amadeo Espinosa, and Paco Guzmán had met with the subsecretary of the interior, Carrillo Olea, who sought the suspension of the strike; it was thought that the state government's recriminations against the three members of the negotiating committee who had met with the President suggested prior agreements with the populists, and the Ministry of Education openly offered to receive a negotiating commission headed by Manuel Hernández in Mexico City (and was equally openly refused).

by militants from the Línea Proletaria Popular (as the Línea Proletaria and Manuel Hernández axis was now called). Hence, it was Línea Proletaria's leaders and the "populists" who would suffer for any dissatisfaction with the conduct or outcome of the strike, which was finally lifted on March 15. The results looked relatively good. The teachers had demanded increases in the cost-of-living bonus across the eighty-five municipalities of the state; the authorities conceded increases in forty-two of them and also agreed to dismiss the Ministry of Education's delegate, Juan Carlos Camacho Salinas. Nonetheless, it was precisely at this moment that the suspicions surrounding Hernández's role came home to roost, and there were immediate accusations of a sellout. Indeed, the municipalities that had not received any increase, and the Trotskyists of course, insisted that the strike must go on until the increase was made general and until they had won their other main demand that state and federal teachers' wages be brought into line. Without doubt there was some general grass-roots anger at the results of the strike, but the most bitter resistance came from the ETAs and the Trotskyists on the sectional committee. The state assembly had to vote seven times on an end to the strike before a clear three to one mandate emerged.

The meeting to announce the end of the strike was held in the main square of Tuxtla Gutiérrez, the state capital, and it was at this scene of some of its greatest triumphs that the movement reached its nadir. When he rose to speak, Rafael Arellanes of Línea Proletaria was roundly booed and pelted with tomatoes, in an ugly display of resentment and dislike. Worse yet, this *tomatazo* took place in full view of the state authorities seated in the governor's palace. In the Trotskyist accounts of the incident it is portrayed as a spontaneous outburst of popular anger against Línea Proletaria and Manuel Hernández, who were seen to "have subverted a coordinated state mobilization" by their mistaken strategy of "tactical retreats" (Corriente Democrática Magisterial 1985). But Manuel Hernández was sure that this was a conspiracy of the "ultra-left" and that the *tomatazo* was premeditated (Hernández Gómez et al. 1985). Línea Proletaria's response, which lamented the aggression of "those elements who seek quite unjustified support in revolutionary theory," remained relatively muted in comparison to the sharpness of the Trotskyist invective, which leveled charges of betrayal. These were then taken up by the yellow press, which rushed to condemn Manuel Hernández as the "Judas" of the teachers' movement. In short, the positive results of the strike paled into insignificance in comparison with the damage wrought by these increasingly visceral confrontations.

A state assembly was convened to assess the strike, and it tried to limit the damage. Its anodyne report reproved the "public exhibition of our political and ideological differences" and noted that "the incorrect method of channelling our internal contradictions prevented bigger gains." Moreover, it condemned the "system of threats and manipulation being used by some comrades" and recommended that the different political tendencies should all present their own particular "projects" in the next meeting so that the movement could once again agree on a "program of unified action." But the damage was extensive. Only 157 of 306 delegates were present, and only 14 of these had brought strike minutes from their union delegations. Despite the calls for a united front, the assembly was obliged to authorize the different tendencies to draw up their own reports on the strike and circulate them to the membership "to enrich the analysis." The Trotskyists pretended they were doing just this when they chose this moment to produce a document that revealed the secret plans of the Revolutionary Vanguard for reconquering the sectional committee. But Línea Proletaria objected that the Trotskyists had kept the document hidden for some months, and its prestidigitatious appearance at this precise moment was designed to defend their own position and discredit Línea Proletaria's good offices with the state government.[14]

Any analysis clearly remained subject to the continuing hostility between the two camps, which the state assembly finally did little to resolve. Each side accused the other of betrayal. The Trotskyists continued to believe that Manuel Hernández made surreptitious deals with the state government. But in Línea Proletaria's view, this concerted attack on its purported "collaboration" simply exposed the movement to manipulation by the *charros* and hampered the struggle at the grass roots. It was chagrin versus resentment. In its fight to recover public sector housing that had been seized by the *charros*, Línea Proletaria found itself accused by the Revolutionary Vanguard of "collaboration with the state government," and this it blamed on the Trotskyists, while they accused Línea Proletaria of disseminating divisive ideas at the base in order to win the political argument. In this way, the war of words in the state assembly turned into a political battle for the loyalty of the grass roots. By October the Trotskyists had decided to avow their Trotskyism and take every opportunity to spread its message. They intended to combat the main enemy, which was now Línea Proletaria, but still seek "the unity of the sectional committee."

## Replaying the main scenes

In retrospect, the mutual recriminations that followed the strike of 1985 look like a dress rehearsal for the organizational schism provoked by the strike of 1987. Once again, Línea Proletaria and the populists led the movement into the strike, and once again the same camp negotiated its solution. The strategic and practical imperatives of conducting the long sixty-five day strike forced all

---

14 Línea Proletaria accused the Trotskyists not only of dishonesty but also of developing a strategy that was dependent on "the analysis of the oppressors." More specifically, Línea Proletaria alleged that the plan had been drawn up by one of the elite groups opposed to the government of Absalón Castellanos in Chiapas and would therefore involve the teachers' movement in "intrabourgeois struggles," which were especially acrid in Chiapas. This was the same charge that the Trotskyists were to level at Línea Proletaria and the populists when they allied with Germán Jimenez and the peasant movement of La Fraylesca (see Chapter 5).

factions in the movement into a temporary cohesion, which was bolstered by the calls for unity from the National Coordinating Committe, but the divisions reemerged toward the end. Almost predictably, the state assembly, which had been in permanent session, finally split between Línea Proletaria militants, who wanted to lift the strike, and Trotskyist sympathizers, who argued for continuing the struggle with the support of the parent and teacher councils. The voting was marred by mutual accusations of manipulation and by apparent attempts by Línea Proletaria to pack the assembly, which led the meeting to reconvene three times before voting could proceed.[15] The assembly stopped the strike, but the beginning of negotiations only served to sharpen the internal disputes.

During the strike no combination of political tendencies had had a clear majority in the state assembly, where internal alliances were in constant flux, but once again the negotiating commission was mainly composed of Línea Proletaria militants. In the Trotskyist view, it was the commission's manipulation of the state assembly that led to the movement's most damaging defeat and the imposition of a "mixed" executive committee, which was in fact dominated by the Revolutionary Vanguard. The commission falsely informed the assembly that it was the movement, not the Vanguard, which would nominate the secretary-general of the committee and so control it, and it was the commission that stage-managed the signing of the agreement. Línea Proletaria rejected such claims and argued that it was simply the unfavorable balance of the forces that led to an unfavorable agreement, which the Trotskyists had invited by disloyal criticism and party politics.

The mutual accusations had not changed, but the situation had. The Revolutionary Vanguard had succeeded in imposing an executive committee, which would be headed by a delegate from the SNTE's National Executive Committee, with the rest of the posts divided between the Vanguard and the movement. The movement's state assembly held elections for the "democratic" posts on this committee, but Línea Proletaria and populist militants abstained at the last moment, thus sending the Trotskyists to the committee to deal with the Vanguard and "administer the defeat." Hence, the predominant presence of the Trotskyists on the Committee (not counting the Revolutionary Vanguard) hardly reflected the real correlation of forces inside the movement. The Trotskyists themselves still had their base in the ETAs but had only a minor presence in primary, secondary, or Indian education, and the internecine strife had left them more dogmatically committed to PRT doctrine. Línea Proletaria still controlled twelve to fifteen substantial cadres across the state. Manuel Her-

---

15 The story may be apocryphal, but the way the Trotskyists tell it is that Línea Proletaria tried to smuggle nonaccredited delegates into the assembly while movies were being shown and the auditorium was in darkness. The whole assembly then had to leave the auditorium twice, the second time only reentering with new credentials, before voting could proceed.

nández and the top populist leaders were in Cerro Hueco prison, but this had
only enhanced Hernández's charisma and the potency of his appeal to the grass
roots. On the other hand, in the argot of popular politics, Ricardo Aguilar had
been "burnt" and left completely isolated. Finally, although a growing number
of teachers had come to avoid any political affiliation, this was not true of the
young recruits to the movement, who tended to join up with the most radical
tendencies. The movement was therefore still fully involved in "ideological
struggle," even if it mainly took the form of rumor and slander, but it was
farther than ever from "political unity." If the different political tendencies
could not agree on their real strategic requirements, such unity could never
come. Despite the rhetoric, all tendencies had been moving inexorably toward
more "institutionalist" positions, which understood the recurrent need for
negotiation; but equally, and this was what made Línea Proletaria smart under
the Trotskyist attacks, no tendency wanted to be "burnt" for collaboration. In
practice, this contradictory constraint led whatever tendency was excluded from
the leadership to promote such radical demands at the grass roots that stable
leadership itself became unlikely, if not impossible. It was an open question
whether the threat to the movement's very survival could lead instead to
reconciliation.

# PART III

# National mobilization and system responses

# 7

# Regional movements

The teachers' movement in Chiapas was the pioneer of political mobilization by teachers nationwide.[1] The militant support the Chiapas teachers gave to this pioneering movement was an example to teachers everywhere, and within a few months Chiapas was sending brigades across the country to win wider support for its campaign. The brigades discovered deep disquiet among the teachers themselves, but they sometimes received a hostile response from the sectional committees. As mobilization spread into other states, especially neighboring Oaxaca, the Chiapas movement became more difficult to contain, and it was a combined protest in Mexico City by teachers from Chiapas, Oaxaca, and Morelos that persuaded the SNTE to concede Chiapas's democratic congress. There is no doubt that this regional victory was partly a result of national mobilization, but, equally, the national movement never escaped its regional origins. The main reason for approaching this movement through a regional perspective is that it was always regionally based and driven.

Although nearly all Mexico's teachers had the same employer, and although they all belonged to the same union, their regional movements were different one from the other because "each of the states which have joined the struggle have done so for their own reasons, in response to a specific situation" (Reyes 1980). These specificities tended to supersede any more general commitment to the national struggle, so that the regional movements remained largely autonomous and the rhythm of regional struggles was driven by the beat of different drummers. In particular, the strength the movements drew from their directly democratic organization also constrained attempts to forge a more unified national strategy, and this was damaging at critical moments of national mobilization. Thus, the National Coordinating Committee remained true to its name, and the national struggle always tended to revert to its regional realities.

The movements in Oaxaca, Hidalgo, Morelos, and the Valle de México soon

---

1 As early as October 3, 1979, the president of the Mexican Academy of Education, Ramón Bonfil, warned that the Chiapas movement "could grow and acquire national dimensions," and within fifteen days Tabasco and the Montaña de Guerrero had mobilized and the ETAs of La Laguna had launched an indefinite strike.

moved into the frontline of the struggle, and, together with Chiapas and Guerrero, they came to constitute the core of the movement at the national level. Elsewhere the dissident organizations had a precarious presence, and they were altogether absent from at least ten states. Most importantly, the movement made no headway in the SNTE's most powerful sections, IX and X in Mexico City. This did not mean, however, that it was confined to the poor rural regions of the country, for it advanced in the heavily urban areas of the Valle de México and Morelos and won strategically placed academic delegations in Mexico City itself, which together rounded out its national presence. But it did mean that the national movement suffered from the "risky isolation of the six regions which have for a long time sustained the weight of the teachers' struggle" (Fuentes Molinar 1983).

To a degree this uneven development reflected the different working and living conditions of teachers in different regions. Bonuses were much lower in the south than the north, and the Indian and bilingual teachers in the southern states of Chiapas, Oaxaca, Guerrero, and Hidalgo were paid lower wages and treated worse than most other teachers (see Chapters 1 and 3). The case of the Valle de México was special, insofar as its teachers suffered the same pressures as the rest but were also deeply frustrated by the dirt, poverty, and lack of public services of the outer urban settlements where they lived (CNTE 1981; Salinas Alvarez 1983). It was precisely in these states that the movements flourished, but others in Michoacán and Puebla met with bitter defeats despite widespread mobilization. Elsewhere, the "movements" were nothing more than small cadres, which led to tensions between their delegates on the National Coordinating Committee and the leaders of regional mass movements, such as Manuel Hernández.[2] How could these Committee men weigh equally in the balance with 25,000 federal teachers in Chiapas?

The leaders of the main movements also differed in style and strategy. It was the strategic combination of mobilization and negotiation that achieved democratic control of the sectional committees in Chiapas and Oaxaca. The more intransigent stance of leaders in Morelos, Hidalgo, and the Valle de México made such an outcome less likely, and it can be argued that it was an insistence on "all or nothing" that led to defeats in Morelos, Hidalgo, and Guerrero. On the other hand, the early movement in Michoacán was defeated not by too much radicalism but by too little. The teachers from Michoacán were as combative as any, but, differently from Chiapas and Oaxaca, their demands were immediately adopted by the delegational leaders within the section, who used

2 Hernández and the populists were especially scathing of fellow *chiapaneco* Ricardo Aguilar, who pursued a narrowly bureaucratic career on the National Coordinating Committee despite a lack of popular support in his home state. Moreover, they alleged that he had been coopted (by a "study grant" from the Ministry of the Interior).

the impetus of the movement for their own purposes, before turning and betraying it. They then proceeded to isolate the movement by forbidding meetings and suppressing the most mobile grass-roots cadres.

Hence, the apparent relationship between the political style of regional leaderships and their variable success may be spurious, or may not tell the whole story. Differences of institutional and political context, and especially in the reaction of the authorities, seem just as important. This reaction was extraordinarily fierce in the case of Section XXVI in the Valle de México because the dissident leaders challenged one of the strongholds of the Revolutionary Vanguard, besides threatening to "contaminate" the populous working-class districts bordering Mexico City. The Valle therefore mobilized intensively to combat systematic repression, and not because the leaders had failed to grasp the strategic efficacy of simultaneously pursuing negotiation (similar arguments can be made for Morelos). Elsewhere, official responses often depended on the political disposition of the state government: Initially compliant governments in Chiapas and Oaxaca stand in stark contrast to those of Hidalgo and Guerrero, which were violently opposed to the movements.[3] Contextual differences of this kind were later accentuated by the program of educational decentralization (see Chapter 8), which created distinct institutional settings in different states.

The net result of these differences was that "each region had its own dynamic with different trajectories and intensities" (Pérez Arce 1987), and consequently these regional movements often failed to coincide in their timing and objectives. The widespread mobilization of 1982 (see The national trajectory: the second phase, below) had already subsided before the struggle peaked in the Valle de México, and therefore this struggle received little national support.[4] Although both Oaxaca and Chiapas were locked in bitter conflicts at the beginning of 1985, one was struggling to renew its "democratic" sectional committee while the other sought bigger bonuses and better social services (see Chapter 6), and thus it was impossible to link their respective negotiations with the SNTE and the Ministry of Education. This general lack of coordination was clearly something the National Coordinating Committee was set up to rectify, but longer-term strategic goals continued to elude the Committee, which had to settle for broad-based mobilization around short-term objectives. In fact, the Committee's lack of strategic initiative tended to compound the intrinsic regionalism of the movements, advertising to the authorities that "we were not the sum of parts but separate parts with different processes" (Fernández Dorado 1982).

---

3  Therefore, to argue that it was simply the radical intransigence of their leaders that sank the movements in Guerrero and Hidalgo is to underestimate the violence of the *charro* response and to demean the courage of the cadres who bore the brunt of this violence.

4  Mobilization had subsided because of the specious resolution of the conflicts in Morelos and Chiapas, but the lack of support for the Valle was also a result of the deepening ideological divide between its leaders and the leadership of the National Coordinating Committee.

Such regionalism could lead to national myopia and occasional failures to appreciate the strategic openings created in inter-institutional disputes within the federal government (see Chapter 9).

## Continuing attempts at coordination

Before the emergence of the teachers' movement, it was the Advanced School in Mexico City that had distilled the traditional militancy of the teacher training schools and coordinated regional dissent. Indeed, its own struggle for democratic self-government and its intensive summer courses had schooled many of the movement's future leaders (see Chapter 3); the Advanced School acted as a bridgehead for the brigades from the Central Struggle Committee of Chiapas, and its militants worked alongside them in stimulating the movement in other states. After the formation of the National Coordinating Committee, the Advanced School served as its operational base, with the regions then using its summer courses to exchange information and explore alliances. This led to recurrent attacks from the SNTE and Ministry of Education, which intended to break up these courses and disperse them to the four corners of the country. When it finally succeeded in 1983, it did not just shut down a school.[5] It destroyed the cradle of the national movement.

But long before this, the new movement had formed its own Coordinating Committee. The original movement in Chiapas had stimulated the first solidarity committee among left-wing teachers' groups in Mexico City as early as August 1979, and the rump of this committee continued to be active in the Valle de México and in the Coalition for the Rights of Education Workers (which preceded the Valle's Central Struggle Committee).[6] In several more states similar initiatives had accompanied the widespread mobilization that followed the first strikes in Chiapas, and these encouraged the Central Struggle Committees of Chiapas and Tabasco to call a national meeting of the SNTE's dissident and proto-democratic organizations. Twenty-five such organizations, including movements, groups, and tendencies (and bringing together delegates from thirty of the SNTE's sections across the country), finally met on December 17–18, 1979, in Tuxtla Gutiérrez (Chiapas). There they agreed on a common platform of economic and political demands, including the democratization of the SNTE through open sectional congresses. Most important of all, they

---

5 The Ministry itself had first set up the summer courses in order to qualify teachers for work in secondary education or in the training schools.

6 The Coalition unified the National Independent Teachers' Front (FMIN), the National Commission of the TV Secondaries, and other groups like the Committee for an Increased Bonus, thus helping to dissolve the differences between these organizations, as well as building bridges to the delegational committees by sending brigades across the region. The Coalition gradually joined forces with the teachers led by Misael Núñez Acosta, and the Central Struggle Committee of the Valle de México was finally formed on June 13, 1980.

agreed to establish the National Coordinating Committee of Workers in Education and Democratic Organizations of the SNTE (as it was first known) in order to coordinate the growing movements in Oaxaca, Guerrero, Hidalgo, Morelos, and the Valle de México, and to lend support to sympathetic organizations across the country.[7]

The initial meeting had been a success, but forging a durable committee from so many disparate elements was to prove difficult. The scale of the problem was measured by the National Assembly of the Coordinating Committee of September 1980, where 600 delegates from twenty-three different organizations debated their diverse approaches to *charrismo,* political alliances, and the conquest of union committees; internal disputes similar to those in Chiapas (see Chapter 6) were inevitably magnified by the syncretism of the Committee itself. Some of this was simple factionalism. The radical stance of parallel syndicalism had been rejected from the beginning, but its proponents continued to attack the "reformism" of the MRM, and the delegates from the National Independent Teachers' Front (FMIN) and the Alliance of Workers in Education (ATE) were especially incensed by the MRM's success in negotiating posts on the National Executive Committee of the SNTE.[8] But as in Chiapas, the

7  The first formal meeting of the National Coordinating Committee on February 14, 1980, provided a clear map of the scale of such organization in different regions. Present were the Central Struggle Committees of Chiapas, Tabasco, and Morelos; the coordinating committees of Guerrero, La Laguna, the Valle de México, Sinaloa, Baja California Sur, Puebla, Querétaro, Tlaxcala, Guanajuanto, Toluca, and Monterrey; the campaign committees of Sections IX and X in the Federal District; and the delegates from the "democratic organizations" such as the FMIN, the MRM, the Independent and Democratic Syndical Tendency (COSID), the Alliance of Workers in Education (ATE), and the Socialist Tendency. Possibly the first action promoted by the National Coordinating Committee took place fifteen days later when teachers from Michoacán and the Federal District marched together in the capital, and so inaugurated a decade of popular protest and political mobilization on the streets of Mexico City. Indeed, it was the second formal meeting of the Committee that called for the first of the multitudinous marches, which took place in the capital on June 9 that year.

8  Anyone can be forgiven for not making much initial sense out of the "alphabet soup" that is the left in Mexico. The range of political groups and tendencies participating in the teachers' movement was impressive by any standard. It included the Revolutionary Teachers' Movement (MRM), linked first to the Mexican Communist Party (PCM) and then to the Unified Socialist Party of Mexico (PSUM, which had absorbed the PCM in the early 1980s); the Democratic and Independent Syndical Tendency (COSID), linked to the Revolutionary Workers' Party (PRT); the National Independent Teacher's Front (FMIN), which was Maoist in orientation; and the Alliance of Workers in Education (ATE), linked to the (Trotskyist) Marxist Workers' League.

   Their leaders vied for influence over the different regional movements and met with variable success. Línea Proletaria did well in Chiapas and Section X (in Mexico City), as did the COSID in Sinaloa and the MRM in Guerrero, Puebla, and, not surprisingly, Section IX (see Chapter 3). As often as not this diverse display of political credentials made little headway in leading the movement, which was the case in Oaxaca, where political control was contested by Línea Proletaria, the left-wing UTE (the Union of Workers in Education), the MRM (with the PCM), the COSID (with the PRT), and the Línea de Masas, not to mention the PRAXIS, a local tendency linked to the Coalition of Workers, Peasants and Students of the Isthmus (COCEI). But where a particular political group did take over the leadership of a movement

factional disputes both reflected and fueled strategic divergences, which at one point threatened to split the Committee into two blocs.

The big debate in the September 1980 National Assembly concerned the future of the national movement. On the one hand, the MRM, the Independent and Democratic Syndical Tendency (COSID), and a handful of supporters wanted a national program and a central apparatus to implement it. On the other, the majority of Struggle Committees, especially those of Chiapas and the Valle de México, rejected such an idea in favor of a minimum coordination of regional movements "around a platform of unifying demands" (Palomino 1983a), which was the formula for combining coordination with regional autonomy. This view reflected the uneven development of the regional movements and their differing political contexts as much as it did the ideological plurality of their leaders, but above all it reflected a fear of factional domination (by analogy with the Revolutionary Vanguard within the SNTE), which could only occur if an apparatus existed to secure such dominance. Once this view had prevailed, it was clear that no such apparatus would ever be built, and the National Committee was confined to a minimalist role. The third meeting of the Committee in April 1981 confirmed this approach but also agreed to set up a Permanent Commission[9] to implement the decisions of the National Assembly and direct coordinated action.

The effort to organize a central executive in the form of a National Struggle Committee had foundered on the directly democratic style of decision making in the National Committee,[10] which referred all strategic issues to the individual Struggle Committees, whose decisions anyway had to be approved by their respective assemblies. But these democratic mechanisms also diluted and filtered the influence of the political factions, and assured the integrity of the movement overall. In some degree it was to remain true that "contradictions and disparities are plentiful inside the Coordinating Committee, while the sectors which support it are riddled with sectarianism, unreal utopias and

(which occurred with the PSUM in Puebla), or where sectarian divisions came to dominate the struggle (which occurred within the Campaign Committee of Section IX in the capital), mass defection and defeat often resulted. Hence, seasoned leaders of the struggle tried to cut through the confusion of political competition to point out that there were only two possible strategic paths: the "pro-government" path promoted by the self-appointed factional leaders, and the independent and democratic path decided by the membership (Fernández Dorado and Palomino Gutiérrez 1986).

9  The Commission was composed of five members from each democratic section and from each Central Struggle Committee, one member from each political tendency, and one from each campaign committee. It was the National Assembly of November 1981 that planned the first such coordinated action at the national level and reaffirmed the role of the Permanent Commission.

10  In June 1982 the decision was taken to try to strengthen the CNTE's organization by promoting joint meetings between grass-roots representatives from different regions, and the first of these took place between Oaxaca and Chiapas in October. But when the first national grass-roots meeting took place in Tonalá (Chiapas) toward the end of the same year, fears were voiced that the initiative might weaken the CNTE's already precarious executive capacity.

*machismo*" (Monsiváis 1981); but once the Committee was consolidated, many of the smaller factions declined, and the COSID and the ATE disappeared altogether. The MRM had no mass presence. The FMIN continued as a cadre-based group with key leaders in the Valle de México and La Laguna. Inside the Committee itself the business of coordination became more routinized, and doctrinal differences consequently became less salient: "the regional leaders greeted each other and did not seem to like or dislike each other any more than usual" (Pérez Arce 1982a).[11]

In this way the National Coordinating Committee survived intact, but it never came close to being a National Struggle Committee. On the contrary, by March 1982 it plainly depended on the core support of the two (legal) sectional committees in Oaxaca and Chiapas, and a further five Central Struggle Committees, besides the twelve "campaign committees" and a few militant delegations. In short, there was no integral national organization, and the regional committees were quite capable of acting against national initiatives. Under the continual prompting of the intellectuals in the capital,[12] the National Coordinating Committee did press for representation on the SNTE's National Executive Committee in order to take advantage of its national infrastructure for its own purposes, but the Revolutionary Vanguard was ruthless in defending its near monopoly of executive posts[13] and the strategy therefore met with little success.

But what the National Coordinating Committee lacked in firm organization it possibly made up for in its capacity for mobilization. Soon after its formation it agreed that where conquest of the sectional committee proved impossible it at least had to promote grass-roots mobilization. In other words, the Committee was not entirely content to coordinate existing organizations but also sought to catalyze new ones, and most subsequent protests were linked more or less directly with the Committee. The Committee soon proved its worth in the months following the February 1980 Assembly by diffusing the demands of the Oaxaca movement, which had erupted onto the streets of the capital with unprecedented force. It worked to link Oaxaca and Chiapas, and to make ten-

---

11 Nonetheless, it can be no surprise that the movement's search for alliances was seen to be difficult, slow, and contradictory "owing in good measure to the heterogeneity of the movement and to the diverse syndical conceptions within the different Central Struggle Committees" (Movimiento Revolucionario del Magisterio 1982).

12 These were grouped in the Instituto Nacional de Antropología e Historia, which was delegation D-III-24 of Section XI in the Federal District. Academic activists like Luis Hernández and Francisco Pérez Arce "carried out a permanent and important job of analysis and systematization of the conflict" (Salinas Alvarez and Imaz Gispert 1984).

13 The eighty or so delegates the Committee was finally able to send to the XIII National Congress of the SNTE in September 1982 were insufficient to drive a wedge into the Revolutionary Vanguard. Although the dissident teachers came to control a large number of delegational committees at the regional level, their representation at the National Congress was systematically contained by fraud, so that the Vanguard never had to concede more than five posts on its Executive Committee.

tative contacts with Guerrero; and grass-roots activists from the Valle de México soon formed joint brigades with the Oaxaca teachers, which reached beyond the industrial periphery of Mexico City to Hidalgo. On this occasion the Committee already provided a skeletal framework that was firm enough to capitalize on the massive impetus from Oaxaca, and in later years it came to express a national "project" that was politically available to teachers on the march.

Such a "project" made solidarity actions make some sense. Hidalgo was exemplary in this respect. It began its movement in solidarity with Oaxaca, it marched and "encamped" in solidarity with Guerrero, it lent full support to the struggle in Puebla, and finally it went on hunger strike in Morelos. Such active solidarity actually catalyzed the formation of campaign committees in Sections IX and X in the Federal District, and, in general, was the key to the Coordinating Committee's successful mobilizations. After a period of relative withdrawal (see next section) the Chiapas movement was especially responsive to the Committee's calls, offering mass support for the national protests of early 1982 and consistent solidarity with Oaxaca in its struggle for a democratic congress. These active sentiments also made the movement national.

## The national trajectory: the first phase

The teachers' movement was therefore a complex result of regional movements that could coincide in moments of national mobilization, and the variable and occasionally contradictory rhythms of the different movements complicates the periodization of the movement at the national level. Nonetheless, the regional movements sometimes converged to produce peaks of mobilization that define the trajectory of the national movement and divide it into discernible phases. The first phase runs from the pioneering movement in Chiapas in the fall of 1979 to February 1981, and its consistency was achieved by the progressive but staged adhesion of different regions to the national struggle: Guerrero and La Laguna in late 1979, Oaxaca in May 1980, Morelos and the Valle de México in late 1980, and Hidalgo early in 1981. It was the entry of Oaxaca that was critical in this first moment,[14] for the mobilization of its 30,000 teachers had a national impact that had been lacking until then: The mass march from the Advanced School to the Zócalo on June 9, 1980, won an immediate 22 percent wage rise for teachers across the country.

---

14  The first strike in Oaxaca was actually led by the SNTE's official leadership in the region (and was complicated by the personal political agenda of the new secretary-general of the sectional committee, Fernando Maldonado Robles). The only objective was the dismissal of the Ministry of Education's delegate, which the Ministry quickly conceded, but the teachers at the grass roots were pressing for higher wages and refused to lift the strike. As the SNTE officials failed to back this demand, they immediately insisted on a democratically elected sectional committee. In just ten days the political contradictions at the state level had propelled the teachers into a new movement, which the intransigence of the authorities then acted to consolidate.

Yet if Oaxaca had achieved a national impact, it was the convergence of long strikes in Morelos and the Valle de México with a mass encampment in Mexico City by the teachers of Chiapas toward the end of 1980 that gave the movement a national profile for the first time. The joint protest in front of the Ministry of Education and SNTE headquarters by contingents of teachers from Chiapas, Oaxaca, the Valle de México, and Morelos was attacked by the police, but when the repression proved ineffective the authorities promised democratic congresses for Chiapas, Morelos, and Oaxaca (with increased bonuses across the board). Any future congresses of this kind were forbidden to the dissident teachers "because they were already liking them just a little too much."

In the new year the movement continued its forward momentum. Guerrero and Hidalgo launched indefinite strikes, and the National Coordinating Committee called for a national stoppage on February 2 to back its platform of national demands for a higher wage, the celebration of the promised congresses, and, most contentiously, the recognition of sectional committees elected by "mass congresses" (as had already occurred in the Valle de México, Morelos, and Hidalgo). In the event, the scheduled stoppage was swelled by protest against Governor Figueroa's violent treatment of the teachers in Guerrero and by the assassination of the Valle de México teachers' leader Misael Núñez Acosta (who had been killed just three days previously). Not only the mass presence of almost 40,000 teachers but also their mood spurred the Ministry of the Interior to convince the Ministry of Education and the SNTE to settle their differences (see Chapter 9) and make the kind of offer the movement could accept. With bad grace the SNTE conceded five extra posts on the sectional committees of Hidalgo, Guerrero, and the Valle de México to the leaders of their Central Struggle Committees.

Whereas the Coordinating Committee had played no part in organizing the protests of the previous November, it had planned this combined offensive and had even tried to conduct joint negotiations. The largely symbolic concession of extra posts may have seemed significant but, in fact, served to protect the legal status of sectional committees, which had been rejected by the majority of their teachers. This was a poor result from months of mobilization and was a clear attempt to reproduce the classical Mexican amalgam of represssion and cooptation (while still conforming to the profile of López Portillo's "political reform," which looked to give dissidents a voice but not a say). Disappointment led some to suggest (Salinas Alvarez and Imaz Gispert 1984) that these three states might have found a legal way to conquer their sectional committees had the teachers of Chiapas mobilized in their support: A lack of coordination, even solidarity, had fatally altered the balance of forces at this critical moment.

Chiapas had won its congress in November 1980 on condition that it respect the SNTE's legal procedures and refrain from extralegal mobilization, and, in effect, it "withdrew" from the national movement just when these other regional movements most needed its support. Its letter of compliance to the

SNTE's secretary-general (see Chapter 6) provoked bitter criticisms from teachers' leaders in Hidalgo and Morelos, who charged that Chiapas was "betraying" the teachers from other states who had previously mobilized to back its objectives. But the Chiapas leadership insisted on the strategic priority of the democratic committee, which would extend the legal boundaries of movements in other states and provide a benchmark for their political aspirations. In the longer run this was almost certainly right (even if it was unfair to suggest that the criticisms had been motivated by simple factionalism). But this did not end the debate, for the newly democratic committee in Chiapas appeared to give merely token support to a national movement that it mainly ignored; Manuel Hernández, in particular, seemed disdainful of the Coordinating Committee, which he saw as a cabal of overambitious leaders lacking proper popular support (see Chapter 5). This relative isolationism proved to be a temporary effect of institutional advance, and by the end of 1981 Chiapas was again mobilizing alongside other states in a new offensive against the SNTE.

## The national trajectory: the second phase

During 1981 the movement withdrew to its bases in the regions. Some regions waxed strong. Chiapas won its committee, and Oaxaca and Hidalgo continued their grass-roots mobilization. Others were on the wane, with the Valle de México, Guerrero, and especially Morelos increasingly wasted by the "war of attrition" (see Chapter 8). The Coordinating Committee held a series of national meetings to plan the kind of combined response that might contain the offensive of the Revolutionary Vanguard, but for most teachers "the retreat meant a return to the silent battles, to the daily defense of paper victories, to the muted conflicts over individual case work" (Pérez Arce 1982b).

The Revolutionary Vanguard had calculated that it could isolate and wear down the movements in Guerrero, Morelos, and the Valle de México, but they were again in the frontline at the beginning of 1982 when they joined Chiapas and Oaxaca in a national stoppage to force compliance with previous agreements: The Valle de México, Hidalgo, and Guerrero were again excluded from their sectional committees,[15] and Oaxaca was still waiting for its democratic congress. The official response was again selective in authorizing the long delayed "mixed commission" for Oaxaca, which finally won control of its sectional committee late in February; but far from being placated, the Oaxacan teachers now joined the Coordinating Committee for the first time and lent their weight to the series of marches and protests that shook Mexico City during the month of March. A demonstration of 30,000 teachers and the occupation of

15 An Extraordinary National Council meeting of the SNTE in February 1982 had expelled the Central Struggle Committee delegates from the sectional committees of these states, thus reneging on the 1981 agreement.

the SNTE's own headquarters finally convinced its Executive Committee to negotiate (to delay any longer would risk the loyalty of teachers in the SNTE's sectional strongholds in the capital), and in the "April Accords" the SNTE again granted extra posts on the sectional committees of Hidalgo, Morelos, and the Valle de México, with the important promise of extraordinary congresses, and therefore democratic committees, to follow.

Oaxaca won its congress because of extensive grass-roots organization and widespread solidarity, and in retrospect it is clear that the national movement would not have rallied in its support were it not for the victory already achieved by Chiapas in the previous year. At the same time general elections were imminent (see Chapter 9) and the ruling party's presidential candidate, Miguel de la Madrid, effectively dismissed the repressive option canvassed by the Revolutionary Vanguard, and even advised its secretary-general to "moderate his will."[16] But beyond Oaxaca the concessions were uncertain, consisting mainly of promises that might well, and eventually did, remain unfulfilled (with none of the three states ever holding a democratic congress). Although the Revolutionary Vanguard had failed to dampen the mobilization by its usual delaying tactics, it had complied with the Ministry of the Interior's insistence on negotiation only on condition that it negotiate with each regional movement separately and had succeeded in persuading the leaders from Chiapas and Morelos to cease their protest in return for firm dates for future democratic congresses.[17] Thus, despite every effort of the negotiating commission from the Coordinating Committee, the Struggle Committees of Hidalgo, Guerrero, and the Valle de México were separately cajoled into accepting a package deal that maintained the institutional hold of the Vanguard.

Inside the Coordinating Committee the political alliances were continually shifting, and if this prevented any one tendency from asserting its own control over the movement, it also made it difficult to agree on a joint agenda for negotiations. This left the national movement susceptible to manipulation by the government and the SNTE, which invariably sought separate negotiations with different movements in order to reduce national confrontations to regional conflicts that could be more easily contained. The precise tactical balance of threat and promise would change with the circumstances, but the general policy was to maintain silent intransigence at the national level while responding with the proper combination of repression and negotiation in each region. This approach proved effective in setting party political tendencies against nonpartisan Struggle Committees, and even the Struggle Committees against each other (and may have conformed to a broader government "reform" strategy for dispersing

16 This did not prevent the Minister of Education, Fernando Solana, from threatening the teachers in flights of violent rhetoric, while the Revolutionary Vanguard sat tight and waited for better days.
17 In the case of Morelos this was the second time that the movement had been promised an extraordinary "democratic" congress, which should have made its leadership more cautious than it appeared to be.

the political left) (Salinas Alvarez and Imaz Gispert 1984). But this was success in a one-sided battle. It must be remembered that, as much in February 1981 as in March 1982, the negotiations that secured the successful "institutional-ization" of the struggle were conditioned by the constant menace of violent repression.

## The national trajectory: the third phase

Despite its occasional successes in dispersing the dissidents, the Revolutionary Vanguard had been on the defensive. But at the end of 1982 it launched a counterattack that rolled back the regional movements and defeated their attempts to elect their own committees. In Hidalgo and Morelos the move-ments were reduced to nuclei of militant cadres with limited popular support, and after Chiapas and Oaxaca the teachers had to wait until July 1989 before they won another sectional committee (see postscript to Chapter 12). These states therefore acquired a special importance for the national movement, but even they found it difficult to consolidate their gains.[18] In Mexico City the teach-ers' columns in the Labor Day 1983 demonstrations were assaulted by armed *charros,* and bloody street battles ensued. In September of the same year the Ministries of Education and the Interior sent in armed and mounted police to close the Advanced School and suppress its summer courses.[19] All this coincided both with the beginning of the Ministry of Education's decentralization pro-gram (see Chapter 8) and with a general government offensive against the right to organize and the right to stike, which targeted the militant unions in the universities and nuclear power industries.

The Coordinating Committee organized huge demonstrations in May and June 1983, but its proven capacity for mobilization seemed ineffective in the face of government intransigence. A key weakness in its campaign was the con-tinuing failure to rouse the teachers of the Revolutionary Vanguard's strong-holds in Mexico City, where dissidents were confined to a few uncoordinated delegations and where the campaign committee of Section IX remained immo-bilized. By the time of the fifth National Assembly of the Committee in June 1984, the Chiapas movement argued that the time was right for an indefinite strike to press their demands but admitted that only Oaxaca and Chiapas were ready to mobilize. Hence, by the end of 1984 the Revolutionary Vanguard's rearguard was secure, and it could now plan its offensive to recover the ground lost in Oaxaca and Chiapas.

18  The Revolutionary Vanguard tried direct intervention to recover control in Oaxaca, sending 200 of its armed minions to surround the headquarters of Section XXII in Oaxaca City. But massive grass-roots mobilization repulsed this attack.

19  As the Advanced School had also acted as headquarters for the teachers of Section IX of the Federal District, its closure meant that they now had nowhere to meet.

## The national trajectory: the fourth phase

On September 19, 1985, the earthquake struck Mexico City, and 1,294 schools were damaged or destroyed. This was one-half of all buildings broken by the tremors.[20] In the previous month, at the Coordinating Committee's sixth National Assembly, the Oaxaca delegates had pressed for a plan of action that might mobilize the national movement to support Oaxaca's struggle for union rights. The Vanguard had used fair means and foul to postpone and prevent the congress scheduled for 1985, and by the beginning of 1986 the SNTE's National Executive Committee felt confident enough to cancel the congress altogether. Then it used the platform of its own National Congress in Baja California to validate this decision "democratically." The Congress was carefully controlled. Delegates from Chiapas were denied entry unless they forswore support for Oaxaca, which they refused to do; the only delegates from Oaxaca itself were the sycophants of the Vanguard. The window dressing was necessary because not even the SNTE could renege lightly on an agreement backed by the Ministries of Education and the Interior. The clear intention was to unseat the democratic committee and impose one of its own choosing. But Oaxaca did not give up. Its teachers stopped work. They mobilized. They camped out. They cut roads. They started a hunger strike in Oaxaca City. More than 30,000 of them marched on Mexico City. And against all odds they won their congress for the second time.[21]

At the beginning of 1987 the Revolutionary Vanguard went on the attack again, and again focused its fire on the democratic committees in Oaxaca and Chiapas. At the same time the efforts of the Ministry of Education and the SNTE to tighten their legal and institutional control of teachers throughout the nation (see Chapter 8) appeared effective in restraining the Coordinating Committee, which entered into decline. Its support for the sixty-six day strike in Chiapas was confined to gestures of solidarity in the form of two thirty-six hour stoppages in January and February, which met with uncertain success.[22] Hence, the Extraordinary National Council of the SNTE had no compunction in dis-

---

20  "Union officials . . . were thrown out of tens of schools because of their failure to deal with the disaster . . . the *charros*, more worried about their posts than about solving problems, have been bypassed by events" (Equipo Pueblo 1986b).

21  The Catholic Base Communities (*Comunidades Eclesiales de Base*), which held their XII National Congress in Oaxaca City at the beginning of February 1986, also lent their full support to the Oaxaca teachers' struggle for their congress. The Archbishop of Oaxaca, Bartólome Carrasco, published a message of solidarity that referred to the rights enshrined in the III General Conference of Latin American Bishops in Puebla (Mexico) in 1979.

22  Despite the National Committee's stoppages and a march of 15,000 teachers in Mexico City, this meant that the Chiapas movement mainly had to go it alone. Even then it enjoyed the support of the Independent Confederation of Agricultural Workers and Peasants (CIOAC), the Emiliano Zapata Peasant Organization (OCEZ), the Union of Unions, and the public sector unions in Chiapas.

missing Chiapas's democratic committee on March 9, 1987, which it could do quite legally by the simple expedient of revoking its mandate (just as it had done in the case of Section IX in Mexico City twenty-seven years earlier). This degree of success against the pioneering movement of Chiapas was a clear sign that the teachers' movement overall had indeed been reduced to separate regional struggles.

Not only was the national movement in decline; its territorial redoubts in the south also appeared to be under threat. But the trajectory of the movement had always fluctuated between crescendos of protest and gulfs of inactivity, and it was much too early in the history of the movement to count it out. Brigades returning to Chiapas from the Valle de México reported a strengthened Central Struggle Committee and widespread disquiet at low wages and lack of respect for basic rights within the union. And other reports indicated, with some prescience, that the movement "in the Federal District was growing stronger, as was clear from the national march of February 19 when a large number of teachers joined up with the contingents of the Student Council of the National University" (Street 1987d). In effect, within two years the teachers' movement would not merely have recovered its traditional regional impetus, but would have succeeded in penetrating the heartland of the Revolutionary Vanguard in Mexico City.

# 8

## Institutional controls

The teachers' movement did not develop in a political vacuum. Rather, it advanced across the institutional terrain linking political actors in civil society with government agencies. Its trajectory was therefore conditioned not only by the changing internal composition of the movement (see Chapters 5 and 6) but also by recurrent shifts in the institutional context of the struggle, which might prevent or promote the movement's organization and demands. These shifts often reflected changing relations between government agencies themselves as they responded to new strategic priorities or, indeed, to the political pressure of popular mobilization (see Chapter 9); and such changes in "internal State organization" (Jessop 1982) were less legal or constitutional than purely political outcomes of a complex process of confrontation and negotiation. Most relevant to the teachers' movement and its strategic opportunities was the relationship between the National Union of Workers in Education (SNTE) and the Ministry of Education, particularly the political strains induced by the latter's program of educational decentralization.

The SNTE occupies a central place in Mexico's political system (see Chapter 3).[1] Traditionally, the intimate connections between the federal government and the union have been cemented by both bureaucratic and political mechanisms. The ruling party has recruited union leaders into the middle ranges of the federal bureaucracy, thus ensuring union influence over the regional administration of the Ministry of Education; and the union has also achieved a political presence in the federal congress and in a large number of state and municipal governments across the country.[2] At the same time, the union bridges the corporative and electoral arenas of the system (see Introduction) and has direct contact with teachers in every community in Mexico (see Chapter 1). It thus

---

1 It organizes about 40 percent of all public employees and is by far the most influential union within the Union Federation of Workers in the State Sector (FSTSE), which is itself the best organized and most powerful element within the National Confederation of Popular Organizations (CNOP) – one of the three massive labor sectors constructed under the political aegis of the ruling party.

2 The CNOP has traditionally controlled more seats in Congress than either of the other main sectors of the ruling party (CTM and CNC). In 1982 the CNOP occupied 48 out of 300 seats in the Chamber of Deputies, and 11 of these belonged to the SNTE itself.

enjoys an unusual degree of political autonomy, which introduces ambiguities into its relation with the government.[3] The political viability of the federal government required an effective SNTE, but, equally, government control could be impaired by a union that grew too strong.

In this regard, it is clear the President Echeverría supported Jonguitud's putsch of 1972 (see Chapter 3) for his own purposes. In return for concessions to the Revolutionary Vanguard, the government expected unconditional support for its own plans, especially for its educational reform. During the 1970s this unwritten pact was buttressed by wage rises that consistently bettered the public sector norm, and it appeared set to continue in the subsequent administration of López Portillo, who made a rare campaign promise to deliver Jonguitud's most cherished ambition of a National Teachers' University. In fact, the change of administration created considerable political friction between the Vanguard and the Ministry of Education, which led indirectly to the early resignation of the Minister of Education, Porfirio Muñoz Ledo, in December 1977, and by the end of the decade economic constraints had added to the tension. López Portillo invited the Vanguard's leaders to his palace on the occasion of the SNTE's XII Congress early in 1980 and warned them that "the State, brother teachers, cannot invent its resources." The leaders listened with that dogged expression reserved for presidential interviews, "a mixture of seriousness, devotion and forced intelligence"(*Unomásuno,* February 5, 1980), but the show of patriotism could not disguise the conflicts.

By the end of the 1970s the Ministry of Education was massive. It employed about 70 percent of all federal workers and accounted for about half the staff of the federal government itself. Nonetheless, its administration could not cope with the huge increase in the number of teachers from 400,000 in 1970 to 900,000 in 1980, and it anyway faced severe competition from the SNTE over the management of education and the direction of educational policy. The new National Teachers' University provoked intense pedagogical debates between the Ministry and the SNTE, which only partially disguised the SNTE's intentions of deepening its clientelistic controls and securing more influence over the Ministry itself (*Unomásuno,* February 12, 1980).[4] The Minister of Education,

---

3 Following the struggles of the late 1950s (see Chapter 3), the ambiguity found constitutional expression in an amendment that created a separate legal status for federal employees and restricted their right to strike. In 1966, however, government and private employees were reunited under one political and constitutional umbrella in the Labor Congress (CT), which was designed to unify the labor movement under the leadership of the Confederation of Mexican Workers (CTM), which comprised at least half the membership of the Labor Congress and controlled its tripartite bodies. The point remains that the federal government had to seek the means, whether constitutional or institutional, to control its powerful and potentially autonomous union ally.

4 The SNTE's project was itself a response to the pressures generated by the teachers' movements. It intended to use the University to create a range of new titles and grades, and so reinforce its rigid pyramidal control of the teachers. In public, the SNTE defended a University that offered mass professional training against the Ministry's "elitist" view of a University offering technical qualifications to future educational managers.

Fernando Solana, temporized with the SNTE's leaders but signally failed to stem their demands; it sometimes seemed as if his long awaited resignation was only postponed to frustrate Jonguitud's longer ambition of filling his ministerial shoes. In reality, Solana had been busy creating the conditions for a much broader conflict between the Ministry and the SNTE through the logistical support he lent to the decentralization program, which from mid-1980 came to define their competing political agendas.

## The educational decentralization program

The reform proposal of the early 1970s had stagnated until Solana became Minister of Education at the end of 1977 and began to make the changes that gave more power to the reformers. In particular, the Sub-Ministry of Educational Planning and Coordination came to play a key role in 1978 when it took over the entire educational budget, and the ministerial staff created new delegations in the regions, which accelerated the administrative decentralization while retaining strong central control over political decision making.[5] By 1982 these delegations already administered most educational services and absorbed 56 percent of the Ministry's budget (De los Reyes 1986).[6] The delegations also sought closer links with state governments, thus extending the scope of the reform and strengthening the regional presence of the federal government in order to streamline the flow of information to the center and to control the flow of resources to the regions.

The reform attacked the traditional separation of the administration and the profession, which had been sustained by the division of political labor between the Ministry and the SNTE. Nonetheless, although the new delegations threatened the prebendary powers of the federal directors (and, below them, the supervisors), they were far from achieving full executive authority. The federal directors could still protect the supervisors, who themselves resisted any attempt to limit their own authority over school directors; just as the delegations tried to influence appointments, transfers, and promotions, so the directors and supervisors demanded more union control of the new administrative apparatus. Thus, the battle lines were drawn between the Ministry and the SNTE, or between the reform program and the Vanguard's clientelism; but the potential conflicts remained largely latent until the accession of De la Madrid, who endorsed the program in his inaugural speech and promised to accelerate it

5 The lines of command had run from the Ministry to the various sub-ministries (one of planning, and one each for primary, secondary, and higher education), to the "chief officers" *(oficiales mayores)*, who controlled finance (budgets and wages), to the "federal directors of education," who ran the school system in each state and managed the supervisors. The delegations were inserted between the chief officers and the federal directors, which meant that the former lost powers to the Sub-Ministry of Planning, while the latter fell under the more direct control of the federal delegation (Street 1983, 1989b).

6 The process of decentralization also involved centralizing all the educational services within each state in one building, and the Ministry built thirty-one new state headquarters for this purpose.

under the new Minister of Education, Jésus Reyes Heroles. This precipitated a double struggle inside the educational sector in subsequent years, as the Revolutionary Vanguard found itself fighting both the teachers' movements and the reformers within the Ministry of Education.

The reform had proposed decentralization but in fact envisaged tighter central control over policy and its implementation in order to domesticate the Revolutionary Vanguard and defeat the teachers' movements. But these two objectives could be contradictory. By attacking the Vanguard's control of regional educational authorities, the program provoked not only the expected conflicts with the Vanguard itself but also the unexpected capture of federal delegations by the dissident movements in states like Chiapas, and this obliged the Ministry to revise its methods. In August 1983, after some months of "consultation" with the SNTE, Reyes Heroles moved to disband the delegations and to replace each of them with several Units to Decentralize Educational Services (USEDs). The plan was to diffuse the disputes in the most conflictual states, thus dissipating the impact of the teachers' movements,[7] as well as to wrest control from the Vanguard by creating a cluster of new USED cadres that would owe no loyalty to Jonguitud. But when Reyes Heroles died later that year, the new minister, González Avelar, allowed nearly all the USEDs to be taken over by Vanguard loyalists, which explains the constant antagonism between the dissident sectional committees of Chiapas and Oaxaca and their USED directors.

## Regional conflicts and national confrontation

The presidential decree of March 1978, which announced the creation of the delegations, was a declaration of war against the SNTE's sectional leaders, and especially the middle-level cadres of the Revolutionary Vanguard, which were viscerally opposed to any attempt to restrict their union prerogatives. The reform itself did indeed damage these cadres in the beginning, as disputes between Ministry of Education and union multiplied at the grass roots; but they responded by fighting for control of key positions inside the delegation, not least that of delegate. This response confused the Ministry's clear lines of command and weakened its control over the directors and supervisors. The outcome of these struggles varied from region to region, and consequently so did the political stance of the thirty-one delegations, but in most places there were more or less open conflicts between SNTE leaders and Ministry personnel, with important implications for the teachers' movements (see next section).

If it was not easy for the Ministry of Education to maintain control of its own

---

7 The simultaneous dispersal of the intensive courses of the Advanced School in Mexico City (September 1983) had the same objective and provided a dramatic metaphor for the real purposes of the reform. It was alleged that the School's building was dangerous because it was located on a geological fault. But when half the city's schools collapsed in the earthquake of fall 1985, this building survived intact. Apparently the fault had been not so much geological as political.

delegations, it was much harder to extend that control to the directors and supervisors who composed the warp and woof of the Vanguard's "huge net of incapacities and corruption"(Partido Socialista Unificado de Mexico 1984). The teachers themselves tended to remain subject to the Vanguard's authority. The Ministry then tried to break this conservative hold on the teachers by initiatives like the Municipal Education Committees (CMEs), which promoted community supervision of teachers and, by extension, the denunciation of corruption.[8] But the Ministry could not dismiss any employee whom the SNTE chose to defend, which clearly limited its powers of local intervention. Moreover, the defense of regional union cadres was taken up at the national level by the SNTE, which insisted on negotiating the implementation of the reform state by state.

The confrontation at the national level peaked during the incumbency of Reyes Heroles at the Ministry of Education,[9] and during this time the delegations in states like Chiapas encouraged the teachers' movements as a way of undermining the union bosses of the Revolutionary Vanguard. But whatever the bitterness between Heroles and Jonguitud, the tussle still took place *within* the corporatist mold of the federal government, and, paradoxically, it was precisely the combativeness of the teachers' movements that catalyzed the fast repair of the corporatist relations between the Ministry and the SNTE. With the death of Reyes Heroles, the Ministry and union soon managed to agree on an informal system of power sharing, whereby the Ministry ceded control of the teachers and their careers, and the SNTE accepted the Ministry's administrative reforms. In short, refurbished mechanisms of central control were superimposed on clientelistic networks, and union and Ministry remained entangled in a close political embrace. *Charrismo* survived the reform, and the SNTE did not suffer direct damage in the way that many had wanted. But the indirect results were another story.

## The reform program and the rise of the teachers' movement

Although the political logic of the corporatist pact won out in the end, it is clear that the reform program created a significant strategic opening for the dissident teachers. Through its delegations the Ministry of Education was soon in direct competition with the SNTE for providing services to the teachers, even if prob-

---

8 The CMEs were used by the Ministry to place its own stamp on the relations between teachers and parents, which created antagonisms with both the *charros* and the teachers' movement. As the president of the CME was also the municipal president, their agendas were closely vetted and their work was confined to matters of small importance. Nonetheless, in rural areas the CMEs were sometimes able to address the real needs of the community; they even acted as organizational cells for broader mobilization in the highlands of Chiapas. They could therefore contribute to the political education of the parents.

9 Reyes Heroles was one of the intellectual authors of López Portillo's "political reform" and had already fought several battles with the *charro* leadership of the oil workers' union.

lems of coordination meant that this service was often inefficient, and the regional *caciques* of the SNTE complained of ministerial staff interfering in their "internal affairs." As a consequence they had demanded the dismissal of Ministry delegates in San Luis Potosí, Morelos, Veracruz, Hidalgo, and Oaxaca. But beyond mere meddling, the SNTE suspected that the Ministry had deliberately provoked the dissident movements within it by systematically delaying wage payments, which not only angered the teachers but also impaired the SNTE's claims to the control of municipal administrations and of state and federal legislative seats. This is why the SNTE's secretary-general, Ramón Martínez Martín, warned in September 1981 that "decentralization is a policy which threatens to pulverize our organization."

The fact was that the reform created a bigger bureaucracy that was chronically underfunded. At the same time the patrimonial pact between Ministry and SNTE obliged the delegates to coordinate their administrative procedures with the union loyalties of the directors and supervisors in the field. As a result attempts to implement the reform often led to administrative disarray and to the nonpayment or late payment of wages. Hence, it was not just inflationary pressures that precipitated the dissidence but the "decentralization . . . which generated an administrative chaos leading to the late payment of wages for thousands of teachers" (Palomino 1983b). This is clear from the original platform of the National Coordinating Committee of Workers in Education (CNTE), which put the "payment of late wages" second only to a general wage hike and before the "unfreezing of the bonus." The problem was not equally serious everywhere, varying with the unequal implantation of the reform program in different regions; but the teachers' movement began where the program was first essayed, in Chiapas.

Late payments were not the only motive for the emergence of the teachers' movements. Demands for wage and bonus increases were common to all the movements, and particular detonators were present in some places.[10] But the reform did catalyze the emergence of the movements by creating alternative channels for negotiation and so promoting a new style of popular leadership: The dissident teachers could now seek to get their wage and labor problems solved directly at the doors of the delegation. Furthermore, the reform was partially successful in breaking the old links between the "chief officials" and the regions, thus hampering the SNTE's centralized controls over many of its teachers at a time of deepening economic crisis. As we have seen, the result was not clear-cut. The Ministry avoided confrontation for the most part and was content to remove any number of delegates provided the administrative reform

10 In Morelos it was the death of a teacher because of inadequate medical provision (see end of Chapter 2). In Oaxaca the *charros* themselves first mobilized the teachers to eject one of the Ministry's delegates (see Chapters 2, 4, and footnote 14 to Chapter 7).

appeared to continue intact. And as long as the *charros* were squeezed between the reform program and the dissident teachers, these bureaucratic ambiguities continued to provide strategic openings to the emergent movements.

## Strategies of institutional control

Once the Ministry of Education's pact with the SNTE had been renewed, the Vanguard's regional cadres moved to occupy the key positions within the USEDs, which were then used to intimidate and repress the teachers' movements. The master strategy that informed their campaigns was one of siege warfare, or what the teachers termed the *juego de desgaste*,[11] and it was a logical strategic response to movements that sought to advance by combining mobilization with negotiation. Its primary objective was to reduce and so divide the movements, setting parents against teachers (Arriaga 1981) and teachers against each other. In Chiapas, it is clear how the Vanguard took advantage of factional strife within the movement to deepen its divisions; and when in 1985 the teachers struck to protest the Vanguard's incursions and reaffirm their unity, the deal was again designed to split the movement by increasing the bonus for some areas at the expense of others (see Chapter 6).[12] Elsewhere, as in Morelos, the Vanguard even succeeded in separating the state teachers from the federal teachers; in the meantime the Ministry of Education was already planning further reforms, including the Law of Civil Service Careers, which would further divide the movements by establishing many new categories of teacher with very different levels of pay and privileges.

The main method of siege warfare was "administrative repression," which used all available means to intimidate the teachers on their home ground. Right from the beginning of the movement in Chiapas, the Vanguard's cadres threatened sackings and offered bribes in order to suffocate the strikes; even at that time these cadres had learned to work in collusion with the Ministry of Education's delegation, which issued the dismissal notices *(actas de abandono de empleo)* and ran a slush fund for the bribes. The delegation warned of mass sackings, which never occurred; but supervisors were demoted to directors, directors were demoted to the classroom, and troublesome teachers were transferred to inaccessible schools in the interior. The way was then open for the Vanguard to impose its own loyalists as supervisors and directors, who coun-

---

11  This phrase has no direct translation into English, but refers to the gradual "wearing down" or exhaustion of the enemy implicit in siege or trench warfare. It was precisely this kind of warfare that Gramsci (1971) wished to invoke in his concept of "war of position."

12  Moreover, the claim of the SNTE's National Committee that such bonus and wage rises as were on the table were a result of its negotiations and not the teachers' mobilization spurred the Trotskyist tendency to turn on the leaders of Línea Proletaria, whom it accused of collaboration.

tered the protests of the parents by refusing to register their children's academic results, with the consequent loss of the school year, and who severely sanctioned all dissident teachers. By this time the SNTE's National Committee had canceled the Permanent Commission agreed upon at the end of the strike and imposed the executive commission, which the teachers accepted for strategic reasons of their own (see Chapter 5) but which they still considered "archi-super-anti-democratic" (*La Puya*, February 1980).

This administrative repression became more comprehensive as the Revolutionary Vanguard established its operational base in the Ministry of Education's delegation and forged regional alliances with the state government, with the sectoral organizations of the ruling party such as the National Peasant Confederation (CNC), and with municipal presidents across Chiapas. Early in 1983 the ex-secretary-general of the SNTE, José Luis Andrade Ibarra, led a large group of the SNTE's political officers into the state, where they proceeded to infiltrate the delegational assemblies and sow discord on the committees. Behind the corrupt cover of the Front for the Demands of the Teachers of Chiapas (FRTECH), they tried to buy back popular support and dislodge the sectional committee (and even set up a parallel and illegal sectional committee). In the short term they intended to exhaust the teachers by constant bureaucratic pressure, which included dismissals and delayed wages, and by the end of 1986 the repression had spawned 186 separate conflicts across the state, many of which were already in the courts. In the longer term, by coordinating their operations with federal agencies, they intended to mount a complete blockade of the movement (*política de bloqueo*) and close down every political space it might use to its own strategic advantage.

This repression everywhere depended on the cooperation of the Ministry of Education, which could manipulate or simply refuse to listen to dissident demands, as well as prolonging negotiations to the point of frustration or diverting them to particular or partial solutions. Hence, it was the Ministry's delegate, Filiberto Gamboa, who played the key role in blockading the movement in Chiapas by simply negating the sectional committee's negotiating rights in order to demoralize the teachers and, more especially, to reassert the Vanguard's monopoly over the union's *capacidad de gestión*. The teachers for their part were only too aware of the long list of independent unions and democratic tendencies within unions that had been badly mauled or completely eliminated by State action,[13] and the strike of 1987 was indeed a "do or die" struggle by a movement that saw itself besieged: The state government of Absalón Castellanos supported all the excesses of the old *caciquismo,* and was not disposed to nego-

---

13 The independent unions on the list included the Union of Workers of the National University (STUNAM) and the Independent Union of the Workers in the Metropolitan University (SITUAM); unions affiliated to the Labor Congress that had experienced internal democratic struggles included the Sole Union of Electrical Workers of the Mexican Republic (SUTERM), the Sole Union of Workers in the Nuclear Industry (SUTIN), and the telephone workers' union.

tiate; the Vanguard had sent in its spies and *agents provocateurs,* and grouped its regular cadres in trouble spots like San Cristóbal and Carranza;[14] and as the strike began the administrative repression bit deeper. More teachers were sanctioned and fewer paid wages. More jobs were at risk, and threats were more violent.[15] And as soon as the strike was over and the new executive commission was in place, over 200 teachers were summarily sacked. More than just conditioning the movement's strategic calculations, this was a clear demonstration that shifts in the institutional terrain might alter its very chances of survival.

## Elements of administrative repression

Cooptation had always been a key form of control within the SNTE and had been used both to assuage dissidence and to divide potential opposition. It had proved effective against the democratic movement in Chihuahua, and the Revolutionary Vanguard saw no reason it should not work equally well in Chiapas. But this movement had begun to change the rules of the game, and its directly democratic forms of organization were mainly successful in preventing defections. A few teachers did succumb to offers of loans, bonuses, and the more attractive city or "double shift" jobs, and many more were in fact "ghost" teachers who worked for the Vanguard but never entered a classroom. In this way the Vanguard used its considerable powers of patronage to create and maintain a phalanx of some 3,000 loyalists within the state, who were joined by strikebreakers from other regions during strikes, and who sowed the kind of conflict and confusion that could "justify" administrative repression.

At the same time, the SNTE initially sought to coopt dissident leaderships in toto by agreeing to mixed executive commissions (Oaxaca, Chiapas) or amplified sectional committees (Hidalgo, Morelos, Valle de México), which might draw them into the institutional structure of the SNTE and bind them

14 In Carranza it was reckoned that some fifty teachers were Vanguard agents and were drawing pay without working, and in nearly every school the dissidents were fighting to throw out the Vanguard's cadres. The repression was heavy here "because it was always heavy in Carranza." Furthermore, the Vanguard routinely used undercover agents. As early as May 1980 the Chiapas teachers had captured documents from the headquarters of Section VII that revealed the Vanguard's plans for infiltrating the movement. The Chiapas teachers estimated conservatively that there were fifteen to twenty such agents in their movement; Oaxaca and Guerrero reported much higher numbers of ninety-eight and fifty-seven, respectively. But, as the teachers proudly said, "they cannot even beat us with political knaves" (*"ni con vagos de la política pueden"*).

15 In the highlands the Vanguard agents of San Cristóbal and Antonio Pérez Hernández, the boss of Indian education, armed their supervisors to police the schools and intimidate the striking teachers. In general, the repression bit harder in small sectors like special education and in the sectors (special, nursery, and primary) where the great majority of teachers are women. There is no doubt that some men used the administrative repression to reassert their personal predominance over the women in their workplace. After the strike it was the authorities who had reason to fear: The Ministry's delegate in the highlands, Ernesto Torres López, asked for protection against kidnapping, and it was reliably reported that Filiberto Gamboa had fled the state.

to its bureaucratic procedures. These initiatives were guided by an initial policy of carefully calibrated concessions, including wage concessions, which aimed to slow the momentum of the movements in their first phase. Mobilization by Oaxaca in mid-1980 won a 22 percent wage increase nationally, and further increases were granted less than six months later; at the height of the struggle in Morelos its teachers were awarded two pay increases in as many months to bolster support for the official leadership. But most concessions were nothing more than a cover for official inaction, and officialdom, whether of the government or of the SNTE, consistently reneged on its agreements and broke its promises.

Just a few days before the movement in Morelos was due to hold its promised congress in March 1981, the Revolutionary Vanguard held a secret congress in Coyocóc where the few select delegates elected a new sectional committee. As a result, the committee that was subsequently elected by a mass congress, and that enjoyed clear majority support, was declared illegal by the SNTE's National Committee. Both the SNTE's "leader-for-life," Jonguitud Barrios, and its secretary-general, Martínez Martín, were present at this act of sheer chicanery, which was typical of the preferably legal but perfectly undemocratic tactics used by the Revolutionary Vanguard to reduce authentic majorities to the status of dissident minorities. Such tactics had been used to defeat the movement in Chihuahua (Luna Jurado 1977 and were repeated in Hidalgo, Morelos, and the Valle de México (see Chapter 7). They were again on display in Chiapas in 1987, when the National Committee of the SNTE denied the teachers their sectional congress and then dismissed the sectional committee on the grounds that no congress had been held as scheduled. This was aptly characterized as "the logic of authoritarian caprice: I forbid you to hold elections; I dismiss you because you do not hold elections" (Hernández 1987a).

The SNTE backed these tactical maneuvers with propaganda campaigns that characterized the dissident movements as illegal organizations that sought to divide the union and destroy it. In an interminable series of Extraordinary National Council meetings, beginning in June 1980, the SNTE decried the movements and demanded strict sanctions from the government.[16] There was loose talk of links with left-wing parties and even of an international plot against Mexico, and the Council's "cold war" warriors encouraged campaigns of vilification against striking teachers everywhere. Considerable resources were invested in negative coverage by press and radio, and the SNTE also dragooned peasant and community leaders and municipal presidents to address school assemblies and parents' meetings for the purpose of denigrating the dissidents. The teachers of Chiapas, in particular, were bombarded with defamatory fliers

---

16 The war of words had begun in earnest at the SNTE's XII National Congress in January 1980, when Secretary-General José Luis Andrade Ibarra had exhorted the delegates to "Smash them! And no thought for the consequences!"

and broadsheets that variously described Manuel Hernández as a criminal, a drug smuggler, a communist, an arms smuggler who gave guns to peasants and teachers, a guerrilla fighter with links to Guatemalan and Salvadorean rebels, and, most damning of all, a coffee grower and landowner! A hostile local newspaper called *Avante* propagated similar calumnies that were countered by the rival *Hoy,* which was firm in its support of the movement. Unfortunately, its editor soon found himself behind the bars of Cerro Hueco, alongside Manuel Hernández.

## The recourse to violence

Where administrative repression was not enough, the authorities were ready to use more direct methods. The assassination of the leading figure in the teachers' movement of the Valle de México, Misael Núñez Acosta, on January 30, 1981, was very exactly timed to turn back the swelling tide of protest in that state, and was closely followed by especially violent evictions of the encampments in front of the Ministry of Education and the SNTE's headquarters in Mexico City.[17] Later that year the leader of the Valle's Central Struggle Committee, Ezequiel Reyes Carrillo, was wounded in a "bank assault," even though he was nowhere near a bank, and then "disappeared." In February of the next year the focus of violence switched to Hidalgo where an assembly of dissident teachers was attacked with rockets and gunfire by a group of SNTE strong-arm men recently arrived from Jonguitud's stronghold in San Luis Potosí. One month later, and just as the SNTE was making empty promises to the Central Struggle Committees of the Valle de México, Morelos, and Hidalgo, one of the Hidalgo teachers, Pedro Palma, died of his gunshot wounds and was laid to rest with the thought that "we do not bury you but sow you like a seed of struggle where our movement will germinate" (Hernández 1983c).[18]

Assassinations and "disappearances" were not uncommon, but some have thought that the more rural and inaccessible regions of the south were less subject to the use of violence than the industrial zones near the capital like the Valle de México. The more than thirty political murders of teachers in Oaxaca in the

17 Moreover, when the suspects in the killing were finally arrested on July 3 that year, they swore that they had been recruited (and paid their 300,000 pesos) by Clemente Villegas Villegas, who acted as a consultant to the SNTE's secretary-general, Martínez Martín, on the National Committee. But before any of this could be verified, the two suspects actually accused of the killing escaped from gaol, with the clear complicity of the prison's chief warden and governor. In fact, none of the other wardens turned up for work that day because they were all sick.

18 Ironically, it is only death that allows such quietly elegaic moments. The mood was different in Morelos in June when the leader of its Central Struggle Committee, Víctor Ariel Barcenas, was seized by thugs from the Revolutionary Vanguard and repeatedly buggered in the back of their car. Bravely, Barcenas reported this attempt to frighten and humiliate him to Rosario Ibarra, the president of the National Front Against Represssion (FNCR) (Hernández 1983c).

first seven years of the movement suggest the contrary, although it is possible that the violence there had less public impact than it did in the Valle or Hidalgo. But Guerrero was notorious for the violence of its police and military response to striking teachers, who suffered a series of "disappearances" that were repeatedly condemned at national meetings of the Coordinating Committee. So widespread was the violence that many of Guerrero's teachers actually fled to Morelos early in 1981, where they were received as "refugees." On the day of Núñez Acosta's assassination in the Valle de México, the governor of Guerrero had made a personal appearance with pistol in hand to threaten the dissident teachers, in a startling display of the kind of authoritarian fury that had earlier prompted a respected newspaper editor to ask, "Is Ruben Figueroa the governor of a Mexican State, or president of a banana republic?" (*Excelsior,* November 23, 1979).

In these violent circumstances it is perhaps surprising that by 1987 the movement in Chiapas had suffered only one murder.[19] But the teachers had nonetheless come to expect the worst from the authorities, whose first response to those claiming their rights was always, "first I lock you up, then I investigate" (Hernández Aguilar 1986). In this way "violence and incarceration walked hand in hand in the countryside," and the teachers came to expect violence because they had seen so much of it, and not, as one wag put it, "because we like them to repress us." Finally, almost inevitably, a young teacher was killed in an armed confrontation with the Vanguard's loyalists in the park of Tuxtla Gutiérrez, the capital of Chiapas. The city's bishop said mass before the open coffin in the main square, but no one came down from the governor's palace to pay their last respects, either to the dead teacher or to the freedom of assembly.

Last but not least, violence was routinely used not simply to intimidate but, more specifically, to prepare the ground for negotiation. Thus, during the national work stoppage of December 1981, the teachers met with the sub-secretary of higher education, Eliseo Mendoza Berrueto, who surprised them by sending in armed police and thugs to break up their demonstration with tear gas and clubs, and "in this way negotiations began" (Fernández Dorado 1982). Similarly, just before negotiations to end the mass mobilization of March 1982 in Mexico City, the Ministry of the Interior sent in armed and mounted police to beat, disperse, and imprison the teachers, and so incline them to accept whatever concessions the authorities were ready to offer.[20] On the other hand, when

---

19  As the great majority of assassinations are privately ordered and funded, the relatively few deaths in Chiapas may in part reflect the dense presence of the "forces of order" in the state. In addition to federal and state police, three army regiments are stationed there to guard the border with Guatemala and control the flow of Central American refugees.

20  On this occasion the effects of the police attack were mitigated by the response of the local populace, who hid the teachers in their homes and, moreover, pelted the police with all the household objects that came to hand. This show of popular solidarity prevented the police from loading any more than 400 of the 4,000 teachers into their paddy wagons.

the thugs of the Revolutionary Vanguard attacked the movement in Hidalgo, their aim was not to prepare for negotiation but to provoke the kind of violent response that might prejudice or stop negotiations already under way with the Ministry of Education. But one way or the other, the violence was used to handicap the movements and reduce their chances of making any significant gains through negotiation.

# 9

## Popular strategies

### Mobilization and the institutional impact of the movement

Just as the trajectory of the teachers' movement was conditioned by the institutional terrain it had to traverse, so the movement itself sometimes shaped the contours of its institutional context and thus extended its margins of strategic maneuver. Where this occurred it was likely to be the contingent result of the movement's pursuit of its own objectives and, in particular, of the teachers' struggle to achieve more control over their own professional lives. This was demonstrated by the encounter between the Ministry of Education's program of decentralization (see Chapter 8) and the directly democratic decision making of the movement's assemblies, which displaced the supervisor and the delegational committee, and so changed the whole chain of administrative linkage from the bottom up. This made a big difference to the teachers themselves. They were no longer fixed objects in the hierarchical universe of union and Ministry but full-fledged political actors (see Chapter 1), who could now seek to resolve their own professional problems nearer their point of origin and in direct dialogue with Ministry officials. It also had a major impact on their institutional environment.

Insofar as both Ministry and movement wanted less corruption and more efficiency, their aims appeared to coincide, and the Ministry of Education initially supported the movement in its battle with the union's supervisors. But the real decentralization implicit in the movement soon clashed with the increasingly centralized political controls required by the reform program. Far from promoting popular participation, as the Ministry claimed, its program was designed to achieve direct bureaucratic control over teachers in the schools and to usurp union prerogatives in the process. The teachers, on the contrary, wanted the unholy corporatist alliance of union and Ministry dissolved altogether, so that their movement might give them a real say in their own affairs. In the field, the Ministry's delegations initially responded more to the movement than to their own central apparatus; in Chiapas no fewer than six delegates were dismissed for failing to marry the political imperatives of the reform with

130

the teachers' demands. In short, the rupture in the Ministry's central lines of command was compounded by the delegation's loss of control over the supervisors and directors who were its own administrative agents, and this regional breakdown threatened the national reform program. Hence, it was not long before the delegations were deployed into the frontline of the battle to destroy the movement.

But the teachers' movement also impaired the traditional division between administrative and union matters, and, by extension, the social supports for the political control of the union's *charro* leadership; it was the National Executive Committee of the SNTE that put steel into the delegations' resistance and insisted on dismissing delegates who had proved too compliant to the demands of the movement. Inevitably the movement's dual threat to ministerial authority and *charro* control finally reinforced the alliance between the Ministry and the SNTE at the federal level, and this was sufficient to defend the delegations, albeit with less reformist impulse. Yet, despite the repair, the movement had transformed the terms of the corporatist relationship between the Ministry and the SNTE by challenging the clientelistic controls that had underpinned it. This was the institutional impact of the fight to defend legal rights and vindicate new professional rules. Among other things it made the SNTE's claims for political rewards in return for *charro* control look a lot less convincing.

The legal rights of teachers to control their own professional lives was at the heart of their cause, and it was administrative repression in all its forms (see Chapter 8) that most threatened those rights. Despite the often conciliatory attitude of the teachers themselves, this repression was used against all the regional movements from the very beginning, and it was intensified at moments of increased combativeness, such as the successful alliance between the teachers of Chiapas and the peasants of La Fraylesca (see Chapter 6).[1] There is therefore no doubt that the intransigence and vindictiveness of the authorities often served to catalyze the mobilization of the dissident teachers; and, equally, the force of the regional movements came to be measured by the resistance they could mount to such repression through mobilization. For the teachers it was critical that they defend both their legal rights and the institutional advances that allowed them to solve their own professional problems, so that mobilization became not a choice but a necessity. For this reason recurrent mobilization, more than anything else, characterizes the political practices of the teachers' movement, and mobilization did the most to consolidate popular organization. In effect, without such mobilization there was no movement.

---

1 In the case of Chiapas the response of the authorities was also impelled by a specific, geopolitical assessment of Chiapas as an energy-rich, frontier state, which was exposed to the political contamination of popular and armed struggles in Central America. But what made Chiapas one of the most politically conflictual states was the recurrent confrontation between the *caciquismo* that characterized its government and society and the popular project of the teachers' movement.

## Forms of popular mobilization

At the beginning of the movement it sometimes seemed as if political support was slow to accumulate, and Chiapas called the pioneering meeting of the national movement in December 1979 (see Chapter 7) to alleviate its sense of isolation. But the movement had already made the key organizational discovery of the Central Struggle Committee, which was to serve as a model for teachers of other regions, which soon had similar "committees" or "commissions." Its dissemination was rapid, but regional alliances were too loose to secure its transfer to other sectors, with the exception of Chiapas.[2] Then, with common forms of organization the teachers were able to develop a common tactical sense of their struggle, and their mutual learning was important in resisting the continuous *charro* attempts to infiltrate and divide the movement in the schools, the delegations, and the assemblies. Piecemeal struggle that avoided damaging defeats was the main tactical touchstone (see Chapter 5), with mobilization being carefully measured to secure partial advances that did not invite repression. All of which was easier said than done.

Within these broad lines the teachers explored the tactics that might create the kind of pressure needed to get their demands met.[3] Early in the movement it was low wages and late payment that provoked strikes of thirty days average in Chiapas, Oaxaca, Guerrero, Hidalgo, and the Valle de México. Thereafter, tactics diversified as the demands came to address professional and political issues such as democratic congresses, the recognition of elected leaders and grass-roots delegates, the fulfillment of agreements, and the use and abuse of constitution and law to deny the teachers' rights as citizens. Many of these tactics were not exactly new, but they were used in novel ways and to novel effect. The rapid advance of the movement in Chiapas and Oaxaca,[4] for example, would have been impossible without the brigades (see Chapter 4), which then

2 In Chiapas the teachers encouraged the *ejido*-based peasants to exercise direct control over their own representatives, and so instilled the democratic mechanisms typical of their own movement. In this way the teachers' movement became a model for peasant community organization, but only so far as the alliance was achieved piecemeal at the grass roots. Peasant sectors began to organize autonomously of the sectoral corporations of the ruling party, and of parties in general, and so were able to offer sustained political support to the teachers' struggles; peasants in the highlands even invented new tactics that were later employed by the teachers. This degree of crossover was unprecedented, but also specific to Chiapas.

3 The teachers soon learned that only recurrent mobilization worked. As Manuel Hernández said to subsecretary Mendoza Berrueto in March of 1982, "No matter how many times you provoke us, we will always fight back."

4 Given the difficult geography of the state, the brigades were even more important in Oaxaca than in Chiapas. There were some 800 brigades criss-crossing the state in the early months of the movement. The broad and radical base of the movement was what made the brigades, but their impact was magnified by the work of the Coalition of Bilingual Teachers and Hispanifiers. The teachers of this key group in this massively Indian state were at first suspicious of how a *charro* union could suddenly change its character, but once convinced by the strike of May 1980 they became the most effective "brigadiers" of all.

took on a broader logistical role in mounting mass mobilizations at the national level; and it was the pressing tactical requirement of the brigades that did the most to refine the organization of struggle committees at the delegational and state level. Similarly, work stoppages were linked to marches and demonstrations in ways that raised the profile and increased the impact of coordinated national initiatives.

The success of such tactics was seen in the mass marches, which repeatedly brought tens and sometimes hundreds of thousands of teachers onto the streets of Mexico City and state capitals across the country. None of these was more impressive than the March 1986 demonstration by Oaxacan teachers in defense of their democratic congress. Every one of the 32,560 teachers marched from Oaxaca to Mexico City, including the old, the sick, and the pregnant, and then from March 3 to March 12 they marched no less than ten times through the center of the capital.[5] The lesson could not have been more clear. It was not the stoppage but the mobilization that was fundamental in promoting participation and creating favorable circumstances for effective negotiation.

It was also the teachers from Oaxaca who first added the encampment, or *plantón,* to the mass march when 20,000 of them pitched their tents in front of the Ministry of Education and the SNTE's headquarters in May 1980. Such was the impact on public opinion that this tactic was adopted by many other movements and was used to good effect in state capitals too; different regional movements would sometimes combine their contingents in a single encampment. A later refinement was the mobile encampment, which would retreat by night to avoid violent eviction by the police; the scope of the mobile encampment was extended by the movement in Morelos, which first marched in "caravan" from one city to another. To give a cutting edge to their protests, the teachers also occupied union buildings, held illegal mass congresses, and even went on hunger strike,[6] usually to insist on the democratic congresses that had been promised but never held. And where they finally got such a congress (Chiapas, Oaxaca), they had to mobilize in meticulous fashion to prevent manipulation by the *charros,*[7] in clear recognition that mobilization of this kind

---

5 These marches generated a rich variety of chants and slogans, including: *"Lo quiera o no lo quiera, Van-guardia va pa fuera"; "con quincena o sin quincena, ésta lucha no se frena"; "si Juárez viviera, con nosotros estuviera"; "aquí, allá, Oaxaca vencerá"; "Gobierno, entiende, Oaxaca no se vende"; "adelante, atrás, a los lados, aquí no hay acarreados"; "Pueblo, disculpa por esta interrupción, pero es que no tenemos ninguna solución"; "las calles son ahora nuestra habitación, no importa el sacrificio, queremos solución"; "Jonguitud, Oaxaca es tu ataúd"; "A Oaxaca no regreso, si no hay Congreso"; "Se ve, se nota, en Oaxaca no hay derrota."*

6 This tactic was taken to its limit by the Oaxacan teachers during their "Encampment of Dignity" in Mexico City in 1986, when tens of teachers placed themselves in mortal danger.

7 In March 1981 in Chiapas the teachers had held "pre-elections" for all posts on the delegational committees, as well as a "pre-congress" to elect their own slate for the new sectional committee, thus resorting to the tactics of the Vanguard to prevent manipulation by the Vanguard. A month later in Morelos, however, the Vanguard succeeded in electing a spurious committee (see Chapter 8), and so when Oaxaca prepared its congress of February 1982 it carefully imitated the Chiapas tactics in order to avoid a *morelazo.*

was never a "war of manoeuvre" but always a "war of position" (Gramsci 1971), or trench warfare "where every school and every delegation was a trench" (FMIN 1981b; Sección XI 1982).

## Popular mobilization and political alliances

None of this mobilization would have been possible were it not for the support of the parents. This was true from the moment of the ETAs movement in Chiapas (Reyes 1980), which showed that even the first weapon in the tactical armory, the strike, could not be sustained without it. But this support could be lost, as it was progressively in Morelos, and in 1985 this led Oaxaca to set up parents' councils to back its struggle for a democratic congress; these councils then came to constitute the core of the Forum for Popular Organizations, which sought "to coordinate different sectors with the common objective of defending popular interests" (Instituto Politécnico Nacional 1985, no. 9). Such was the identity of purpose between parents and teachers in Oaxaca that they went on hunger strike together in the state capital's cathedral, and together were assassinated for their pains.

But the firm alliance forged with the parents in Oaxaca was an unexpected development in a movement that had vociferously rejected all links with any organization, political or otherwise; and the alliance strategy of regional movements was always complicated by a general rejection of party alliances, whether of the left or right, on the grounds that "the mass organization must take its own decisions" (Sección VII 1982b). The intellectuals of the national movement had it as a point of principle that their organization remain "autonomous of every party and group in power" (Palomino 1983a), and the rights of individual teachers to their own political views were recognized only on the condition that militants of whatever political hue abide by the decisions of the assembly (Salinas Alvarez and Imaz Gispert 1984). Struggle Committees in regions like the Valle de México were even reluctant to ally with the peasant (CNPA) or urban popular (CONAMUP) movements, insisting that all initiatives take place at the grass roots, and not at leadership level.

But if the picture was patchy at the regional level, it was yet more confused at the national level, where the movement's alliance strategy was never adequately defined. In particular, it remained unclear whether the teachers' movement should join forces with other popular movements like the peasant and urban movements, or whether it should collaborate with independent unions. Nonetheless, the teachers' own Coordinating Committee did emerge early in the general process of the national coordination of popular struggles,[8] and it

---

8 It was over the years 1976 to 1982 that the popular movements managed to construct their coordinating committees such as the National Front against Repression (FNCR, in 1977), the "Plan de Ayala" National Coordinating Committee (CNPA, in 1979), and the National Coordinating Committee of the Urban Popular Movement (CONAMUP, in 1981).

joined one of the first intersectoral demonstrations at the national level when it marched with the "Plan de Ayala" Coordinating Committee (CNPA) from the Advanced School to the Ministry of the Interior in May 1981. Early in 1982 it played a big part in organizing the National Meeting of Syndical Solidarity, which founded the National Syndical Coordinating Committee (COSINA), and then in March of that year, joined the COSINA in the Grand March of Teachers and Workers. It later served as a mainstay to the large and loose-knit confederation of the FNDSCAC (National Front for the Defense of Wages and Against Austerity and Need); mobilized its members for the "national civic stoppages"; and became the backbone of the FNDSCAC's successor, the ANOCP (National Popular Assembly of Workers and Peasants). But the large alliances tended to dissolve into internal squabbles that severely limited their impact, and the overall results of these ambitious initiatives were uncertain. So even if it may safely be said that the teachers' movement became the obligatory point of reference and the occasional organizational axis of popular struggle in Mexico, it never really had much success in securing solid cross-sectoral support for the movement itself.

## Mobilization and institutionalism

For the teachers' movement, mobilization was necessary but not sufficient to achieve an institutional impact. Beyond the tactical ground of mobilization lay the strategic terrain of engagement with the institutional environment. The ·original preference for negotiation over confrontation in the emerging movement of Chiapas showed an early recognition of the strategic need for an institutional connection of some sort. The Central Struggle Committee provided effective organization, but it was illegal, and this is why the primary objective came to be the legal conquest of the sectional committee. Once the committee was won, the leadership was quite clear that it "must seek political agreements with the federal government and the state political apparatus" (Sección VII 1982a). If these links provided the kind of negotiating leverage, or *capacidad de gestión,* that secured the leadership's own position,[9] they would also underpin the development of the movement itself. Thus the regional leadership became "a valid interlocutor" for the authorities, in a way that was inconceivable in the 1950s, but this almost never occurred with the National Coordinating Committee.

Despite the initial successes of the Chiapas leadership, its compliance with the mixed executive commission (see Chapters 4 and 5) led to criticisms that further mobilization now depended on the approval of the SNTE (Salinas Alvarez and Imaz Gispert 1984). Such a purist approach was decisively rejected by

---

9 This same leadership was clear that the Chiapas strike of 1985 "defeated the strategy of dismantling the movement by damaging the capacity of the union to get its demands met" (Hernández Gómez et al. 1985).

the national movement, which insisted that the teachers "must go on transforming the juridical structure of their union, which means legalizing each stage of the struggle for the democratization of the SNTE" (National Assembly, January 1982). In effect, nearly every regional movement tried to dismiss its official sectional committee and call a congress to elect a new one,[10] in an effort to form links with the political system of which the SNTE was a key part. It was unfortunate that the strategy often led to the "minority institutionalization of the dissidents" (Salinas Alvarez and Imaz Gispert), with the movement's mobilization outmaneuvered by the elite pacts of the Revolutionary Vanguard (see Chapter 7), but the movement went on demanding official recognition at the very doors of officialdom. This was the point of the Oaxaca movement's encampment of May 1980, of the unsuccessful insistence on national negotiations with the SNTE in March 1982, and the clamor in the capital of Chiapas for a meeting with President Miguel de la Madrid (who happened to visit the state during the strike of 1985). In short, where the authorities refused recognition, the movement tried to leapfrog to the top of the system. In the marches to Mexico City, geography was merely the metaphor.

The key perception underlying this institutionalist strategy was that the State was not monolithic, but was rather a contradictory ensemble of complex institutions. The Ministry of Education sometimes seemed disposed to respond to economic demands; it not only agreed to negotiate with "valid interlocutors" from legal sectional committees but also carried on occasional negotiations with "illegal" representatives, which certainly sharpened its differences with the SNTE in Oaxaca and Hidalgo. At other times the Ministry could easily refuse negotiation, insisting that the SNTE was the only legal representative and supporting the SNTE in its administrative repression. The SNTE, on the other hand, was usually more openly intransigent because its own position within the political system, and its leverage in the process of elite pacts, clearly depended on its monopoly control of the teachers. But the key point is that Ministry and SNTE did not always respond in the same way at the same time, in part because of the complexities of their own interactions, which were compounded by the reform program (see Chapter 8); this sometimes enabled the teachers' movement to bypass the SNTE and approach the Ministry of Education, or other federal departments, and state governments in the struggle for institutional advance. In the most favorable of circumstances the movement might calibrate its institutionalism by targeting different state agencies in different moments.

These different moments refer to what might be called "political time," and are partly defined and fixed by the relations between the government agencies themselves. In Chapter 5 it was observed how the strategic choices and internal

---

10 Even when backed by massive mobilization these maneuvers were never very likely to succeed. On one infamous occasion in Morelos the SNTE's secretary-general had met with the movement's leadership and had given his signed permission for a democratic congress, but in fact he had forged a signature that was not "his own" and later denied being present at the meeting at all!

dynamics of the movement might contribute to the configuration of a political "conjuncture," and this notion is now complicated by the external dynamics of the institutional environment, not to mention the interaction between the two. This was already clear in Chapter 8 in the specific context of the Ministry of Education's reform program, which extended the movement's margins of political maneuver in the regions, but sometimes drew particular movements into damaging and strategically unjustified confrontations. Now the intention is to expand the range of institutional reference to see how other government agencies and policy priorities have conditioned the trajectory of the movement. The field of reference is mainly federal, but contradictions between state governments and federal agencies have also been important in some moments. In particular, there were strong tensions between the state governments of Chiapas (see Chapter 5), Oaxaca, Morelos, and Hidalgo, which were broadly sympathetic to the movement in its early years, and the Revolutionary Vanguard in the person of its "leader-for-life," Carlos Barrios Jonguitud. The governors of these states clearly resented the incursions of another governor into their political territory, as well as the influence that the Vanguard everywhere tried to exercise over the municipal presidents and federal senators and deputies.

## Moments in political time

Besides the Ministry of Education and SNTE, the key federal actor for the fledging teachers' movement was the Ministry of the Interior. The friction between the Ministry of the Interior and the National Executive Committee of the SNTE was no secret,[11] so the Ministry might have been expected to favor the movement in some degree; and because its first priority was public order, it might be ready to respond to new forms of mass mobilization. Hence, when it first intervened in negotiations between the protesting teachers of Oaxaca, the SNTE, and the Ministry of Education in June of 1980,[12] it played a conciliatory role in the recognition that the SNTE had lost control of a large number of its teachers. The intervention brought the promise of a democratic congress for Oaxaca and a wage rise for teachers across the country, and the Ministry of the Interior continued to press for the kind of economic concessions that might assuage grass-roots agitation, at the same time urging the state governments of Guerrero and Morelos to seek negotiated outcomes rather than pursuing more violent options.

Beyond conciliation the Ministry of the Interior had a yet more important

---

11 It was rumored that the Minister of the Interior was committed to reducing the power of the SNTE as part of his play for the presidential succession.

12 The Ministry of the Interior was responding to the impact on public opinion caused by 20,000 Oaxacan teachers and their Encampment of Dignity. At the same time, the dissident teachers had invited the Ministry to resolve the political divisions between their state government, on the one hand, and, on the other, the SNTE's sectional committee and the Ministry of Education's delegation in Oaxaca.

objective: to coordinate the responses of Federal agencies, which had so far failed to act in concert. Just before the June protest it had promoted a tripartite commission from the Ministry of Education, the Ministry of Programming and Budget (Minister de la Madrid), and the SNTE to study the wage question, and once the commission was established in November that year it was successful in getting the Ministry of Education and the SNTE to present a united front to the striking teachers. The problem with the front was its intransigence, with the Ministry of Education threatening to stop pay and the SNTE refusing to recognize the negotiating initiatives of the dissident Coordinating Committee. It is true that the commission had announced increased bonuses at the beginning of 1981, but by now the teachers were demanding recognition for the sectional committees elected by mass congresses in Hidalgo and the Valle de México, and a provisional democratic committee for Guerrero. Once again, the March for Teachers Dignity took the dissidents directly to the doors of the Ministry of the Interior, which again brought the Ministry of Education and the SNTE to the negotiating table, with results that are already known (see Chapter 7). In this way the Ministry of the Interior made sure that the teachers got something because it wanted to clear the streets, but it made equally sure that they did not get everything because this would invite more regional mobilizations.[13]

The actual Minister of the Interior during this period and in the run-up to the 1982 general elections, was Enrique Olivares Santana, who belonged to the political clique that had controlled the SNTE prior to Jonguitud's coup of 1972, which ushered in the Revolutionary Vanguard (see Chapter 3). His loyalties had made a difference to the outcome of the first democratic congress in Chiapas, which took place at a time (March 1981) when the Vanguard was at odds both with the Ministry of the Interior and with the Ministry of Education, whose delegate in Chiapas had been director of the rural training schools and was fully committed to implementing the Ministry's reform program and responding to the teachers' demands. As we know, the governor of Chiapas at this time, Juan Sabines, belonged to the same political family as Santana (see Chapter 5), and in this case the combination of political contradictions at federal and state level, and the way they cross-cut, created the teachers' strategic opportunity.[14]

With the presidential succession of 1982 looming large, many more regions

---

13  The Ministry of the Interior continued to favor negotiated solutions that avoided damaging confrontations. In October 1984 it set up a joint commission, composed of representatives of the Ministry of the Interior, the Ministry of Education, the two state governments, and the SNTE, to resolve the conflicts in Chiapas and Oaxaca.

14  On the other hand, the SNTE strongman in the region, who headed the mixed commission that had been imposed in the wake of the 1979 strike, aspired to the post of secretary-general and was therefore implacable in his defense of *charro* control. But at this moment even the hostility of the Vanguard proved salutary in binding together a potentially divided movement (see Chapters 5 and 6).

experienced deepening political divisions as rivalry intensified between political cliques at the federal level. Both the Ministries of the Interior and of Education were recalcitrant to the demands of an SNTE that was seen as ever more ambitious but ever less effective, insofar as it resisted reform (see Chapter 8) but failed to control the teachers. Moreover, as the teachers' movement was now focusing on political rather than economic demands, and thus posing a more direct challenge to the Revolutionary Vanguard, it proved useful to those federal departments that needed a stick to beat the SNTE. Most critically, the Vanguard had no links to the political clique of the eventual presidential candidate, Miguel de la Madrid, and sought in vain to secure some political advantage from the presidential campaign.[15] As a measure of its desperation, it resorted to accusing state governments of financing the dissident teachers.

In February of 1982 a commission from the dissidents' Coordinating Committee was received by Fernando Elias Calles, who was federal director of the Ministry of Education's regional delegations. The agenda focused on the administrative problems caused by the reform program, and both sides saw an advantage in doing some effective casework and reducing the level of regional conflict. But the negotiations appeared to recognize the leaders of the main Central Struggle Committees as the effective representatives of the teachers in their regions, and this point was not lost on the Revolutionary Vanguard. In the wake of the Hidalgo ambush (see Chapter 8) it launched a scathing attack that sank both Calles and the negotiations but added more impetus to the mass mobilizations during the month of March in Mexico City (see Chapter 7). Once again it was the Ministry of the Interior that finally obliged the SNTE to begin negotiations,[16] whereupon the Revolutionary Vanguard immediately accused the Coordinating Committee of complicity with government officials. By this time, relations between the Vanguard and the personnel of both Education and the Interior had reached their nadir.

The big turnabout came late in 1983. The movement had been forced back to economic demands that made no headway against the new government's austerity policies, and its defense of the intensive summer courses in the Advanced School had led to confrontation and defeat (see Chapters 7 and 8). In the congressional and municipal elections of 1983, on the other hand, the government had suffered serious reverses that suddenly put a new premium on the SNTE's cooperation and convinced both the Ministry of the Interior and the ruling party that they needed the SNTE machinery to recover their electoral

---

15 The yawning gap between Jonguitud and Miguel de la Madrid was dramatically displayed in the embarrassing failure of a huge reception of teachers and primary school pupils whom Jonguitud had dragooned to greet the candidate in his home state of San Luis Potosí.

16 The Ministry of the Interior took this initiative after a meeting between its undersecretary, Fernando Gutiérrez Barrios, and the representatives of the teachers' movement. One of the members of the eventual negotiating commission of the National Executive Committee of the SNTE was Elba Esther Gordillo, today the SNTE's secretary-general.

fortunes in the north of the country. Hence, when the architect of the reform program, Reyes Heroles, chose this moment to die, President de la Madrid seized the opportunity to send the new Minister of Education, González Avelar, to court the Revolutionary Vanguard and remake its marriage of convenience with the government. In this way the teachers' movement lost the political space it had enjoyed at the federal level because of renewed government reliance on the traditional role of the teachers in mobilizing and controlling the vote (see Introduction and Chapter 1).

In refurbishing the pact González Avelar had tried to placate Jonguitud by conceding control of the National Teachers' University and surrendering the regional USEDs to Vanguard loyalists. Jonguitud himself quickly moved to recover the ground he had lost. He reneged on the promise of a democratic congress for Oaxaca, even though the Ministries of Education and the Interior were both signatories to the agreement; he delivered a public snub to González Avelar at the SNTE's National Congress; and he renewed the Vanguard's offensive in Chiapas. The fact that all this coincided with a general goverment offensive against organized labor, which led to the resounding defeat of the university and nuclear power workers, only served to reinforce the conclusion that the change in the fortunes of the teachers' movement reflected a genuine conjunctural shift. And now that the movement was possibly the only political force capable of mobilizing popular opposition to austerity, it became the government's priority target.

During the conflicts that surrounded the shift, the Ministry of the Interior continued as the federal agency of last resort, but its attempts to arbitrate were neither so successful nor so plausible as before. The Minister of the Interior, Manuel Bartlett, failed to prevent the national strike that brought 300,000 teachers onto the streets in June 1983, and although he again tried to intervene in the endless dispute over Oaxaca's second democratic congress, he "never sought to resolve the conflict so much as to prevent the federal government and the president from being seen as responsible for it" (Instituto Politécnico Nacional 1985, no. 13). Thus, the Ministry of the Interior underwrote the agreement signed in March 1985, but the congress promised for the following month never took place; and the Ministry was again witness to the next empty promise of February 1986. The hard truth was that together the federal government and the SNTE had tightened their institutional hold throughout the national territory and were trying to strangle the teachers' movement. The teachers from Oaxaca led a silent and funereal march through Mexico City to show that "democracy was dead in Mexico."

The impact of this shift in conjuncture varied between regional movements, depending *inter alia* on the political color of the state government. In Chiapas, where the state government still responded to mobilization, the movement continued to believe that it could take advantage of institutional contradictions at the time of the 1985 congressional elections. The Ministry of Education was under some pressure from the SNTE at the federal level, and the federal executive preferred to pursue negotiations through the state governments, which suited the movement well enough. But factional disputes within the movement prevented it from capitalizing on these partial openings (see Chapter 6), and after October that year the Ministry of Education, a new state government, and the National Committee of the SNTE combined their forces in a coordinated assault on the movement. The Ministry's new delegate, Filiberto Gamboa Guzmán, opened the campaign with a broadside against the teachers' professional rights and union prerogatives. He refused point blank to negotiate with the sectional committee; he canceled all transfers and promotions agreed with it, and decided them unilaterally; he imposed his own *charros* as supervisors throughout the section; he tried to oust the leaders of the movement by sacking them; and he also sacked all Ministry employees who had shown any sympathy for the movement, which was most of them.

The strike of 1987 took place before the next presidential election of 1988, and the moment might have provided further openings for the movement. In the event, both the Ministers of Education and the Interior were reluctant to intervene for fear of prejudicing their presidential chances, which gave less room for maneuver to the movement than it did to the Vanguard in a state where the governor, Absalón Castellanos Domínguez, aspired to be Minister of Defense and the Ministry of Education delegate aspired to be governor. Hence, despite the sixty-five day strike, the strength of the parents' support, and the permanent encampment in front of the governor's palace, the movement was roundly defeated. Moreover, when the SNTE's National Committee finally dismissed the sectional committee, it took the opportunity to accuse the Ministers of Education and the Interior of responsibility for the strike, thus doing its utmost to disqualify them as presidential candidates. But the Ministry of Education's delegate and the state governor warmly welcomed the SNTE's intervention, and it had clearly been the unprecedented degree of cooperation between these three that had assured their "victory."[17] The result was especially pleasing for the SNTE's special emissary, José Luis Andrade Ibarra, who had been secretary-general of the SNTE when the teachers of Chiapas first began to mobilize.

17 José Domingo Guillén, among others, was convinced that the authorities' master plan for defeating the movement had been drawn up with the help of research done in the region by students of the Harvard School of Education, which had found its way into the offices of the Ministry of Education.

# PART IV

# Popular movements and political change

# 10

## Institutional linkage

### Linkage: autonomy and representation

In discussing the linkages between the teachers' movement and the Mexican political system, this analysis has tended to emphasize the ways in which the system has shaped the trajectory of the movement, rather than exploring the influence of the movement on processes of institutional change. In the preceding chapter some attempt was made to correct this bias, but, in general, the influence of popular organization on political change in Mexico has been difficult to discern, and the literature has only recently begun to address the issue (Foweraker and Craig 1990). Research and writing has usually focused on the two poles of the relationship between popular struggle and the political system, with scant attention to the relationship itself. This is partly a result of the conceptual problems posed by popular movements, which aspire simultaneously to more autonomy and more representation. But the lessons of the teachers' movement suggest that this contradiction in terms is more apparent than real and that its resolution may reveal the political content of popular "linkage politics."[1]

There is no doubt that popular movements are reluctant to form alliances with political parties (see Chapter 9), just as they are wary of cooptation by the State. But a lateral autonomy separating popular movements from political parties is different from a vertical autonomy separating them from the State, and while the former has been the general rule, the latter has not. Yet it has been argued that anything less than a complete autonomy from the State leads to a "constant destruction of democratic channels and spaces" (Zermeño 1987a), which means that the only movements to survive will be those "with restricted identity." Implicit here and elsewhere is the notion that popular struggles can be divorced from the realm of institutional politics[2] and left to inhabit an Arcadian world where popular experiments in social life create a

---

1 I have (mis)appropriated this term from the title of the book on *Linkage Politics* edited by J. Rosenau.

2 This is tantamount to divorcing the struggles of "particular peoples" from those of the "people in general" (or what Rousseau might have called "the general interest"). In popular-democratic theory these struggles are the same struggle "since the extension of democratic control requires the creation of specific material and social conditions favourable to the exercise of various formal freedoms" (Jessop 1980).

"small-scale counter culture" (Evers 1985) uncontaminated by relations of political power.[3]

The reality is less comfortable. The political exclusion of popular organization may be increasing, and this will leave popular movements "condemned to sterility" (Marion 1987), especially if they lack the protection of a large coordinating committee or union confederation. Similarly, independent union organizations have tended to prosper less than movements within State-chartered union corporations. Hence, an insistence on total autonomy suggests a "jacobinism" (Laclau 1977) that seems unrealistic in the political conditions created by the historical success of State transformism (see Introduction), which has consistently deepened and complicated the institutional penetration and control of Mexican civil society. In these conditions, popular movements depend for their survival and success on the political representation they can achieve, and on the ways their organization and strategy condition their insertion into the political system overall. There is no denying that popular movements may seek a strategic defense of their autonomy (Marván 1988), but more as a condition of effective representation and never as an absolute end in itself.

However, equal care must be taken with the concept of representation, which can imply that interests are defined *a priori* in economic and social life, and then represented in another place called the political (Laclau and Mouffe 1985), rather than being defined through popular struggle itself. There are real problems in researching the pre-political life of interests (which are explored in Chapter 12), and it has anyway been suggested (Castells 1983) that what really matters are the demands that emerge from the processes of popular organization and strategic invention. Everything in this study of the teachers' movement supports this conclusion, with the corollary that popular representation means pressing demands that relate increasingly to the nature and forms of linkage to the political system. Economic and social demands become political, and union struggles automatically take on political objectives. Clearly, this process can be catalyzed by State incursions and institutional controls (see Chapter 8), but, equally, popular movements themselves seek linkage with the system and struggle to get it on their own terms because they cannot do without the *capacidad de gestión,* or the kind of institutional insertion that can get demands met and problems solved. The alternative is the sterility of exclusion and the organizational decline that follows loss of confidence in popular leadership.

## Institutionalism and legalism

The search for institutional linkage is necessarily "characterized by a pattern of negotiation with the State" (Boschi 1984), and the dissident teachers consistently tried to solve their problems by negotiation with the delegations of the

---

3 Evers asserts that "the innovating capacity of these movements appears to lie less in their political potential than in their ability to create and experiment with different forms of social relations in everyday life."

Ministry of Education. Where the regional obstacles were insurmountable, they marched to Mexico City and claimed direct linkage at the doors of the federal government (see Chapter 9). But the kind of "practical legality" they achieved in this way was not enough, and both regional and national leaders came to see that only legal forms and statutory procedures could cement new means of representation, and so convert political advances into more secure linkages. In other words, they came to accept the inevitable institutionalism of the struggle.

Institutionalism may be understood to limit the aims and constrain the political scope of popular movements, but it certainly does not imply a lack of conflict (see Chapters 7 and 8). On the contrary, the widespread conflict both inside and outside the corporative institutions of the system (Cook 1990; Harvey 1990b) shows that there is little popular conformity to institutional controls, whether of a formal or an informal kind. The movements may try to avoid confrontation, but they still have to struggle for representation, in the process challenging the exclusionary policies of the ruling party in particular and the clientelistic patterns of political control in general (see The popular impact on institutional change, below). Popular movements are therefore both institutionalist and nonconformist.

Similarly, just as the institutionalist approach may be conflictual, so the popular struggle for legality is sometimes pursued by illegal means. The struggle against the *charrismo* of the SNTE has often resorted to illegal methods to restore respect for the statutes (Pérez Arce 1990), and the very origin of many urban popular movements is an illegal act of land invasion, for which the movement nonetheless seeks legal sanction and government approval (Ramírez Saiz 1990). The government, for its part, always insists on the rule of law while often abusing it in order to stop the movements and repress political dissidence. Hence, the strategic combination of legal and "extralegal" struggle (see Chapter 6) emerged in a context that is itself legally ambiguous. Although popular movements tend to appeal to the law, their support for it can never be unconditional.

The political potency of legalist appeals in Mexico has deep historical roots and goes some way toward explaining why this *democracia bárbara* compares quite favorably with most other political regimes across the continent over the past thirty years. In particular, such was the "civilizing capacity" (Gramsci 1971) of the Mexican Constitution of 1917 that popular demands for the simple application of the law still have radical implications (see Introduction), which are important to the institutionalism of the teachers' movement. On the one hand, shifts from mobilized militancy to legalism and negotiation do not indicate the changing character of popular organization so much as moments of strategic choice. On the other, the insistence on professional, and therefore legal, rights led the teachers to combat *charrismo* and fight for political control of their union, thus strengthening the institutional impact of their movement (see The popular impact on institutional change, below).

## Institutional terrain and war of position

Institutionalism recognizes that popular movements must learn to live in the real world of institutional politics, and that popular organization and mobilization can occur at all only in intimate interrelation with State laws and institutions. Thus, like every other political struggle in modern societies, the teachers' movement had to advance across a specific legal and institutional terrain; this terrain shaped and conditioned the development of the movement, which responded to its variable pattern of political constraints and opportunities (see Chapter 9).[4] In large measure this pattern reflected the shifting institutional relationships of the political system itself (see Chapters 8 and 9), but specific institutional forms, such as the SNTE's sectional structure (see Chapter 3) or the Ministry of Education's municipal education committees (see Chapters 4 and 5), were also important,[5] as were the laws that made some demands more possible than others and so influenced the movement's objectives (Ramírez Saiz 1990; Craig 1990). Laws and institutions not only mold popular organization but also generate discourse, which may itself change the terms of political argument and even the content of political demands.

The notion of legal-institutional terrain is broader than Stepan's "political society,"[6] as well as being less constitutionally orientated and more sensitive to the balance of social forces in the society at large. Popular struggle has to take place here, if only because there is nowhere else, and so it is clear that popular movements do not struggle in conditions that are of their own choosing. But this does not mean, as Zermeño (1987a) seems to suggest, that all popular movements must meet an equal fate in the procrustean bed of State laws and institutions. Just as the specific contours of the terrain may be created by government policies and priorities (see Chapter 8), so popular movements struggle to modify their institutional environment through mobilization and strategic calculation. In other words this is, above all, a strategic terrain that is continuously shifting under the impact of both popular organization and State initiatives.

4  For this reason the theorists talk of popular movements "creating spaces of interaction within existing structures" (Boschi 1984) and insist that they "respond first and foremost to State intervention," rather than to the initiatives of other political actors in civil society (Touraine 1987).

5  The first democratic councils of the teachers' movements in Chiapas and Oaxaca, which were designed to cement the alliance between teachers and parents, were formed through the municipal education committees of the Ministry, which sought to extend its lines of vertical control. Institutional forms are often more important to popular struggles than the content of particular government policies (compare Foweraker 1989b).

6  "By 'political society' in a democratizing setting I mean that arena in which the polity specifically arranges itself for political contestation to gain control over public power and the state apparatus . . . a full democratic transition must involve political society, and the composition and consolidation of a democratic polity must entail serious thought and action about those core institutions of a democratic political society — political parties, elections, electoral rules, political leadership, intra party alliances, and legislatures — through which civil society can constitute itself politically to select and monitor democratic government" (Stepan 1988).

This is the terrain where Gramsci (1971) sees social forces waging their "war of position," and what finally configures the terrain is the war itself, in all its organizational and strategic variations. If it is true that "popular-democratic struggle is first of all a struggle to form the people" (Jessop 1980), then the State will seek to lead and discipline this formation, and to control the "political spaces" (Laclau 1985) opened up by popular initiatives. But the effects of government policy are sometimes contradictory and always contingent, so that Echeverría's attempt to ally with the alternative leadership of the electricians' union ended with military intervention, and Reyes Heroles's encouragement of the teachers' movements ended with the Ministry of Education and the SNTE combining to tighten legal and institutional control throughout the national territory (see Chapter 8). Popular leaders, on the other hand, seek to promote popular organization and secure political advance, with no guarantee that the efforts expended at the grass roots will ever bring about broader political changes (Mainwaring 1987), or that legal recognition of their progress will make it permanent (as in the SNTE's dismissal of legal sectional committees by simply revoking their mandate). In sum, the linkages between popular organization and the political system are inherently unstable and are only as predictable as the results of the "war of position."

## Government policy and institutional terrain

Every federal administration of the past twenty years has taken major initiatives to shape the legal-institutional terrain to its own advantage (see Introduction). Echeverría's political opening aimed to revitalize the role of State-chartered union corporations, whereas López Portillo's political reform and de la Madrid's moral renovation switched the strategic emphasis to the electoral arena. In the short term these initiatives seemed successful. Despite some setbacks, the policies of the 1970s bound many independent unions to the corporate bias of government through the incentives and sanctions of the Labor Congress, where even recalcitrant union tendencies found some margin of maneuver;[7] and if the political reform did not finally divide the electoral left, it did considerable damage to the cohesion of some popular movements. But the strategic displacement of the priority channels of representation from the corporative to the electoral arena was to prove counterproductive (see Chapter 11).

The priority objective of federal policy was clearly the institutionalization of popular struggle. In the case of the teachers' movement, the implementation of

---

7 In general, the changing relations between federal executive and union corporations express important shifts in the terrain. In the early 1970s independent unionism meant parallel unionism, as exemplified in the democratic tendency of the electricians' union. After 1978, however, the managers of *charrismo* sought a new consensus by bringing independent unions into the Labor Congress. The dissident teachers in the CNTE, the university workers in the STUNAM, the Volkswagen workers' union, and the National Pensioners Movement joined many smaller independent unions to form a Council for Union Cooperation (*Mesa de Concertación Sindical*) in order to make more effective use of the Congress.

this policy combined major reform projects like educational decentralization with pseudolegal *démarches*, such as the reduction of authentic majorities to the status of dissident minorities (see Chapters 7 and 8). At the same time the government and the SNTE tried to disarticulate and disperse the movement through the complex and effective *juego de desgaste* and the many forms of "administrative repression" (see Chapter 8). These hybrid initiatives seem to lend support to Kowarick's (1985) observation that State bureaucracies usually operate to dilute and segment the institutional advance of popular groups, but it is equally true that every government initiative that increases the "density" of the legal-institutional terrain not only adds to the constraints on popular movements but also multiplies their strategic opportunities for achieving more advantageous forms of linkage. Thus, there is little doubt that the bureaucratic disputes and disruption of the educational reform project actually provoked heightened popular struggle in some instances (see Chapter 8).

## Popular movements and institutional terrain

The government's policy of institutionalization of popular insurgency and the institutionalism of the popular movements themselves are two halves of the same strategic coin, but this does not return institutionalism to the "political participation" of the modernization paradigm. When Manuel Hernández ironically suggested that the leaders of the teachers' movement had once been radicals (see Chapter 1), he did not mean that they had now come to accept the system as it was; rather, he meant that they had achieved a more modulated approach, flexible in tactics but firm in the strategy of conquering the legal apparatus of the SNTE. Thus, institutionalism does not reflect passive participation so much as the active projection of grass-roots changes into the political system where they can find a more permanent expression. This optimistic interpretation is supported by the impact of the movement on the delivery of the Ministry of Education's reform project (see Chapter 9).

In this connection it has become clear that the forms of organization and strategic choices of popular movements can influence the nature of their linkages to the political system. The teachers sought to make their principles of organization directly democratic to ensure an accountable leadership that could not easily be coopted[8] and that would be sufficiently decentralized to resolve union problems close to their point of origin and to avoid the insidious separation of the base and the leadership existing in the SNTE itself (see Chapter 4). On the evidence, the active engagement of an organized base was more effective in preventing the quick decapitation of the movement than in assuaging

---

8 The dangers were not only external. Directly democratic procedures might also mitigate the influence of political (party) groups inside the movement, and so prevent capture by partisan interests. But the factional infighting suffered by the movement shows that controls of this kind can never be complete.

internal divisions, which were often exacerbated by assembly-led democratic mechanisms (see Chapter 6).

In this regard it is equally clear by now that the teachers' movement was not the political expression of some pure democratic demiurge but was permeated by ideological disputes and political confrontations that reflected internal and often personal power struggles. Insofar as these internal struggles created much of the energy and impetus of the movement, they were a necessary evil; but factional competition for support at the grass roots contained a clear potential for division and decline (see Chapter 6). In the present perspective, moreover, it is apparent that many of the disputes turned on the question of institutionalism, with "basist" and "ultra-democratic" leaders claiming any contact with the State as collaboration or betrayal, and more moderate leaders defending negotiations as essential to the resolution of their demands (see Chapter 5). Indeed, possibly the most important effect of the factional infighting has been on the definition of political strategies.

The two key choices to define the strategic thrust of the movement were, first, the decision to work within the union corporation and with the administrative agencies of the State (institutionalism and the promotion of linkage), and, second, the search for alliances (combatting transformism and assuaging the negative effects of linkage). The movement adopted both strategies simultaneously, knowing the need for a *capacidad de gestión* and seeking to broaden resistance to administrative repression. It has been noted that national alliances were always politically and operationally precarious (see Chapter 9), but it was recognized that they never envisaged organization so much as mobilization, which was the essential complement to the institutionalism of the movement.[9] In other words, even where legal linkage was the final goal, any political advance had to be impelled by the pressure of mobilization.

This mobilization was difficult to coordinate nationally because the different regional movements had different trajectories and different contexts (see Chapter 7). To a degree this heterogeneity was an effect of the legal-institutional terrain, which was itself not uniform; the SNTE in particular was inserted differentially into specific regional power systems, or *cacicazgos,* through different forms of political alliance. The overall situation was complicated by the administrative frictions provoked by the reform program (see Chapter 8), by the hostility of some state governments to the SNTE in the person of its leader-for-life

---

9 The internal organization of the teachers' movements encouraged direct participation and catalyzed successive mobilizations. Even where the movements had achieved some form of legal representation, it was nearly always through mobilization that they won their demands, especially wage rises and bigger cost-of-living bonuses. (The leadership of the SNTE continued to argue, on the contrary, that it was official negotiation that got results.) Documents of the National Independent Teachers' Front (FMIN), which directed the movement in the Valle de México, suggest that this was a clearly conceived combination of legal and extralegal struggle; but the logistical limits of most movements anyway favored recurrent mobilization over increasing organization.

Jonguitud, by the intrinsic organizational regionalism of some movements, and by the State strategy of divide-and-rule. The result was a movement that was unable to construct a permanent national leadership or advance anything more than a minimalist political platform. These were not fatal weaknesses, but they did lead to a certain lack of political initiative and, in particular, to an incomplete appreciation of the potential strategic openings created by interbureaucratic divisions within the State.

These divisions were mainly created by shifts in the internal relations of a State that was constantly engaged in internal organization and reorganization; as was evident from the complex relationship between the SNTE and the Ministry of Education, such relations were often non-constitutional and non-normative. The implicit support given to the teachers' movement in its first phase (see Chapter 7) reflected federal dissatisfaction with the prepotent position of Jonguitud and the Revolutionary Vanguard, as well as responding to a broad strategy of cooptation. Moreover, the Ministry of the Interior intervened recurrently in negotiations between the movement, on the one hand, and the Ministry of Education and the SNTE, on the other, once it became obvious that the SNTE was failing to discipline the dissidents (see Chapter 9). In large measure this favorable moment was the result of Reyes Heroles's reform project, which sought to marry administrative modernization with an attack on union *charrismo*,[10] but the moment changed with electoral rebellion in the north and the loss of benign state governments in Chiapas and Oaxaca. With the institutional realignment of the terrain, the movement's "institutionalist" strategy became deadlocked. But the important point is that both the favorable and the unfavorable conjunctures had been shaped in some degree by popular mobilization, first in the south and then in the north of the country.

## The popular impact on institutional change

It is often admitted that changes in popular organization are not automatically transmitted into institutional changes within the political system overall (Mainwaring 1987), and the impact of the teachers' movement might seem to have

---

10  Reyes Heroles saw that any effective "political reform" would entail confrontation with union *caciques*, and he confronted not only Jonguitud but also Joaquín Hernández Galicia (La Quina) of the oil workers' union. His career now appears as an historical dress rehearsal for President Salinas's more recent assault on the feudal bastions of union power. Salinas moved quickly to oust the oil workers' boss in January 1989, but this was less the beginning of the political reform of the union regime and more an act of pure political revenge for La Quina's support for Cuauhtémoc Cárdenas during the presidential campaign. And when just five months later the "leader-for-life" of the SNTE, Jonguitud, was also forced to resign, it was a result of the massive protests by dissident teachers on the streets of the capital (see postscript to Chapter 12). In general, it appears that Salinas has chosen to avoid a direct confrontation with the entrenched *charro* establishment of the State-chartered union corporations in favor of a strategy that seeks to outflank it: The traditional union leaders are left to their own devices while government pursues direct links with new popular clienteles through its so-called Solidarity Program (PRONASOL), which has recently been elevated to a full-fledged Ministry of Social Development.

been muted by the successful institutionalization of its struggle. But if institutionalism is part of this same process, it appears plausible that the movement itself may also have had an important impact "on the forms and margins of maneuver of State institutions" (Marván 1988). Institutionalism means the incremental negotiation and renegotiation of the links between popular movements and the dominant institutions of national political life, and it is precisely in seeking and shaping their linkage with the political system that popular movements have contributed to changes in its institutional configuration.

Just as popular movements seek linkage with the political system (and try to get it on their own terms), so *caciquismo, charrismo,* and clientelism more generally act to deny this linkage and so prevent effective representation. Hence, the secular impact of the movements is rooted in the continuous challenge they mount to these traditional mechanisms of political control. This challenge is specific, gradual, and differentiated, and only rarely signaled by spectacular effects. So even if it is not exactly invisible, it can pass unperceived. In the corporatist arena it is the phenomenon of *charrismo,* above all, that condenses the contradictions of linkage politics, and at first the extensive clientelistic network of the Revolutionary Vanguard seemed to present an insuperable obstacle to the teachers' movement precisely because it refused to take up the movement's demands. But, equally, the movement gathered impetus wherever it became apparent that official representatives were failing to represent, and thus inviting the struggle to establish or restore linkage.

Some commentators argue that there is nothing new in all this and that *caciquismo* has always been under challenge (Rubin 1990; Knight 1990); in this view Mexico's corporatist State has been a "Swiss cheese State," shot full of holes created by such challenges. But only in the past decade has this corporatism entered into general crisis, which is simultaneously a crisis of the social pact (undermined by economic decline and fiscal pressure) and a crisis of the clientelism that was always its political sinew (see Chapter 11). This change is at least partly a result of popular mobilization, and especially of the strategic search for political alliances, which render clientelistic forms of control increasingly less effective. If in the past *caciquismo* may sometimes have had a popular base, this is now less likely to be so; and corporatist structures are under attack for camouflaging the operation of *caciquismo* and clientelism.

Inevitably, this comprehensive challenge to the clientelism that has traditionally informed the main ways of doing politics in Mexico has had repercussions on the configuration of the institutional and legal terrain. Urban popular movements in particular have rejected the patrimonial culture of petitions and concessions in favor of popular projects and political confrontations (Ramírez Saiz 1990). After the 1985 earthquake in Mexico City, the government was obliged to abandon its own reconstruction plans in the face of popular mobilization and organization, and to recognize alternative projects proposed by popular movements in the technical and legal language of the State. This was a convincing demonstration of a popular potential for policy initiatives that countered the clientelistic assumptions of the government, and this successful challenge carried over into the formation of neighborhood committees, the election of delegates to the Assembly of Representatives, the dissemination of the demand for an authentically elective government of the Federal District, and, last but not least, a clear electoral triumph for the opposition throughout the capital in July 1988 (see Chapter 11).

But it is the teachers' movement that best exemplifies the challenge in its constant struggle to defend and promote professional rights (see Chapters 3, 5, and passim). This assertion of legal rights lies at the heart of the challenge to clientelism and *charrismo* precisely because these predominant forms of political control deny such rights. Indeed, they are intrinsically vested in a particularistic and non-normative exercise of power, which rejects the very possibility of juridical authority. Thus, in asserting the rights that they hold in common because there is something called the law, popular actors may begin to lay claim to their citizenship. In the teachers' movement it was the fight for professional rights, more than anything else, that catalyzed the shift from syndical to political struggle; and it is in challenging clientelism that the teachers changed from political subjects to political actors (see Chapter 1).

Nevertheless, the challenge appears as something of an historical paradox. Uniquely in Latin America, the popular masses in Mexico played a key role in the construction of the corporatist State and in the formulation of public law (labor law, agrarian law, electoral law). But, consistent with the pervasiveness of clientelism, the use of this law is often discretional, so that even plainly illegal government initiatives may be legalized *ex post facto* (Tamayo 1990). In other words, Mexican law is at the disposition of the political authorities and always has a casuistic content, being applied only if and when the authorities ordain it. In short, it is the "institutional charisma" of the regime that has most provoked popular movements to challenge its political boundaries. For many years the challenge contested the particularism of clientelism and was therefore concentrated in the corporatist arena. Now it has moved into the electoral arena, where government control of the electoral commissions had traditionally meant that virtually any result was possible, and "legal."

Here it is worth recalling that popular movements, and the teachers' movement in particular, have insisted on distinguishing different arenas or "fronts" of struggle; the clearest divide was drawn between struggles to defend their rights in the community and the union, on the one hand, and, on the other, electoral struggles over the policies and legitimacy of the government. Indeed, there may be some strategic ambivalence in popular movements that organize to negotiate "corporate" demands while participating in electoral and post-electoral campaigns for citizens' rights. But on one reading the political struggle for "effective suffrage" and against electoral manipulation is an extension of traditional struggles for legal rights and against clientelism, and the principle of continuity from sectoral to electoral struggle is provided by the common goal of an *Estado de Derecho,* or the simple insistence on the rule of law.

The government itself had encouraged entry into the electoral arena through the political reforms of 1977 and after, but all politics is finally local politics, and it took constant mobilization and a recurrent search for intersectoral alliances before sectoral demands could be generalized at the national level. In particular, it was only after 1985 that some popular movements seemed to lose their deep-seated suspicion of political parties, and even began to build alliances with them, if only at the regional level (Tamayo 1990). But it still required the historical contingencies of a split within the ruling party and the subsequent presidential candidacy of Cuauhtémoc Cárdenas (the son of the revolutionary president of the 1930s) to encourage popular movements to resolve their differences by shifting the focus of their political activity and by condensing their demands into a broad electoral coalition against the ruling party. These developments will be explored in greater detail in the following chapter, but it is worth insisting on two key points for the purposes of the present argument. First, the split in the ruling party, and the emergence of the National Democratic Front (FDN) in electoral opposition to it, were themselves provoked in large degree by the pressure of popular mobilization. Second, although it is clear that the vote for Cárdenas's National Democratic Front in July 1988 was more than the sum of the popular movements, there is no doublt about the diverse and massive presence of these movements in the coalition.

The Front's rapid rise to electoral prominence appears to indicate a dramatic political advance, which has disseminated popular demands and legitimated popular leaders. But electoral defeats and continuing electoral "alchemy" may erode this legitimacy, and the phenomenon of *neocardenismo* (the neologism that characterized Cárdenas's campaign) may still lack a more permanent and positive principle of unity beyond a radical rejection of austerity policies or, indeed, beyond the *caudillismo* of Cárdenas himself (Zermeño 1990). And despite Cárdenas's appeals to nationalism, a "national-popular will" (Gramsci 1971) to replace the historical project of the ruling party will be difficult to forge in such a heterogeneous nation as Mexico. For these reasons it is open to debate whether the entry into the electoral arena expresses a substantive shift to electoral politics and a demand for liberal democracy *tout court,* or rather reflects a strategic choice to forge new alliances in this arena and extend the scope of popular struggle, while continuing to build sectoral organizations and press more immediate demands.

In this connection it is vital to emphasize the strategically central role of the SNTE in Mexico's "corporatist democracy" (Aziz 1987) (see Introduction and Chapter 1). In effect, since the 1950s it was SNTE machinery and SNTE cadres that mobilized the vote and controlled elections across the country, as well as doing whatever was necessary to return the traditionally overwhelming majorities of the ruling party. But during the last decade this assured pattern of vertical and corporate control has been fractured by the continuous struggles of the teachers' movements, so that today the government can no longer guarantee the same degree of electoral discipline, and consequently electoral outcomes are far more uncertain. This is one of the main changes that popular pressure has provoked in the political system. The following chapter will characterize the scope and direction of these changes, and thus place these electoral developments in their proper context.

# 11

## The political system

There are no guarantees that political changes achieved in civil society will necessarily be extended into the institutional organization of the political system (see Chapter 10), and popular claims to legal and political rights may not be recognized by government, which, on the contrary, may respond with more repression. In the Mexico of the past twenty years, in particular, the pressure of popular movements has prompted the political system to undertake a halting and contradictory process of "liberalization," with results that have not in fact been very liberal, let alone democratic. In historical perspective this should cause no surprise. Mexico has no tradition of liberal democracy (Meyer 1983), and no regime initiative is likely to begin one (Whitehead 1988; Cornelius 1986a); in effect, the "democratic openings" and "political reforms" of these years have wrought no real change in the political practices of the ruling party (Gentleman 1987b), which by the middle of 1986 seemed to have recognized that the "liberalization" had reached a dead end (Cornelius 1986a). In this sense the process of "liberalization" can be seen as a true measure of the constraints on the reform of the system (Alvarado 1987), or as an attempt further to institutionalize the regime of the Institutional Revolutionary Party (the PRI) in circumstances of fiscal and economic crisis, and increasing popular pressure.

This thumbnail account conforms to the general recognition of the resilience of the political system, which is demonstrated in its flexible and effective response to independent unionism, in its containment of democratic tendencies inside union corporations, and in the cynical manipulation of the electoral process (Gentleman 1987b). There could be no better example of the political practices that underpin this resilience than the war of attrition waged against the teachers' movement by the Revolutionary Vanguard of the SNTE. Consequently, the system itself has not been under threat (Carr 1983; Needler 1987), and most popular movements have continued to suffer temporary reversals and defeats, if not permanent ones (Rubin 1987). But this does not mean that opposition to the system has been so "very weak" (Camp 1986a) that it has brought no change at all. On the contrary, the system has been changing, but the most significant changes have been less visible and more incremental than those signaled by the regime itself in its efforts to liberalize.

This conservative assessment of the pace of political change may have been plausible until 1988, but the highly visible, indeed spectacular, electoral events of that year, which occurred under close international scrutiny, appear to invalidate it. The sudden and dramatic loss of electoral support for the ruling party seems to require quite new interpretations of the changes in the system. But the elections of 1988 do not stand alone, and they can only be understood in the context of the changes that preceded them. Indeed, it is only the secular tendencies within the system overall, and the pressure points they created, that will reveal the causes of 1988's events and so elucidate the content of Mexico's political crisis. Thus, although there is no intention of denying the importance of the 1988 elections, especially as they appeared to herald the eruption of popular movements into the electoral arena, the inquiry takes a long-term view that rejects an apocalyptic reading of their impact.

## Secular changes in the system

The ruling party had largely succeeded in maintaining discipline within its "single social base" (Meyer 1983) of affiliated union corporations, but it had begun to push other popular organizations to the far horizons of the legal-institutional terrain. Thus, the system no longer responded to popular mobilization by the teachers of Chiapas except by administrative repression and violence (see Chapters 5, 6, and 8), and the teachers began to talk of a *cordon sanitaire* that surrounded them and their peasant allies. In short, the system was becoming more exclusionary. Fiscal crisis had led to a general rejection of demands for higher wages or land redistribution, even if demands from production or marketing cooperatives might still be countenanced (Fox and Gordillo 1989). As a corollary, demands that were originally economic were rapidly becoming politicized, as occurred in the case of the teachers, in a vicious circle of popular mobilization and official intransigence. In consequence, the traditional tactical priorities of political control were often reversed, especially in the countryside, with repression now a first resort rather than a tactic used after cooptation had failed.

In some degree this increasing exclusion simply describes the political effects of changing forms of political mediation, which were themselves both cause and consequence of the challenges to clientelistic control (see Chapter 10). Partly as a result of popular mobilization, the traditional "structures of mediation" (Bartra 1975, 1977) were decomposing and in some sectors were in dangerous disrepair, and government had to impose new, and eventually more centralized, forms of representation and control. The government's main aims were to reinforce central command of political patronage and to disarticulate the popular movements, but its initiatives tended to saturate the legal-institutional terrain with federal agencies, as well as altering the political practices of the State-chartered unions.

In previous analyses of this process I focused on the ways in which policy-making prerogatives and political control in the countryside began to cluster in the federal departments responsible for agriculture and agrarian reform (Foweraker 1988, 1989a), with government also increasing its direct presence in the production, financing, and marketing of food through its agencies such as the BANRURAL, CONASUPO, INMECAFE, and TABAMEX.[1] But the imposition of more centralized forms of mediation was equally evident in the control of popular districts in the cities, especially Mexico City (Jimenez 1989); and at the regional level, in Chiapas in particular, it was apparent that the power of local *caciques* was being displaced by the expanding federal bureaucracy (Harvey 1988). At the same time union corporations like the National Peasant Confederation were now used to repress recalcitrant peasant groups and intimidate communities offering support to the dissident teachers.[2]

Nonetheless, it must be recognized that many recent policies were speciously designed to decentralize the public administration. The political reforms of 1977–9 aspired, in principle, to strengthen federalism, and the February 1984 reform of Article 115 of the Constitution sought specifically to devolve power to the municipalities. In fact, these policies had the different effect of allowing the federal executive and the topmost echelons of the ruling party to assert closer control over state-level administration and political personnel (Alvarado 1987), thus centralizing political recruitment and subverting the main purpose of the reforms (Martinez Assad 1987). Similarly, the policy of educational decentralization in fact reinforced the presence of federal bureaucracy in the regions and tightened central lines of political command (see Chapter 8).

This change to more centralized and concerted forms of mediation must be understood as a propensity and not as an uncontested result. After all, the traditional strength of the political system was the very variegated insertion of federal government agencies into the politically and culturally specific power systems of the regions. The change inevitably provoked tensions between the central government and these *cacicazgos* in a process of renegotiation, readjustment, and occasional conflict. A good example, once again, is the resistance of the SNTE to the educational reform, which finally allowed the Revolutionary

---

1 The shift was signaled by the anti-*caciquismo* discourse of the Echeverría administration, which attempted to preempt the autonomous organization of recently mobilized peasant populations for whom the *cacique* represented generations of manipulation. In place of the *caciques* came the centralized corporatism of the CONPA (a standing agrarian conference), which tried to tie the peasant unions more closely to the National Peasant Confederation (CNC), and so build support for government policies. This approach was reinforced by the "productivist" policies of the López Portillo administration, which also sought to reorganize the *ejido* sector to allow greater governmental control and more effective legal-bureaucratic mediation of land disputes.

2 In Chiapas the National Peasant Confederation was showing signs of strain precisely because of its dependence on local *cacicazgos*. Its administration of SAM (Mexican Food System) monies began the process that was to tie it more closely to central bureaucratic agencies (Harvey 1988).

Vanguard to regroup and take over the key positions created by the reform (see Chapters 8 and 10). But the SNTE itself, as a State-chartered union, had anyway derived its resilience from its variable engagement with regional patterns of *caciquismo,* and it is clear that the teachers' movement advanced faster in regions like Chiapas and Oaxaca where the Vanguard had relatively little grass-roots support and relied on its cadres of supervisors and directors to maintain control.

In general, the resistance of regional *cacicazgos* further complicated the topography of the legal-institutional terrain (see Chapter 10). But the example of the SNTE immediately demonstrates that the tensions induced by increasing centralization were not simply external to a political system that confronted regional *feudos* of political power. On the contrary, the regional *cacicazgos* were more often than not the domain of the "managerial" bosses of the union corporations, and so were intimately connected with the corporatist institutions of the system. Economic and fiscal crisis had in fact strengthened the hand of this official labor leadership, which was the element of the ruling coalition most resistant to political change (Needler 1987). The result was a more conflictual relationship between federal executive and the union *caciques,* which, under pressure of popular mobilization, could lead to a much looser insertion of federal agencies into regional power systems.[3] Not only did the teachers' movement disrupt relations between federal departments and the SNTE in general, but in San Luis Potosí, a powerful civic movement called *navismo* challenged the political control of the state governor and the SNTE's "maximum leader," Carlos Jonguitud Barrios (Márquez 1987).

The resistance of the regional *cacicazgos* explains what the political reforms have always failed to reform, which is the internal organization of the ruling Institutional Revolutionary Party (PRI) itself.[4] According to Bailey (1986, 1987), the PRI's centralized and sectoral organization has created a permanent structural tension between the national leadership and the regional bosses, with the labor sector the prime culprit. It is not just that the party structure meshes

---

3 Once again, the case of Chiapas provides an especially rich illustration of these cross-cutting effects. Here, as in the southeast of the country overall, the Revolution was bitterly resisted by the *caciques* of the landed class, and the Cárdenas reforms of the 1930s were diluted or reversed (see Chapter 1). When the federal government finally began to displace local forms of clientelistic control, it inevitably damaged its relations with local power brokers, and as centralizing incursions intensified during the 1980s, tensions began to build up between federal and state governments, as well as between federal departments and agencies themselves (see Chapters 5, 8, 9, and passim).

4 On more than one occasion in the past, the central apparatus of the PRI government had seen its reform initiatives reversed by the resistance of regional and local *caciques* within the union corporations and the regional headquarters of the ruling party itself. This goes far to explain the failures of the Madrazo reforms of 1965 and the De la Madrid reforms of 1983–5. On both those occasions the failures provoked popular protest. The difference today is that popular mobilization and protest has been accompanying the imposition of more centralized forms of bureaucratic mediation, which seems to be advancing despite the opposition of the *cacicazgos* inside and outside the PRI's union corporations.

imperfectly with the configuration of the electoral arena but that the regional bosses (most often the conservative union *caciques*) are not representatives but power brokers, who insist on delivering majorities through the traditional mechanisms of political patronage and manipulation. This tension has been heightened not only by economic crisis, which has provoked deeper intersectoral conflicts inside and outside the PRI (Carr 1983), but also by the more centralized forms of mediation, which inevitably remove powers of patronage from regional brokers. At the same time the federal executive has tried to retrieve middle-class support by strengthening the "popular" sector of the party, which has meant pushing aside local party bosses in the cities to make way for middle-class representatives (Jimenez 1989). The result has been increasing disaffection among the party's power-brokers, which led to intra-elite splits in the party at the regional level long before the emergence of the Democratic Current at the national level (see next section) (Salinas Domínguez 1987).

Just as the institutional strains within the PRI were partly a result of more centralized forms of mediation, so the centralizing effort itself was partly a response to more general problems of "internal State organization" (Jessop 1982) in a context where "a myriad of local-level organizations and special interest groups were aggregated into a sprawling State apparatus" (Roxborough 1984). In other words, the presence of the *cacicazgos* had led to significantly less government unity, which exacerbated problems of policy implementation and impaired the federal capacity for neutralizing popular mobilization in particular. The federal government had become less coherent, less effective, and more isolated from some of the stronger but largely unrepresented social forces in civil society (Cornelius 1986a).

It is in this context of an increasingly divided government apparatus that the teachers' movement discovered its strategic opportunities. For the pioneering movement in Chiapas, in particular, the favorable disposition of the state government (see Chapter 5) was overdetermined at the federal level by the modernization drive of Reyes Heroles (see Chapters 8 and 9), who was ready to negotiate with any "valid interlocutors," whether or not they owed allegiance to the Revolutionary Vanguard. This was a classic case of the move to new forms of mediation conflicting with a *cacicazgo* contained within the corporatist structure of the ruling party itself. This strategic opening was then closed again when the failed electoral reforms of De la Madrid pushed the federal government back into bed with the Revolutionary Vanguard. The ruling party may have preferred a more tractable leadership (like that of Hernández Suárez of the telephone workers) and may have overestimated the SNTE's continuing ability to turn elections around (see Popular movements and the 1988 elections, below), but it had to make do.[5]

---

5  This style of analysis clearly runs counter to notions of a cohesive, sophisticated, and Machiavellian political class at the center of a tightly organized State apparatus, which conducts political experiments in Oaxaca,

## Loss of popular support for the government

In the transformist project of the ruling party (see Introduction) the relationship between government and people was always contradictory. On the one hand, the government had sought alliances with the people and had deployed a broad range of social benefits and opportunities to secure these alliances. On the other, it had sought to control and manipulate the people in corporatist and authoritarian fashion (Basañez 1981; Zermeño 1978; Sirvent 1973). The contradiction was then between a revolutionary nationalism built on an image of popular sovereignty and the government's commitment to dependent capitalist accumulation, with all the social and political controls this entailed. Government legitimacy had been secured *inter alia* by long-term commitments to agrarian reform and mass education (Basañez 1987), but even if this legitimacy was not threatened directly, the government itself was fast losing support as its policies became increasingly less popular in content.

This loss of support was evident in the electoral arena where the PRI's share of the national vote had fallen from 90 percent to about 65 percent over the previous twenty-five years (Needler 1987). Moreover, the rate of decline had accelerated more recently (Alvarado 1987), with support falling below 50 percent, or rates of abstention climbing above 55 percent, in fifteen of the twenty most populous cities in the country (Molinar 1987). Clearly, the economic crisis had constrained the scope of clientelistic politics, but it was popular mobilization and the popular challenge to clientelistic controls (see Chapter 10) that most directly contributed to the decline; and just as the challenge in the corporatist arena was driven by the assertion of professional and legal rights, so the extension of the challenge into the electoral arena was sustained by the affirmation of political rights. In other words, the diminishing popular content of the PRI's historical project had as much to do with the lack of respect for the people's rights as it did with failing populist policies. Very different popular movements in different parts of the country might then vote against the PRI for fundamentally the same reason.

The fact that there are elections at all is a sign that the PRI takes the popular part of its Revolutionary project seriously. But the popular will had been distorted by decades of systematic and occasionally blatant electoral fraud. During the 1980s the bitter protests of the National Action Party (PAN) at the manipulation of the electoral process, and the consequent demystification of the PRI's electoral dominance, had brought business groups, the Church, and the urban

with the Coalition of Workers, Peasants and Students of the Isthmus (COCEI) (Rubin 1987), or in Chihuahua, with the National Action Party (PAN), in order to measure the strength of popular opposition or test the effectiveness of new forms of mediation. But there is more disagreement with the notion of the State, which is not a unified, anthropomorphic actor with "intentions," than there is with the description of the political class.

middle classes into more open opposition to the ruling party, especially in the north of the country (where even the official unions sometimes voted with the opposition). At the same time the PRI's partial and conflictual efforts to respond by modernizing the party had increased the intransigence of local party bosses and further restricted the representation of popular opinion. It is a telling point that the Democratic Current within the PRI itself, which unsurprisingly sought to make the party more democratic, emerged partly in response to the Democratic Electoral Movement, which was pledged to defend the Revolutionary promise of "effective suffrage." It was Cuauhtémoc Cárdenas, the leader of the breakaway Democratic Current, who became the 1988 presidential candidate of the National Democratic Front (FDN), and the electoral coalition that backed his candidacy included small parties such as the Socialist Workers' Party (PST), the Authentic Party of the Mexican Revolution (PARM), and the Popular Socialist Party (PPS), which were previously seen as electoral stalking horses for the PRI.

But the electoral force of the FDN can only be understood in relation to the profile of political opposition to the PRI prior to 1988. The political reforms of 1977–9 may not have been designed to allow the opposition parties to win power (Gómez Tagle 1987), but they were successful in enticing the opposition into the electoral arena; and the brief attempt to combat electoral chicanery in the 1983–5 period provided an historical glimpse of this profile. It was apparent that the bulk of support for the main opposition party of the time, the National Action Party (PAN), was in the north of the country, where the system looked effectively bipartisan. It was therefore alleged that the real opposition challenge was not a national but a regional one (Needler 1987). It was equally clear that opposition throughout the country was concentrated in the urban middle classes, especially in their younger generation (Guillén López 1987), which seemed to indicate that the challenge was also one of class and generation. Yet, in the context of the secular tendencies within the system overall, these different orders of opposition all reflect and reveal the increasing strains at the *points of intersection* between centralized forms of mediation and the regional or local *cacicazgos,* which have traditionally delivered the PRI's majorities.

It was not simply that increasingly fragile forms of clientelistic control had begun to influence electoral outcomes (Guadarrama 1987), but that the pressures acting on the system and the contradictions within the system tended to converge at these points of intersection. The pressures included the popular movements, which had escaped the confines of corporatist control, and the opposition parties, which mobilized to contest electoral results (as they did massively after the presidential elections of 1988); the contradictions included the intra-elite dissensus at the local level and the institutional rigidity within the ruling party itself (see preceding section). Hence, there was little analytical advantage in debating whether it was popular pressure or intra-elite conflict that posed the biggest threat to the system (Gentleman 1987a), when it was the coincidence and combination of the two that was the real problem.

In some degree these influences within the system have been debated in terms of the deepening divisions between the so-called *técnicos* and *políticos,* that is, the conflict between a "modernizing, technocratic government" and "old-style politicians" entrenched in the ruling party's local and regional organizations (Cornelius 1987). It is alleged that the government was so concerned at the internecine strife between the two groups that it returned to its traditional electoral alchemy in 1985 to avoid a serious rupture in the party (Cornelius 1987), and there is little doubt that the continuing strength of the divisions has put current attempts to reform the party in jeopardy. Thus, the analysis corresponds to the argument developed here, except for a misinterpretation of the political aspirations of the *técnicos,* who are not so much a new breed of political reformers looking to liberalize the system as a group of apparatchiks closely committed to more centralized forms of mediation and administration. Their reform of the PRI would make it more consistent with these forms but not necessarily more democratic, and their reform of the system, if ever it comes, would be unlikely to look very liberal.

Just as the institutional strains within the system cannot adequately be described as a political competition between liberal reformers and conservative fixers, so it is inappropriate to force contemporary Mexican politics into a procrustean division between the left and right of the political spectrum. The purely ideological appeal of left and right was rapidly exhausted in the 1980s (Camp 1986b), but only because it was never very great anyway. Support for the PAN in particular probably had far more to do with "effective suffrage" and real political participation than it did with right-wing politics (Aziz 1987). Circumstantial evidence for this is found in the regional and national political alliances between left and right that had formed to combat the PRI, contest electoral fraud, or both. In 1986 multiclass mobilizations occurred in several regions, and a multipartisan political front that united left and right emerged to field a common candidate against the PRI, while the Democratic Electoral Movement brought both ends of the political spectrum together in its aim of establishing a national organization to oversee elections and eliminate electoral fraud.

## Popular movements and the 1988 elections

If left-right divisions offer only a very imperfect picture of Mexican politics, this is not simply because the PRI occupies a broad political center, but because politics are predominantly shaped by the relations between civil society and the political system. In this perspective popular movements express social forces that have not found proper political representation and are struggling to achieve it, while government responses seek to mitigate the growing isolation of the government by changing and thereby refining its control of the institutional and legal terms of representation (see Introduction).[6] The accumulation of popular struggles since 1968 has precipitated a more intensive contest to define these terms, as well as to organize the previously unorganized; consequently, as the story of the teachers' movement makes abundantly clear, the relations between system and society have become more fluid and volatile, and thus constitute a more complex and contradictory terrain for the rule of the PRI regime.

This is the proper context for examining the electoral force of the National Democratic Front (FDN) and its vertiginous rise to political prominence. Moreover, the results of the presidential elections of July 1988 appear to demand a reassessment of the "liberalization" of electoral politics and the strategic displacement of political representation from the corporative to the electoral arena (see Chapter 10). It is no longer simply a question of whether the ruling party has shot itself in the foot. That the PRI won a bare majority of votes cast, and did so only after agonizing days of apparent electoral alchemy, is not just a sign of the PRI's weakness but also an indication of the growing strength of the opposition within Mexican civil society. But in what sense? Was the FDN the privileged vehicle for the entry of popular movements into the electoral arena?[7] If so, there must be some possibility that electoral *neocardenismo* will overdetermine "linkage politics" (see Chapter 10) across the range of organized popular contact with the political system and will condense the institutionalism of popular movements into some version of party politics.

In this connection, there is no doubt that the most recent rise in the rhythm of popular mobilization coincided with the emergence of the Democratic Current and its split from the PRI. Indeed, the election year was ushered in by the first mobilization in Mexico City of the National Front for Mass Organizations.[8]

6 A recent interpretation has characterized the process as the "bureaupolitics" of the PRI government, which absorbs and atomizes popular organization, denying civil society the space to develop and defend its own "identities" (Zermeño 1990), with radically pessimistic implications for political democracy. The question of political "identities" and democracy was explored by Pizzorno (1985), who argued that "there is a value that democracy alone realizes: it isn't the freedom of political choice . . . but the freedom of political identification. That is, the right these identifications have to exist, their right not to be nullified or even determined solely by the authority of the national State."

7 Before the July 1988 elections this interpretation was favored by the intellectuals of the MAS (Movement Toward Socialism), who saw the FDN as the first national expression of the popular movements that had emerged since 1968 and, consequently, as the potential representative of many of the unrepresented social forces within civil society. But even were they right, this could not be understood as a sudden "resurgence of civil society" (O'Donnell, Schmitter, and Whitehead 1986); rather, it was the result of a progressive process of convergence of the popular movements through alliances, "national coordinating committees" *(coordinadoras)*, and coalitions of coalitions (Alonso 1988).

8 The National Front for Mass Organizations was preceded in 1987 by the Metropolitan Front, which included the Coordinadora Única de Damnificados, the Coordinadora de Luchas Urbanas, and the CONAMUP. The National Front itself brought together more than 150 union, peasant, student, and popular groups, and its first demonstration in the capital in January 1988 was joined by the CNTE, the CNPA, and the CONAMUP (Alonso 1988).

Nor is there much doubt that the Democratic Current itself was a response to popular mobilization, insofar as electoral protests in the north spawned the Democratic Electoral Movement, which catalyzed the formation of the Democratic Current. Moreover, although the two had been moving slowly closer together at the regional level since 1985 (Tamayo 1990), the elections of 1988 mark the first time that popular movements were prepared to ally with political parties at the national level, if only to prevent the PAN from capitalizing on popular discontent (Ramírez Saiz 1987). In many cases it was grass-roots activists who convinced their leaders to take this crucial step, and in nearly all cases the political tendencies within the movements backed the initiative. Leaders of urban popular movements themselves ran as candidates to Congress or, in Mexico City, to the Assembly of Representatives. Furthermore, these popular essays in electoral politics coalesced around the nationalist and progressive platform of the FDN, which itself called for the electoral convergence of the popular opposition. Hence, it seems undeniable that the FDN had become the principal political expression of the popular movements.

Nonetheless, there are reasons to be skeptical of this conclusion. On the one hand, as mentioned earlier the PRI had been suffering a gradual decline in electoral support caused by rising rates of urbanization and literacy that slowly eroded the social bases of conservative politics (Torres 1987; Soares 1986). Its core vote was now concentrated in rural areas, which no longer carried the same weight in general elections, and by 1985 it could secure the votes of just 31 percent of the electorate. On the other hand, the fraudulent defense of the PRI's majorities meant that elections in Mexico had taken on a plebiscitary character (Cammack 1988), whereby the opposition voted not to win power but to protest against government policies. On both counts it seems plausible that the FDN captured a vote that was "already there" among the disaffected middle classes of the major cities, rather than providing an electoral vehicle for the popular movements. Equally, it may have been the unprecedented abstention rate of almost 50 percent that recorded the growing political opposition implicit in popular mobilization.

What is sure is that popular movements have usually fought for sectoral or neighborhood demands rather than addressing general issues in the electoral arena (Ramírez Saiz 1987), and although the politics of the corporatist and electoral arenas are not mutually exclusive, as the PRI has long since demonstrated, the evidence for popular political "crossover" is still very spotty. Therefore, the electoral impact of the movements may still be indirect, achieved mainly by the wedge they have driven into the corporatist flank of the PRI's "corporatist democracy" (Aziz 1987). In particular, it is certain that a decade of struggle by the teachers' movement has irreparably damaged the capacity of the SNTE to mobilize and deliver the vote in the way it always did in the past, and this made Jonguitud's promise of eight million votes for the PRI candidate appear completely unrealistic (*Proceso,* February 22, 1988).[9] At the same time, popular mobilization to protest election results has raised the political costs of electoral fraud and has made it more difficult. In this way, popular movements have dramatically reduced the PRI's ability to manage the electoral arena, but not necessarily because they have invaded it. In short, although the movements may not have found political expression in the FDN, they may indeed have created its electoral opportunities. To put it another way, free elections will be the result and not the starting point of democratic struggle.

None of this implies that the FDN did not attract many votes from members of popular movements. The mobilizations that accompanied the campaign and the popular protests over the electoral results show clearly that it did.[10] But the FDN was not an organic expression of the movements nor, as some have suggested, was it a grand popular movement itself. After all, it began within the PRI itself and built its platform from the top down around demands for a fair vote and a nationalist response to economic crisis. Its populist approach was confirmed by the invocation of a golden age: Lázaro Cárdenas had returned from the dead to purify the Revolutionary project.[11] This might or might not be a good thing. Popular demands coincided with the platform of the FDN (now the Party of the Democratic Revolution or PRD) in opposing the government's austerity measures and its compliant attitude to foreign bankers. But a populist project like *janismo* in the Brazil of the 1960s or *aprismo* in the Peru of the 1980s could lead popular movements into a political cul-de-sac that would constrain their chances of institutional advance. The PRD is now trying to construct a durable political organization from the electoral moment of 1988, while the popular movements carry on with their institutionalist struggles (see Chapters 9 and 10). But the relationship between them remains an open question.

9  It must be emphasized that by 1988 the teachers' movement counted about a third of the SNTE's massive membership among its direct supporters. Moreover, although the movement had never won control of more than two sectional committees, it won a number of posts on many more and controlled hundreds of delegational committees.

10  In the light of the electoral results it is probable that urban popular movements contributed most to the FDN's strong showing, even if it was the demonstrations led by the peasantry of La Laguna and elsewhere that prompted Cárdenas to declare that "the popular response has overtaken the Front."

11  It has been argued that if Cárdenas is a populist figure in this sense, then he must have achieved direct and charismatic links with the unmediated masses as the candidate of the "disorganized society" (Zermeño 1990). This would imply that the slow and conflictual construction of popular movements in civil society had no necessary bearing on the political mobilization that accompanied his candidacy. But, historically, populism has assumed rather than denied prior popular organization, and in Latin America overall populist projects have often been underpinned by those mass sectors that are best organized (as Murmis and Portantiero's [1971] critique of Germani's [1962] notion of the "disposable masses" made clear for the Argentine case).

## Popular movements and political change

The elections of July 1988 seemed to mark a sea change in Mexico's political culture. Despite its modernization platform, the PRI only managed to scrape home on votes from the most backward regions of the country. Presidentialism was impaired, the one-party system was irreparably damaged (Cornelius, Gentleman, and Smith 1989), and history appeared to be leaving the ruling party behind. But the ensuing months of mobilization and protest suggested that political culture cannot be changed overnight, and most subsequent elections showed that the PRI was unwilling to embrace a new political pluralism. On the contrary, the push for pluralism was met by more intolerance. The political repression of popular movements was unremitting, and public assassination became commonplace. Hence, although politics was increasingly defined by competition between different democratic projects, including that of the PRI, whether democracy had entered the historical agenda remained deeply uncertain. In the meantime, no one in Mexican civil society was ready to assert that the emperor had no clothes.

There is no doubt that the government was discredited. But it survived, and the ruling party has now embarked on a double program of political and economic reform. The political reform seeks to streamline the machinery of the party and change the role of the official union leadership. It is recognized that the party needs to relegate the regional power brokers and recruit new middle-class cadres to organize its urban constituencies. The economic reform seeks to modernize the economy by reducing government intervention and allowing the free play of market forces,[12] so preparing Mexico to join the United States and Canada in a form of common market. Much could be said about these reforms, but the important point for the present purpose is that both orders of reform seem to require the dismantling of the corporatist mechanisms that have served the PRI so well in the past. In short, the reforms are exclusionary in effect and can only deepen the divide between the people and the government.

Against this others argue that the PRI seeks to refurbish and rationalize corporatism, not dismantle it (Ramírez Saiz 1990). Indeed, the government has already begun to use new forms of consultation and social "concertation" to target opposition groups, rather than the old corporate sectors. In this perspective the political system will continue to repose on economic-corporate groups and collective representation rather than citizenship and parliamentarianism, and to the degree that neoliberal reforms further undermine clientelist forms of

---

12 The most coherent political project to emerge from Mexican civil society in the recent period came from the entrepreneurial groups that have pressed for a more restricted and neoliberal State. Indeed, it has been argued (Marván 1988) that the entrepreneurial mobilization and organization that succeeded in shifting the terrain in this way are unprecedented in Mexican politics, and that the shift itself is even more significant than the political reform of the late 1970s (which itself altered essential elements of the regime, such as the monopoly of representation by the PRI).

political control (see Secular changes in the system, above), the government will extend the deployment of more centralized and concerted forms of political mediation,[13] as well as refining its repressive capacity. But whether or not this new corporatism works, the PRI still has to win elections in a more competitive electoral arena, and this makes the impact of the reforms ambiguous. Just as it is not clear whether the *neocardenista* PRD is a party of citizens or a party of popular movements, so it is no longer clear whether the PRI aspires to a government of citizens or a government of corporations.

This signals the present political importance of the popular movements. The results of the July 1988 elections certainly came as a political surprise, but in fact, they were the cumulative results of twenty years of popular mobilization (from July 26, 1968, to July 6, 1988, to be precise). This mobilization now persists not only in the defense of the vote but also in the continuing defense of the corporatist system and against the exclusionary effects of the government's neoliberal project. It may appear contradictory for popular movements to defend in the present the very institutions that have so often ignored their demands and denied their rights in the past, but it is soon apparent that they struggle to defend corporatism for the social pact it enshrines and not for the clientelistic lines of control it contains and organizes. In short, the defense of corporatism conforms to the overall institutionalism of the popular movements, which nonetheless continue to combat the arbitrary power of *caciquismo* and *charrismo* (see Chapter 10). Whatever the effect of the reforms, this popular challenge will continue to induce incremental changes in the political system.

The consensus of opinion indicates that the regime will continue and so will popular opposition. The government may have little to offer its new corporatist constituencies, but the opposition has no alternative economic project. Yet a significant historical residue was left by the events of 1988, and this was the unprecedented encounter between popular movements and middle classes. In 1968 there had been minimal contact between the mobilized students and other mass organizations, but in 1988 students and popular movements mobilized and marched together. In 1968 the government crushed the student movement without compunction (see Introduction), but in 1988 its frenetic attempts to separate the "integrated" from the "excluded" (Zermeño 1990) met with uncertain success.

The differences between the two historical moments are clear. In 1988, unlike in 1968, the government was laboring under a chronic economic crisis,

---

13 Contrary to the view of some commentators (Gentleman 1987b; Carr 1987), there is no intrinsic contradiction between the neoliberal economic project, on the one hand, and, on the other, a strong State "rectorship" of civil society, including closer control of official labor organizations. This contradiction exists only in the discourse of Monterrey industrialists who want democracy to the degree that it removes public sector controls from their freedom to accumulate. It is perfectly possible for neoliberal economic policies to be accompanied by a continuing expansion and centralization of the State apparatuses required for regulating economic activity and mediating political struggle.

was facing a civil society with an unprecedented capacity for mobilization, and was losing charisma and conviction because of a series of broken revolutionary pledges. Madero's promise of liberal democracy had never been fulfilled, but widespread protest at electoral fraud made the present government responsible. Lázaro Cárdenas's vision of social justice had finally disintegrated under the impact of unending austerity measures. And even Alemán's program of constant economic growth had collapsed. The government has responded with a neoliberal project of economic and political reform that nevertheless strikes at the heart of the most enduring of all Revolutionary pledges – that of national sovereignty. This is the reason that *neocardenismo* was able to unite middle classes and popular masses, if only temporarily, on the common ground of nationalism, and this is also the reason that 1988, like 1968, may signal an historical turning point.

# 12

## The political meaning of popular movements *

The rise of popular movements in contemporary Mexico began with the students' movement of 1968 (see Introduction). Since that time these movements have grown and multiplied in every region and sector of the country, and have discovered new forms of political organization and new political strategies. Mexico is not unique in experiencing an upsurge in popular mobilization during this period; popular movements have also become increasingly important in Western Europe and North America, not to mention their impact on democratic struggles elsewhere in Latin America. The activities of the "new social movements," as they are usually called in the literature, have generated a series of complex, and occasionally arcane, debates over the definition and significance of popular political organization, but these have often done more to confuse than to clarify our understanding of the phenomenon.

There is no intention here of reviewing this rather extensive literature, if only because this has already been done quite adequately elsewhere (Cohen 1985; Klandermans 1986; Tarrow 1986, 1988; Klandermans and Tarrow 1988). Nor is there any inclination to address the intricacies of the academic debates in all their gothic splendor. On the contrary, I wish to focus directly on the lessons of the teachers' movement in order to reach a practical understanding of popular movements and how they move. This will require a critical response to specific issues in the literature, without aspiring to an alternative explanation of "collective action" in general (après Tilly 1978 or Touraine 1988). In particular, the teachers' movement suggests different interpretations of the key questions of popular strategy and popular identity, which together indicate the need for a new analytical approach to popular mobilization.

One reason that the literature must be treated with caution is that it is mainly concerned with "new social movements" in North America and Western Europe, and does not therefore refer to popular organization among the huge majority of humankind living beyond those borders. Hence, an uncritical application of its conclusions to this majority may distort and disfigure our understanding of popular politics in the underdeveloped world, where not only their context but also their content may be very different. Because of these differences, even very sophisticated inquiries into "new social movements" in the

* The first few pages of this chapter draw directly on the argument of an unpublished essay by Gerry Monck, "Identity and ambiguity in the politics of democracy".

developed world can appear vulgar outside of it,[1] and even seasoned social observers in the underdeveloped world may force native phenomena into a foreign perspective by imitating their "developed" colleagues.[2] A case in point is the current vogue of the writings of Alberto Melucci among observers of popular movements in Latin America.

Nonetheless, the main problems are not empirical but analytical, and however salutary it is to insist on the specificities of popular movements in Latin America, for example, this is not the same as asserting that popular movements in the developed and underdeveloped worlds are finally incommensurable (Feyerabend 1978). Indeed, the preference for the use of the term "popular" over "new social" movement reflects an emphasis on political practices, which are perfectly comparable, rather than social and cultural origins and composition, which may not be. The emphasis here is both on the political, which merits an explanation that is not necessarily reduced to the realm of the social or economic, and on the practices, which give analytical priority to the actions of political actors rather than to the structured context of their actions (or to the experience of passive objects). In short, "movement commonly means action" (Tilly 1978). These practices are popular to the degree that they constitute the people as political actors (see Chapter 1 and passim).

The nature of these popular practices is not transparent, but they must imply a process of political learning. This implication is reflected in the literature's sometimes obsessive inquiry into the question of popular identity, which, whether it is seen as irrelevant or essential to strategic choices, is anyway seen as separate from strategy. But the emphasis on practices recognizes that they may be directed either to the actors themselves, insofar as they achieve organization, leadership, and goals (identity), or to the political environment, insofar as the movement struggles to advance these goals (strategy). Thus, these practices can be characterized as both *intrinsic* and *extrinsic* to the movement (see Introduction), and the continual methodological concern of the present study has been to focus on the interaction between them. The underlying contention is that this is the best way to discover what makes popular movements move because it is this interaction which condenses the "ecology of learning" (Levitt and March 1988) that catalyzes the change of people into political actors.

---

1   By way of illustration, the nature of time is changing for Melucci's social movements because "the experience of the seasons melts on our dining-room tables, where foods lose all reference to seasonal cycles; or in our holidays, which offer us tropical sun or snow at all times of the year" (Melucci 1989, p. 105); for this fortunate minority even "death is becoming something to banish from the social scene" (p. 111). Melucci clearly cannot be referring to the populations of El Salvador, Peru, or Brazil, and so it is inescapable that his analysis stops short at the borders of the developed world.

2   Even if there is skepticism regarding theses on "cultural dependency," it is noticeable how theories and concepts that become influential in the developed world are subsequently passed on to underdeveloped nations. By analogy with the "product cycle" of international political economy, it may be said that these ideas thereby enjoy a longer life, but not necessarily a more useful one.

Such grand statements can be seductive, and it is worth recalling that most popular movements express local struggles that are very uncertain of success. Indeed, in one view their principal strategic dilemmas stem precisely from their geographical, social, and political isolation (Castells 1982). Moreover, it remains true that both context and content of popular political practices are very different in different times and places, with an especially wide variation in the degrees of engagement with the political environment. Hence, there is little point in pursuing a general theory of popular movements. But it may be possible to discern analytical analogies between different processes of popular mobilization and, in particular, to discover analogous modes of strategic choice. The main schools of interpretation have tried to do this either by the assertion of a determining rationality or by making strategy tightly conditional on identity, but it is clear that it is the contingencies of strategic choice and political outcome that best characterize the process of the teachers' movement in Mexico, and in my view it is this contingency that is central to the most significant analogies.

## The strategic content of popular mobilization

The investigation of popular movements in North America has been led by the so-called resource mobilization school, which explains the collective action implicit in such movements in terms of rational choice theory (Oberschall 1973; McCarthy and Zald 1973, 1977, 1979; Zald and McCarthy 1987). The intellectual history of this approach stretches back to the methodological individualism of J. S. Mill, but most recent work is imbued with Mancur Olson's reading of strategy as the outcome of strict calculation by single, self-interested, and rational actors (Olson 1965). Hence, although most of the school attempts to take into account collective interests and group cohesion, collective action itself is still seen to derive from forms of cost-benefit analysis (Klandermans and Tarrow 1988; Cohen 1985; Birnbaum 1988).[3] In this way the resource mobilization school takes individual motivation to be the key to causation, and its method requires privileged access to the intentions of individual actors.

The most common critique of this approach is founded on its inability to explain actors' interests. It is asserted that the approach has "nothing to offer concerning preference formation" (Elster 1982), and so these interests have to be taken for granted, and taken as fixed. In short, the analysis of intentions lacks a proper sense of the ways in which the social and political context may shape

---

3 There is much more to the resource mobilization approach than the "free rider" problem and the Prisoners'
  Dilemma. There is a salutary emphasis on organization and other collective resources, and a variety of
  attempts to resolve the "free rider" problem by including political entrepreneurship in the analysis. Here
  I am simply characterizing its core explanation of what makes popular movements move.

collective identities and aspirations. As a corollary it is suggested that the igno-
rance of interests means that the goals of collective action remain equally
opaque, which is deeply damaging to a theory that seeks to explain popular
movements in terms of means-ends calculations (Munck 1990). Although this
is all fair comment, it seems to miss the main point, which is that the (unknown)
interests of individual actors in popular movements are taken to be the same,
and that this identity of interests accounts for the movement itself as a unified
actor with a singular and undivided rationality. In other words, this approach
simply assumes the coherence of the movement, which is really one of the first
things to be explained. This is recognized by those commentators who insist
that popular actors be seen as forging and maintaining a sense of unity, and so
slowly achieving identity (Mainwaring 1987; Touraine 1988; Melucci 1988);
but there are reasons to doubt whether such identity can ever be fully
constituted.

Even those critics who allege that the resource mobilization school remains
ignorant of actors' interests may themselves believe that such interests can be
known (Munck 1990) and, by implication, that they are formed and fixed
socially or economically, or anyway prior to politics. But the view that "actors
are defined, organized, and capable of action before they have any channel of
political representation" (Touraine 1988) is categorically rejected by those who
assert that "political practice constructs the interests it represents" (Laclau and
Mouffe 1985); at the very least, it is difficult to deny that organization and
mobilization may modify the interests that give rise to them in the first place,
so that actual interests may even come to conflict with the original (Michels
1949). The inescapable conclusion is that interests may be socially unattached,
are always politically malleable, and are anyway difficult if not impossible to
establish.[4]

The story of the teachers' movement lends strong support to the argument
that interests are constructed through the very process of mobilization, but in
the belief that the concept itself has become analytically untenable, this study
has referred consistently not to the movement's interests but to its demands.
These demands emerge through popular organization and strategic choice (see
Chapters 2, 4, 5, and passim), and their content changes from economic to legal
and professional to political as a complex outcome of the organizing effort itself
and of interactions with other actors in civil society and with the agents and
institutions of the political system. In this way popular political practices (both
intrinsic and extrinsic) generate and modify demands, just as the demands influence the practices, and this means that the motivation of popular mobilization
is contingent, and therefore intractable to easy "modeling."

---

4 The only way they can be established, according to Tilly (1978), is by dubious inferences that either return
  us to an assumed connection between interests and social position or force us to accept the verisimilitude
  of the statements of the political actors themselves. Even then, within Michels's perspective, it will be
  impossible to establish what *a priori* interests subsist and how far these have been transformed by organization and mobilization.

In this connection it is clear that the nature of strategic choice is really very different from the way it is described within rational choice theory, and hence within the resource mobilization model. To put it succinctly, although there is certainly agency and intentionality, there is no unified agent with an intention or a singular rationality that can make such choices. This point has been amply illustrated by the pervasive influence of competing factions within the teachers' movement on the shaping of political strategy (see Chapter 6), which is always a contingent result of intrinsic practices of organization and leadership (just as organization itself is conditioned and changed by strategic choices). At the same time, the critical strategic moment[5] for any popular movement is always its engagement with its political environment, and its extrinsic practices necessarily multiply the contingencies of strategic choice. This conclusion applies *a fortiori* where the institutional configuration of the environment itself is shifting (see Chapter 9), partly under the impact of popular movements (see Chapters 10 and 11).

In this regard there is little disagreement that strategic choice is closely conditioned by the relations between popular movements and the State, but the abstraction of State theory (Boschi 1987) leads it to "survey the terrain of collective action from so high an altitude that crucial processes and internal variations cannot be seen" (Tarrow 1988). Thus, despite more modulated approaches that attempt to specify the "selectivity" of the State (Offe 1985; Jessop 1985), State theory itself has contributed very little to the analysis of popular mobilization. For this reason the present study deals directly with the terrain in question, which is the legal and institutional terrain where popular organizations and government agencies and policies meet.[6] This is the strategic terrain par excellence (see Chapter 11), where popular actors struggle to find some political purchase in specific parts of the political system (Piven and Cloward 1979). Similarly, the use of the less discrete notion of political system rather than that of the State helps to blur the sharp distinction that is too easily drawn between State and civil society.[7] My approach therefore emphasizes the linkages between popular movements and the "institutional ensemble" of the State (Jessop 1982), which may themselves influence the institutional relations

5 In the 1857 Preface to the Introduction to the Contribution to the Critique of Political Economy, Marx referred to the different "moments" that mutually constitute and condition each other within the "totality" of capitalist economy. Finally dominant among the different moments was production. By analogy, the totality of the popular movement has its different moments such as organization, identity, leadership, strategic choice, etc., although in the present perspective the dominance of any one moment will depend on the conjuncture, or the passing of "political time" (see Chapter 9).

6 The notion of legal-institutional terrain is more neutral than the more commonly used "political opportunity structure" (Tarrow 1988) and is untainted by game-theoretical implications. It is neutral in the sense that it provides both constraints and opportunities to popular movements, which face a complex and shifting set of legal and institutional rules and practices, some normative and some not.

7 The distinction is made sharper than it should be because it is inscribed in one of the main teleological themes of the literature, that of "society against the State" or the "resurrection of civil society" (O'Donnell, Schmitter, and Whitehead 1986).

of the system (see Chapter 10). Such an approach is especially appropriate for Mexico, where the transformist project of the State (see Introduction) has created a mutual and complex permeation of State and civil society, which are conjoined on a densely textured terrain that is unique in Latin America.

## The identity of popular actors

European theorists have propounded an alternative approach to the "new social movements" that focuses on the collective identity of popular actors and provides a critique of the resource mobilization model. In particular, they reject the easy assumption of the empirical unity of popular movements (Touraine 1988) and complain that the model cannot analyze the process of identity construction. In their view, this process must take priority over explanations of strategic choice, if only because "in order to evaluate interests – that is to calculate costs and benefits – the calculating subject has to be assured of an identifying collectivity" (Pizzorno 1985). In short, only on the basis of a constructed identity does it make sense to talk of political strategy[8] because such an identity can explain the political goals of popular organization and so "complete" the means-ends calculations of rational choice.

There are problems with this position. First and most obvious is the survival of a constricted notion of strategic choice in terms of a singular rationality. Second is the elusive nature of the identity itself, which remains empirically ungrounded.[9] But the main problem is that popular identity, however it is understood, cannot exist prior to, and therefore cannot explain, strategic choice. On the contrary, just as popular demands emerge through the process of popular mobilization, so identity is collectively constructed through organization, strategic decision, and the ensuing interactions with the political environment, especially the political system (Craig 1990). In this way popular actors are always actively making their own identity through their own political practices and, in particular, through their always contingent strategic choices; as the analysis of the teachers' movement made clear (see Chapters 5 and 6), an identity cannot simply be taken as coterminous with a political or strategic unity. In other words, there is never complete identity but only a more or less conflicted process of identity formation. A pristine and *a priori* identity only returns to the fixed preferences of rational choice theory.

In Mexico it seems especially important to locate identity in the context of

8 These theorists also argue that such an identity, once achieved, has a political value that cannot be reduced to the terms of rational and instrumental choice. "Collective action is never based solely on cost-benefit calculation and a collective identity is never entirely negotiable" (Melucci 1988).

9 This has been recognized by Melucci, who has criticized the thinking of his European colleagues. "The identity appears as a datum, a sort of essence of the movement, in the case of Touraine; in the case of Pizzorno, the concept seems to be founded on shared interest, in accordance with the Marxist tradition" (Melucci 1988, p. 346).

the political practices that link popular movements to the political system. In particular, it was suggested that the popular insistence on autonomy does not reflect an absolute value or aspiration so much as the practical condition for effective representation (see Chapter 10), and in the present perspective such practical autonomy would indicate that popular organization and strategic discovery were capable of achieving a collective or community identity, depending on the movement's variable and sometimes conjunctural success in resisting vertical imposition and control. In general, only when it is recognized that identity is a dependent and not an independent variable (to use the behavioralist vocabulary) will it be possible to operationalize it.

## Popular identity differentiated

At the heart of this active vision of a constructed identity is an equally active view of the self-constitution of popular political actors, who form themselves through the political choices and organizational commitments implicit in popular struggle (Lechner 1986; Przeworski 1977; Foweraker 1989b). The teachers in struggle were fully aware of the passage from historical object to political actor inscribed in the movement (see Chapters 1 and 4); they were also aware that such learning is self-taught, with every delegational committee and assembly becoming a "school for democracy." But if the change in political subjectivity is individual, the struggle is collective, and so the process of self-constitution can only take place in a group context. Hence, for Tilly (1978), "a set of individuals is a group to the extent that it is both a category and a network," and it is not only common "beliefs" that matter but also the networks that construct inclusiveness and underpin the "unifying structure" of the organization. This conclusion is strongly supported by my own work on popular struggle in Spain during the Franco era (Foweraker 1989b). But both that study and this account of the teachers' movement also demonstrate that some individuals are much more important than others (see Chapters 4 and 6), and all popular movements depend in some degree on political leadership to define identity and encourage its formation.[10]

But if individual identity is clearly "relational" in this sense, so is group iden-

---

10 The resource mobilization school highlights the role of these "political entrepreneurs" in solving organizational problems, in an attempt to resolve the analytical dilemma of combining individual and collective interests, presented in Mancur Olson's (1965) classic analysis as the "free rider" problem. Olson treated collective action as the effort to produce collective goods. In this way he could apply the economic theory of public goods to the new domain of social organizations. One result was his challenge to the common assumption that the activity of such organizations flowed naturally from the rational pursuit of shared interests. According to Olson's analysis, in most circumstances the average group member's estimated additional return from participation in the group effort will be less than the cost of the effort itself. Thus, if collective action does take place, its explanation must lie beyond the rational self-interest of the average participant.

tity insofar as every strategic choice must always take into account the action and reaction of other agents and organizations in civil society and the political system. Indeed, it is very often the principle of difference, or the construction of "otherness," that is crucial in affirming and reinforcing identity, as the story of the teachers' movement illustrates repeatedly. Thus, the teachers and parents of the rural communities of Chiapas were identified by their opposition to the local *caciques;* the Indian "hispanifiers" of the highlands of Chiapas, by the disdain of their white bosses in the State apparatus; the women teachers, by their difference from the male supervisors and directors; and the teachers in struggle as a whole, by their enmity toward the *charros* within the official union, who condensed all "others" of the region in one figure. Finally, for the Trotskyists within the movement, the core of their political identity was constructed partly by their intransigence toward the State as the principle of domination writ large and partly by their increasingly bitter rivalry with the militants of Línea Proletaria (Chapter 6).

But the central debate over the principles of difference that compose the identity of popular movements concerns the continuing claims of class analysis. In the European context explanations of the movements have tended to favor either the "pull" factors of objective needs in determinate structural conditions or the "push" factors of new values and new concerns that make new cultural issues (Cohen 1985; Offe 1985), and class references have tended to suggest that at least some popular movements continue to have a material base and make material demands. This seems to be the kind of compromise favored by Touraine (1988), who stresses that most social conflicts are currently cultural yet insists that "the notion of social movement is inseparable from that of class."

In the Latin American context, on the other hand, where material demands appear to be universal, the debate has focused more on the social location of these demands. The collective consumption thesis of Castells (1983), in particular, suggests that popular movements have taken material demands out of the class sphere of production into the community sphere of reproduction, as newly organized movements seek to defend or promote a minimum level of infrastructure and service provision. But this argument does not beg the corollary that popular movements have therefore superseded class struggles or that the two are mutually exclusive. It is then but a small step to the recognition that popular movements may articulate both class divisions and other orders of cultural and political difference, and so combine both class and non-class identities. In the case of the teachers' struggle it is clear that their original material demands were fused with ideas of community, ethnicity, gender, profession, and citizenship to form a movement that was simultaneously syndical and popular.[11] In general, it is safe to conclude that the class content of popular movements is an empirical question.

---

11 The peasant movements of Chiapas did not hesitate to forge class alliances with the dissident teachers.

Material needs are increasing in Latin America and material demands have never been more important, but it is worth insisting that these demands do not exhaust the political agenda of popular movements. In Mexico the teachers' struggle for material survival (see Chapters 1 and 2) soon spawned further demands that their professional and legal rights be respected (see Chapters 3 and 5), and popular movements throughout the country have come to claim a cluster of inalienable and often constitutional rights. In this regard popular aspirations in contemporary Latin America are analogous to those of the European social movements in their classic period of the nineteenth and early twentieth centuries, insofar as they struggle to vindicate specific rights that have come to constitute the political elements of modern citizenship. Today these rights are both recognized and established in Western Europe and North America, but they are far from being so in Mexico. This is not so much a question of political forms, the Mexican Constitution being one of the most advanced in the world, as of their real political content, which is consistently defended and promoted by popular mobilization. This, then, is the universal content of the teachers' constant battle against "administrative repression" (see Chapter 8), as their movement struggled both for the satisfaction of material needs and for the achievement of citizenship.

## The parochialism of postmaterial theory

The presence or absence of material needs continues to condition discussions of popular mobilization and even to determine the definition of popular movements. It is therefore instructive to consider the radical postmaterialism of Alberto Melucci (1989), who argues that contemporary popular movements are no longer preoccupied with struggles over the production and distribution of material goods and resources, but inhabit a postmaterial world of codes, values, and meanings; that the significance of their political practices is their non-institutional and more-than-instrumental character, which does not require engagement or confrontation with the institutions of the State, and which in this sense is therefore "non-antagonistic";[12] that they are mainly drawn from the middle classes, and possibly the unemployed and students, but emphatically not from the working class (here Melucci follows Claus Offe); and that these movements are overwhelmingly concerned with issues of identity (gay rights, women's movement, ethnic movements) or with the planetary dimension of life in complex societies (environmental and nuclear issues).

All this may appear perfectly plausible if the political context is Western Europe, and *a fortiori* if the principal empirical reference is Milan, one of the

---

12 Whereas popular movements in Mexico have contested the government's neoliberal project by mobilizing to defend the social pact inscribed within the corporatist institutions of the political system (see Chapter 11), in Europe a similar neoliberal or conservative project to restrict the political arena has coincided with popular aspirations to autonomy and a non-institutional style of politics (Offe 1985).

most prosperous cities in Europe. But none of it applies one iota to most popular movements in Latin America, which continue to be driven by material needs and demands; which are obliged to direct their activities to the institutions of the State and are predominantly "institutionalist" in their strategies (see Chapters 9 and 10); which are mainly drawn from workers, peasants, residents of low-income neighborhoods, and State employees such as teachers who are paid less than skilled workers; and which are increasingly concerned with wages, services, and finally survival in the face of savage economic crisis and stringent austerity policies.

This radical difference in the descriptions of a First World characterized by cultural needs and a Third World driven desperate by material needs leads to an equally dramatic difference in the very definition of popular movements. Melucci's assertion that "the cultural dimension of needs supersedes their material determination and opens up new unexplored territory" (Melucci 1989, p. 177) serves as the premise for a far-reaching defense of popular movements as political messages that challenge the neutral logic of the political system on cultural grounds. Furthermore, because popular movements qualify as such only if they challenge or break the limits of the system, Melucci deliberately excludes any movement that seeks inclusion in a system of benefits or rules. Touraine (1988) is equally adamant that the notion of a social movement "must be reserved for truly central conflicts" that challenge society's basic rules.

Now there is no doubt that popular movements in Latin America are engaged in cultural struggles, if legal and constitutional rights are a question of political culture; and it might be argued that the popular challenge to clientelism and *charrismo* in Mexico is a challenge to the basic rules of the political system, if not to the society as such (see Chapters 10 and 11). But by Melucci's definition there are no popular movements in Latin America, where cultural needs, in his sense, run a very poor second to physical survival for most individuals; where traditional struggles for a more equitable distribution of diminishing material benefits still hold sway; and where every popular movement must seek some form of inclusion in the legal and institutional system of government if it is to extract the minimum benefits that may ensure its own reproduction and survival. Moreover, it is precisely their institutionalism that compels these popular movements to fight for their legal and political rights, and encourages the continual refinement of political organization and political strategy.

Nonetheless, Melucci's iconoclastic vision of popular movements as "nomads of the present" (Melucci 1989) reverberates with the social and political realities of contemporary Latin America, but more for reasons of analytical coincidence than anything else. Melucci uses the phrase to suggest the specificity of modern social movements. Unlike the movements of the century past with their historical personality and historical role, those of today have no program, no future, and no universal plan of history. In place of personality there is heterogeneity, and Melucci rejects teleology in favor of contingency. In Latin America too, popular movements are deeply inserted in the present because they have no material or political guarantee of tomorrow. Theirs is presently a precarious struggle for material survival, and the parallel struggles for legal and political rights aspire to protect present physical integrity and defend present dignity, rather than reflecting an imagined political community or reaching for a more perfect political future. In Latin America history has been thrown into reverse as economies shrink and the dispossessed see the little that they have taken away, while political authority becomes more arbitrary and dangerous, and life itself becomes increasingly cheap.

## The political ambiguity of popular politics

None of this is meant to imply that popular movements do not seek and occasionally achieve institutional and political change. This quest was an integral part of early definitions of the movements (Wilkinson 1971; Tilly 1978), and it is clear that popular movements have had some impact on political change in Mexico (see Chapters 10 and 11). But this change is not a response to a doctrinal program of political renewal or to a popular vision of democratic government. On the contrary, the change has come, if at all, in response to concrete and immediate demands for the satisfaction of material needs and for respect for professional and legal rights. The combination of these demands has encouraged popular efforts to achieve linkage with the political system through a range of institutionalist strategies, which have led inexorably to a struggle over the terms of representation within this system overall (see Introduction and Chapter 11).

This struggle presents a persistent challenge to the legitimacy of government institutions, to the effectiveness of traditional forms of political control, and to the prerogatives of the politically powerful. But it should not be overstated as a struggle for democracy in the sense of a full-fledged liberal democratic system. The political horizons of most popular movements do not reach so far. Nonetheless, in contrast to a postmodern vision of Western Europe, where popular organization mainly expresses political differences and so lays claim to rights that can no longer be universalized (Mouffe 1989), it is clear that popular movements in Mexico still struggle to defend common civil liberties and to achieve equal and universal rights. They are certainly reformist and not revolutionary, yet they struggle to salvage the legacy of their own Mexican Revolution.

These ambitious assertions should not be construed to mean that popular movements are guided by pure ethical principles, or are themselves more democratic or politically pure than the political culture that surrounds them (although both may occasionally be the case). What it does mean is that these movements have to defend their own organizational integrity and operational autonomy while simultaneously achieving sufficient political purchase within the political system to get their demands met. This strategic tension between autonomy and representation (see Chapter 10), or between institutionalism and institutionalization (see Chapters 9 and 10), can by its very nature never be resolved; this is especially true on the transformist terrain linking State and civil society in Mexico (see Introduction). The historical result is the pervasive ambiguity of popular politics in Mexico, which imbues every strategic choice with an element of political risk and a sense of political loss. This ambiguity reveals the real meaning of popular movements in Mexico because only by popular mobilization can the tension be maintained and the ambivalence contained. Thus, paradoxically, popular mobilization is what creates the conditions for popular organization in the form of popular movements that approach the political system through a *fuite en avant*.[13] The recurrent reversals and defeats of recent years must mean that they can never be sanguine about the possibility or persistence of success, but in the words of the Spanish proverb, "if they stumble, it means they're walking."


## Postscript

The teachers of Chiapas and most other regions of the country had "stumbled" in the spring of 1987. But just two years later, in April and May of 1989, the National Coordinating Committee of Workers in Education (CNTE) launched a massive national mobilization to back traditional demands for wage rises and an unprecedented demand for the dismissal of the SNTE's "leader-for-life," Carlos Jonguitud Barrios. With the capital of the country paralyzed by the dissident teachers, President Salinas summoned Jonguitud and told him he had to go.

On this occasion the teachers who led the protest came from Section IX in the Federal District, the heartland of the Revolutionary Vanguard, and their advance was consolidated in the assemblies and congress that followed in June and July. On July 18, 1989, the new secretary-general of the SNTE, Elba Esther Gordillo, ratified the election of a new and democratic sectional committee for Section IX, so setting the seal on the teachers' movement's most important victory. Not one Vanguardist had been elected in Section IX, and the dissidents now controlled the executive committees of Sections IX (Federal District), VII (Chiapas), and XXII (Oaxaca), as well as sharing executive authority in three other sections.

Some months before the 1989 mobilization President Salinas had ousted the head of the oilworkers' union and ordered the arrest of the director of one of Mexico's largest stockbroking houses. Both men were charged with fraud,

---

13 Translated literally as "fleeing forwards." Similarly, the act of walking can be thought of as a process of continually falling down, which is always prevented by continuing to walk.

which sent out a clear message that *charrismo* and its attendant corruption were no longer immune to political attack; and the signal was not lost on the dissident teachers when they dared to demand Jonguitud's head. But his dismissal did not mean that the Revolutionary Vanguard itself had suddenly disappeared. The composition of the National Executive Committee of the SNTE remained largely unchanged and was clearly Vanguardist in its loyalties. Indeed, at both national and regional levels the Vanguardists were too strong to succumb to frontal attack.

The new secretary-general herself had been one of the Revolutionary Vanguard's hardline apparatchiks, but appeared ready to bend with the political wind and, in particular, to comply with the new administration's plans to modernize the educational system (a hardy perennial of the policymakers in the Ministry of Education). To do so, she sought to build her own power base of ex-Vanguardists, ex-dissidents, and intellectuals wedded to the Ministry of Education's reform project. But the way forward was not easy. On one flank were the Vanguardists, practiced in the ways of corruption and fighting to retain power within their union *cacicazgos*. On the other flank was the teachers' movement, whose historic leadership had just won its most significant battle, and which still aspired to capture overall control of the union. Moreover, Elba Esther was under strong pressure from both the Ministry of Education and the political management of the Federal District, neither of whom was satisfied that order had been restored in the profession.

It was at this moment (June 15–16, 1989) that the teachers of Chiapas held their long-delayed sectional congress, which, it was expected, would return Section VII to democratic control. But even though the movement in Chiapas had remained under attack from the Revolutionary Vanguard and the state government, it had also remained as divided as ever between Línea Proletaria and the Trotskyists (and the sundry groups that coalesced around these two factions). The only exception was Ricardo Aguilar Gordillo, who was now a firm follower of the new secretary-general. The congress was accompanied by the usual mutual accusations of collaboration, and its progress was as conflictive as ever. By the time the conflicts had run their course Línea Proletaria and the historic leadership of the movement had been defeated.

The SNTE's new secretary-general, who was a native of Chiapas, had not expected this result. In fact, she had been courting the historic leadership, especially members of the original Central Struggle Committee, whom she had invited to help her in the national reconstruction of the union. But the state government had been viscerally opposed to this leadership because of its advocacy and practice of teacher-peasant alliances, which posed a severe threat to public order in this predominantly rural state. This gave the Trotskyists a strong political advantage and, it was rumored, the means to offer material incentives to the Indian "hispanifiers," whose votes were able to swing the contest in the Trotskyists' favor. Once Elba Esther Gordillo saw the groundswell of support for the Trotskyists, she immediately ditched her erstwhile allies in order to secure her own position in her home state.

This division between the "radicals" and the historic leadership of the teachers' movement was not peculiar to Chiapas, but had come to pervade the movement overall. At the national level the radicals had wanted to reject the presidential imposition of Elba Esther, whereas the historic leaders saw a strategic opportunity to resolve a series of regional disputes (knowing that the historic force of the movement always lay in the regions). By the fall of 1989 the movements within the two most conflicted states at that time, Guerrero and Michoacán, had become radicalized, and radicals at the national level insisted on launching a strike prior to the President's "state of the Union" address at the beginning of November. The moment for the strike was not propitious, and the predictable result was a new wave of "administrative repression," which succeeded in reversing some of the achievements of earlier in the year.

But the new secretary-general's ambitions were also damaged. She had been promoting a "broad front" within the SNTE that could reconcile its different tendencies, but the repression made her resemble Jonguitud. With her political project in jeopardy, Elba Esther had no choice but to seize the initiative, which she did in December 1989 by convening the SNTE's first Extraordinary National Congress for the following month. Many of the dissident sections and tendencies decided to send representatives, even if they stopped short of competing for posts on the National Executive Committee (for fear of turning *charro*). The National Coordinating Committee (CNTE) of the teachers' movement again demonstrated a lack of unified national direction, and, as a result, the dissident's representatives attended the Congress without any clear strategic goal. Therefore, although they often had the best of the argument, they could make no impact on the decision-making process itself, and eventually left the Congress in protest.

Nonetheless, the Congress did carry through some reforms that responded to long-time demands of the movement. All reference to the Revolutionary Vanguard was to be removed from the statutes. The SNTE was obliged to be independent of all political parties. Union funds had to be more evenly distributed. Individual sections and delegations were to gain greater autonomy of the National Executive Committee, and the formerly illegal meetings of school representatives were now encouraged. Moreover, there is no doubt that the teachers' movement in the shape of the CNTE, which now represented about a third of all teachers, received an unprecedented degree of official recognition.

However, the main institutional business of the Congress was to legitimize a leader who had been imposed by presidential fiat, while simultaneously excising Jonguitud's costly *cacicazgo*. Elba Esther Gordillo was duly elected as secretary-general, and she could then proceed to tighten the lines of political command within the union, binding some sectional committees to her reform project and pushing others to the sidelines. This had the desired effect of securing her own position, and the contingent effect of reinforcing the coexistence of three distinct factions within the union: a strong phalanx of unrepentant Vanguardists, the new secretary-general's own supporters, and the teachers' movement itself. These three factions all had different short-term objectives and different long-term aspirations. Since none of them had any real prospect of easily eliminating the others, they would have to learn to live together. Thus, another chapter had been written in the life of the teachers' movement, but it was clear that this could not be the end of the story.

# Bibliography

## Primary sources


Alonso, Ana María. 1986. "The Effects of Truth: Re-Presentations of the Past and the 'Imagining of Community.'" Mimeo. Center for U.S.-Mexican Studies, University of California, San Diego.

Alonso, Jorge. 1988. "El Papel de las Convergencias de los Movimientos Sociales en los Cambios del Sistema Político Mexicano." Paper presented to conference on *Mexico's Alternative Political Futures,* Center for U.S.-Mexican Studies, University of California, San Diego, March 22–25.

Altamirano, Juan J. 1986. *Balance Político y Perspectivas de Lucha del Magisterio Nayarita.* FMIN/CNTE/Comisión Promotora de la CNTE en Nayarit. Noviembre.

Arellanes Caballero, Rafael, Librado Santiago Constantino, and Julio Peralta Esteva. 1985. *Radiografías y Diagnóstico de un Proceso Sindical: El Movimiento Magisterial Chiapaneco.* Comité Ejecutivo de la Sección VII del SNTE. Febrero.

Balboa, Juan. 1987a. "El Convenio deja las Puertas Abiertas a Maestros de Vanguardia Revolucionaria." *El Observador de la Frontera Sur,* 21 de abril.

Bartra, Armando. 1978. *Apuntes sobre la Cuestión Campesina.* Departamento de Estudios Económicos y Sociales, Universidad de Yucatán, Merida.

*Chispa Sindical.* See Consejo Central de Lucha de las Escuelas Técnicas Agropecuarias de Chiapas.

CIACH (Centro de Información y Análisis de Chiapas). 1986–7. *Resumen Informativo,* nums. 2–5. San Cristóbal de las Casas, Chiapas.

CNTE. 1980. *Proyecto de Programa y Plataforma de Acción (que servirá de material central en la Conferencia Nacional de los días 19/20 de septiembre de 1980).* Agosto.

    November 1980–October 1981. *El Movimiento Magisterial* (fortnightly reports on movement at national and regional levels by the Asessoría de la CNTE).

    1981. *Misael Nuñez A.: Biografía de Una Lucha/Relato de Una Infamia. Información Obrera,* 27 de julio.

    1982. *Un Primer Balance. Tácticas para la Democratización del SNTE.* Documento de la Asamblea Nacional de Acapulco, 17 enero.

    1983. *III Foro Coordinadora Nacional de Trabajadores de la Educación,* 5/6 de marzo.

    1987a. *Caminemos,* IV num. 16. Mexico D.F., junio.

    1987b. *Convocatoria a los Normalistas del País.* Tuxtla Gutiérrez, 21 julio.

    nd. "El XIX Consejo Ordinario del SNTE." Mimeo. Comisión Permanente.

Comisión Nacional de Maestros Coordinadores de Telesecundarias. 1979. *Al Magisterio Nacional. Unomásuno,* 13 diciembre.

Comisión Promotora del Consejo Central de Lucha de la Sección X del SNTE. 1981. *Balance y Perspectivas del Movimiento Magisterial Nacional.*

Consejo Central de Huelga del Magisterio Chiapaneco. 1979a. *Actas de Asambleas* de los días 8, 17, 24, 29 de septiembre y 1, 2, 4 de octubre.

    1979b. *Alto a la Represión!* (Al CEN del SNTE, Al Congreso de Trabajo, Al Magisterio Nacional), 28 septiembre.

    1979–80. *La Puya* (Órgano Informativo), 1 and 2, septiembre 1979; 3, febrero 1980.

Consejo Central de Lucha de las Escuelas Técnicas Agropecuarias de Chiapas. 1978. *Carta Abierta al C. Secretario de Educación Tecnológica Agropecuaria.* Tuxtla Gutiérrez, marzo.

    1978–86. *Chispa Sindical* (Órgano Informativo), 1, marzo 1978; 2, mayo 1978; 3, septiembre 1978; 4, mayo 1979; 5, junio 1979; 6, noviembre 1979; 7, abril 1980; 8, 1 mayo 1980; 9, 10 mayo 1980; 10, febrero 1981; 11, marzo 1981; 12, abril 1981; 13, 1 mayo 1981; 14, enero 1982; Suplemento, 28 octubre 1982; 15, julio 1983; 16, octubre 1983; 17, noviembre 1983; Suplemento, 14 enero 1984; 18, 25 febrero 1984; Especial, febrero 1984; Especial, marzo 1984; Suplemento, 13 octubre 1984; Especial, noviembre 1984; Especial (II), noviembre 1984; Suplemento, 25 octubre 1985; 19, marzo 1986; 20 Especial, 24 mayo 1986; 21 Especial, 16 junio 1986; 22, octubre 1986.

    1981. "Línea Proletaria: una Dirección que ha Traicionado al Movimiento en Chiapas." *Boletín Independiente,* febrero.

Consejo Central de Lucha del Magisterio Chiapaneco. 1980a. *Manifiesto al Magisterio en General,* 11 marzo.

    1980b. *El Movimiento Magisterial Chiapaneco: Materiales de Discusión y Análisis* 1, 10 octubre.

    1981. *Plantón del Magisterio de Chiapas: Materiales de Discusión y Análisis* 2.

Consejo Central de Lucha del Magisterio de Guerrero. 1985. *Juicio Político a "Vanguardia Revolucionaria."* Oaxaca, 30 enero.

Consejo Central de Lucha del Magisterio Hidalguense. 1981. *Documento de Discusión: Balance y Perspectivas.*

Consejo Central de Lucha Magisterial del Valle de México. 1981. "Al Magisterio Nacional y al Pueblo de México." *Unomásuno,* 23 febrero, p. 7.

Consejo Central de Lucha Misael Nuñez Acosta. 1982. *Balance del Movimiento Magisterial del Valle de México.*

Corriente Democrática Magisterial. 1985. *Elementos para un Balance de la Jornada Magisterial,* Primavera.

Corriente Revolucionaria. 1979. *Conciencia,* num. 1, febrero.

Cortina, Regina. nd. "Women in the Teaching Union of Mexico City." Mimeo.

    1985. *Power, Gender and Education: Unionized Teachers in Mexico City.* School of Education, Stanford University, Stanford, Calif., May.

Delgado, Hector. 1979. "El Éxito, Gracias a las Bases." *Oposición,* 21 octubre.

Equipo Pueblo. 1984a. "Balance de la CNTE 1984." *Pueblo,* VI, num. 118–19, noviembre-diciembre.

    1984b. "Organización y Democracia Sindical: Sección 7 del SNTE en el Estado de Chiapas." *Pueblo,* Folleto num. 1.

    1985. "Organización y Democracia Sindical." *Pueblo,* Folleto num. 2.

    1986a. *Maestros: Una Historia por Contarse.* Cuadernos de Insurgencia Sindical.

    1986b. *Oaxaca: Los Maestros en Lucha Continua. Pueblo,* abril.

Fernández Dorado, Rubelio. nd. *Las Luchas Magisteriales del '56–'60.* Cuadernos de Insurgencia Sindical.

    1982. *El Auge Magisterial de Marzo de 1982: La Jornadas de Lucha del Magisterio Dirigido por la CNTE.* Frente Magisterial Independiente Nacional.

    1984. *El Nuevo Sindicalismo y la Lucha Magisterial en Michoacán,* febrero.

    1985. *Informe a los Trabajadores sobre el 10 de Mayo.* Coordinadora Nacional de Trabajadores de la Educación.

Fernández Dorado, Rubelio, and Teodoro Palomino Gutiérrez. 1986. Comentario sobre el Documento "Consideraciones sobre la Situación y Breve Esbozo de Perspectiva para el Movimiento Magisterial Chiapaneco" por Ricardo Aguilar Gordillo. 16 Junio.

FMIN (Frente Magisterial Independiente Nacional). 1981a. *¿Que es el Charrismo y Como lo Está Combatiendo el Magisterio Nacional?* Cuadernos de Educación Sindical Clasista, I, mayo.

1981b. "Congreso Charro: Lo Mismo de Siempre." *Educador Socialista,* num. 13, mayo.

1981c. *Chiapas: Testimonios de Dirigentes del Movimiento Magisterial,* abril.

1982. "Estatutos y Reglamento General de Asambleas del SNTE." *Educador Socialista,* num. 22, noviembre–diciembre.

1984a. "El Viejo y el Nuevo Sindicalismo. Ayer y Hoy del Sindicalismo en la Sección 7 de Chiapas." *Educador Socialista,* num. 27, febrero.

1984b. "Informe sobre el VIII Congreso de la Sección 7 de Chiapas." *Educador Socialista,* num. 28, marzo–abril.

1984c. "Crónica de la Reciente Lucha Magisterial en la Región Petrolera de Chiapas." *Educador Socialista,* num. 29, julio.

1986. "Oaxaca y Chiapas: Extragos de un Informe a la Asamblea Nacional del FMIN." *Educador Socialista,* num. 38, mayo–junio.

1987. *El Disidente* (que ni come niños ni mata gente), nums. 19, 20.

Harvey, Neil. 1990a. *Corporatist Strategies and Popular Responses in Rural Mexico: State and Opposition in Chiapas, 1970–1988.* Ph.D. thesis, University of Essex, Colchester.

Hernández, Luis. nd. "Ante la Ofensiva contra el Magisterio Chiapaneco: Las Bases Tienen la Palabra"; "El Congreso Seccional Chiapaneco: una Sopa de su Propio Chocolate"; "Un Baño de Agua Fría"; "El Amargo Sabor de la Derrota"; "Chiapas: Germina la Semilla de la Rebelión"; "Una Larga Marcha"; "El Camino de la Resistencia"; "La Quinta Oleada del Movimiento Magisterial"; "Chiapas: Recuperar la Initiativa"; "Una Carta/Un Compromiso"; "Construir la Unidad de las Fuerzas Populares"; "Sentimientos Desconsolados"; "Organizaciones Autónomas de Masas: Notas para la Discusión." Undated manuscripts.

1984. "Maestros Democráticos: Guerra Social el Próximo Febrero" (diciembre).

Hernández Gómez, Manuel, et al. 1985. *Un Antes: Acerca del Por Qué de las Contradicciones de Esta Etapa de Lucha Magisterial en Chiapas* (20 abril).

Instituto Politécnico Nacional (Grupo La Tuerca). 1985. *La Tuerca,* nums. 1–13, marzo de 1985 a abril de 1986.

*La Puya. See* Consejo Central de Huelga del Magisterio Chiapaneco.

López R, Octavio, and Simon Castillejos. 1987. "Chiapas: gran reto para el magisterio democrático." *Bandera Socialista,* num. 351, 18 mayo.

Marván Laborde, Ignacio. 1988. "Tendencias Actuales de los Movimientos Sociales en México: Expresiones Nacionales y Regionales." Mimeo. Instituto de Investigaciones Sociales, UNAM, México D.F.

Meyer, Lorenzo. nd. "Las Elecciones en México: La Fuerza de la Tradición." Mimeo. El Colegio de México, México D.F.

1986. Various articles in *Excelsior,* August.

Movimiento Revolucionario del Magisterio (MRM). 1982. *Política de Alianzas de la Coordinadora Nacional de Trabajadores de la Educación,* junio.

Organización Magisterial 27 de Abril. 1984. "Análisis del Movimiento Magisterial." *Camarada,* Complemento, Tuxtla Gutiérrez, abril.

Organización Revolucionaria de los Trabajadores de la Educación. 1982. "XXII Congreso Extraordinario de la Sección XXII de los Trabajadores de la Educación en Oaxaca." *Insurgente,* Cuadernos Políticos, num. 1, julio.

Partido Socialista Unificado de Mexico (PSUM). 1984. *Documento Central de la Conferencia Nacional de la Rama de los Trabajadores de la Educación miembros del PSUM,* mayo.

Reyes, Ramiro (MRM). 1980. *Manuscrito sobre El Movimiento Magisterial Chiapaneco*. Mexico D.F., julio–agosto.

Sánchez Sánchez, Samuel, et al. 1985. *Al Magisterio Bilingue; Al Magisterio en General*. Tuxtla Gutiérrez, abril.

Sección VII (SNTE). 1977. *Manifiesto al C.Lic. Fernando Solana – Secretario de Educación Pública y al C.Dr. Rolando W. de Lasse, Director General de Educación Tecnológica Agropecuaria*. Delegaciones D-II-10, D-II-11, D-II-12. Tuxtla Gutiérrez, diciembre.

———. 1978. *Al Magisterio de Chiapas*. Comité Ejecutivo Seccional, 13 abril.

———. 1981. *Germen* (Órgano de Información y Análisis de la Sección VII del SNTE), num. 1, diciembre.

———. 1982a. *Germen*, num. 3, junio.

———. 1982b. *Diferencias Ideológicas?* Discussion documents for Asamblea Estatal de Representantes Sindicales, 17/18 septiembre.

———. 1983–4. Interviews with leaders of Coordinadora Regional del Centro (Chiapas).

———. 1984a. *Reseña del PreCongreso/Congreso de Marzo de 1984*.

———. 1984b. *La Profundización de la Democracia Sindical*.

———. 1985a. *Respuestas a Nuestras Demandas en Esta Etapa de Lucha*. CES, Subcomisión de Difusión y Propaganda, marzo.

———. 1985b. *Consideraciones, Acuerdos y Tareas*. Asamblea Estatal de Balance, 20/21 abril.

———. 1987. "Proyecto de Balance, Análisis y Propuestas Políticas y Organizativas." Chiapas, 12 junio.

Sección VII (SNTE), Coordinadora Regional de la Costa. 1983. *Un Proyecto de Lucha basado en la Experiencia de Nuestro Movimiento Magisterial*, agosto.

Sección VII (SNTE). E.S.T. 17. 1987. *Pensamiento Democrático 1*. Mimeo.

Sección VII (SNTE). Bloque Democrático. 1985. *Proyecto de Balance del Reciente Período de Movilizaciones Magisteriales*. Tuxtla Gutiérrez, 22 marzo.

Sección VII (SNTE), Colectivo Seccional. 1985. *Nuestros Primeros Pasos en la Unidad, Organización y Solidaridad Campesina*, julio.

Secciones VII, XL, and XXII (SNTE). 1983. *Primera Asamblea de Representantes Sindicales Delegacionales y de Centros de Trabajo de los Trabajadores de la Educación de Oaxaca y Chiapas*, 22/23 octubre.

Sección XI (SNTE), Delegación D-III-24. nd. *Tácticas de Lucha para la Democratización del SNTE*.

———. 1980. "Las Luchas Recientes de los Trabajadores del SNTE." *Folletos de Educación Sindical*, num. 5, agosto.

———. 1981. "El Movimiento Magisterial Democrático: La Lucha continua." *Folletos de Educación Sindical*, num. 7, marzo.

———. 1982. "Balance: La Quinta Oleada del Movimiento Magisterial." *Folletos de Educación Sindical*, num. 10, mayo.

———. 1983a. "Vanguardia va a la Guerra." *Folletos de Educación Sindical*, num. 12, mayo.

———. 1983b. La Toma de la Sección XI del SNTE. *Folletos de Educación Sindical*, num. 13, octubre.

———. 1984. "Vanguardia va a la Lona" (Luis Hernández and A. Manuel Hernández). *Folletos de Educación Sindical*, num. 15, abril.

———. 1985. "Oaxaca la Fiesta de los Maestros; El Juicio a Vanguardia; El Sabor del Asfalto" (Jorge Belarmino Fernández and Luis Hernández). *Folletos de Educación Sindical*, num. 17, junio.

Sección XXII (SNTE). 1985. *Por la Educación al Servicio del Pueblo*. Comité Ejecutivo Seccional, Oaxaca, mayo.

Secretaría de Educación Pública. 1987. *Esquema de Educación Básica: Documento de Formalización*. 13 Mayo.

Solana, Fernando. 1981. Letter to Ramón Martínez Martín, Secretario General del CEN del SNTE, 19 enero.

Street, Susan. 1987a. "Los Maestros Chiapanecos y la Calidad Educativa." *Excelsior*, 25 marzo.

1987b. "Maestros Chiapanecos: La Lucha que Vendrá." *Excelsior*, 1 abril.

1987c. "Defienden los Maestros de Chiapas sus Ideales y el Derecho a la Dignidad." *Excelsior*, 10 abril.

1989a. "El Projecto Educativo desde la Base." Jornadas de Reflexión: Magisterio, Universidad y Cambio. Universidad Pedagógica Nacional, octubre.

STUNAM. 1986–7. *Consideraciones*, nums. 1–10, Mexico D.F.

Treviño Carrillo, Ana Helena. 1984. *El Movimiento Magisterial en México: el Caso de Morelos (1980–81)*. Masters Thesis, FLACSO, México D.F., July.

Valdez Vega, María Eugenia. 1986. *Participación de los Maestros de Primaria del Distrito Federal en la Insurgencia Magisterial de 1979–1983*. Masters Thesis, FLACSO, Mexico D.F., July.

Whitehead, Laurence. 1988. "The Consolidation of Fragile Democracies: a Discussion with Illustrations." Mimeo. European Consortium for Political Research, Joint Sessions. Rimini, 5–10 April.

Yescas Martínez, Isidoro, and Gloria Zafra. 1985. *La Insurgencia Magisterial en Oaxaca, 1980*. Instituto de Investigaciones Sociológicas de la Universidad Autónoma Benito Juárez de Oaxaca.


## Newspapers

In Mexico City: *Excelsior*, September 1979 to February 1980; *El Universal*, June to October 1979; *Diario de Mexico*, October 1979; *El Día*, September to December 1979; *Novedades*, June to October 1979; *Avance*, December 1979; *Ovaciones*, September and October 1979; *Sucesos*, April to December 1980; *Unomásuno*, September 1979 to February 1980.

In Chiapas: *El Heraldo*, September 1979 to January 1980; *El Sol de Chiapas*, September and October 1979; *Diario Popular*, October 1978; *El Ahuizote*, October 1979; *Cuarto Poder*, September and October 1979; *Boletín Independiente*, July 1978; *La República en Chiapas*, April 1978 to May 1980; *La Tribuna* April 1978 to September 1979; *Reflexión* (fortnightly), September 1979.

## Interviews

Interviews were carried out with leaders, intellectuals, and militants of the teachers' movement, mainly but not exclusively in Chiapas. The principal informants are listed here, but none of them are responsible for the content of my argument or its conclusions.

David Torres, Alberto Arnaut, Gerardo Peláez, Luis Hernández (2), Manuel Hernández Gómez (2), Jésus López Constantino (2), Jácobo Nazar Morales (2), Gustavo Zarate, Arturo Velasco Martínez, Rafael Arellanes Caballero (2), Francisco Guzmán López, Amadeo Espinosa Ramos, José Antonio Hernández, Víctor Manuel Anchaita, Manuel Valda, Alfredo, Ricardo Aguilar Gordillo, Russell Aguilar Brindis, Rosario Guadalupe de León Roblero, Sara Gladys Espinosa Utrilla, Julieta de Paz Ramos, Octavio López Ruiz (2), José Domingo Guillén, Leonidas Ojeda Fierro, Manuel de Jésus Navarro, Jaime del Toro Lozada, Guadalupe Guzmán Zwart, Jorge Hernández Gutiérrez, Jose María Fino, Hernán Villatoro Barrios, Gabriel Cruz Hilerio (El Chino), Carlos Misael Palma, María Lucia Yervas Leydon, Mariano López Díaz, Andrés Fábregas Puig, Angel Fonseca Vallenas, Reynaldo, Rodrigo Ochoa Aguilar, Samuel Sánchez Sánchez, Eufrosino Sánchez Sánchez, Felix Toala Albores, Pedro Miranda Matías, Teodoro Palomino Gutiérrez, Francisco Pérez Arce, Miguel Lanz, Juan Balboa

## Secondary sources

Alvarado, Artur, ed. 1987. *Electoral Patterns and Perspectives in Mexico.* Center for U.S.–Mexican Studies, University of California, San Diego.

Alvarez, Alejandro. 1986. "Crisis in Mexico: Impacts on the Working Class and on the Labor Movement." In *The Mexican Left, the Popular Movements, and the Politics of Austerity. See* Carr and Montoya 1986.

Anderson, Benedict. 1983. *Imagined Communities.* Verso/New Left Books, London.

Anderson, Bo, and James Cockroft. 1972. "Control and Cooptation in Mexican Politics." In J. Cockroft et al., eds., *Dependence and Underdevelopment.* Anchor, New York.

Angell, Alan. 1982. "Classroom Maoists: the Politics of Peruvian Schoolteachers under Military Government." *Bulletin of Latin American Research,* vol. 1, no. 2.

Arau Chavarría, Rosalinda. 1987. "Organización de los Pueblos y Colonias del Sur." *Revista Mexicana de Sociología,* vol. 49, num. 4, octubre.

Arriaga, María de la Luz. 1981. "El Magisterio en Lucha." *Cuadernos Políticos,* vol. 27, pp. 79–101, enero–marzo.

Asociación Nacional de Educadores Salvadoreños (ANDES). 1980. *Las Luchas Magisteriales en El Salvador.* Ediciones y Impresiones Pedagógicas, México D.F.

Aziz, Alberto. 1987. "Electoral Practices and Democracy in Chihuahua, 1985." In *Electoral Patterns and Perspectives in Mexico. See* Alvarado 1987.

Bailey, John. 1986. "What Explains the Decline of the PRI and Will It Continue?" In *Mexico's Political Stability: the Next Five Years.* See Camp 1986c.

—— 1987. "Can the PRI Be Reformed? Decentralizing Candidate Selection." In *Mexican Politics in Transition. See* Gentleman 1987c.

Balboa, Juan. 1987b. "De la Madrid prometió Respuesta; la sección de Chiapas, desconocida." *Proceso,* num. 541, 16 marzo.

—— 1987c. "Cede la SEP a reclamos en Oaxaca y Chiapas; rechazo a propuestas del SNTE." *Proceso,* num. 543, 30 marzo.

Bartra, Roger. 1974. *Estructura Agraria y Clases Sociales en México.* Ediciones ERA, México D.F.

—— 1975. "Campesinado y Poder Político en Mexico." In R. Bartra et al., *Caciquismo y Poder Político en el Mexico Rural.* Siglo Veintiuno Editores, México D.F.

—— 1977. "De la mediación no democrática a la democracia sin mediación." *Estudios Sociales Centroamericanos,* vol. 6, num. 16.

Basañez, Miguel. 1981. *La Lucha por la Hegemonía en México 1968–1980.* Siglo Veintiuno Editores, México D.F.

—— 1987. "Elections and Political Culture in Mexico." In *Mexican Politics in Transition.* See Gentleman 1987c.

Birnbaum, Pierre. 1988. *States and Collective Action: The European Experience.* Cambridge University Press, Cambridge.

Boschi, Renato. 1984. "On Social Movements and Democratization: Theoretical Issues." *Occasional Papers in Latin American Studies,* no. 9. Joint Center for Latin American Studies, Stanford University–University of California, Berkeley.

—— 1987. *A Arte da Associação.* Vertice & IUPERJ, Rio de Janeiro.

Britton, John A. 1976. *Educación y Radicalismo en México: los Años de Cárdenas.* Secretaría de Educación Pública, México D.F.

Camacho, Manuel. 1985. *La Clase Obrera en la Historia de Mexico: El Futuro Inmediato.* Instituto de Investigaciones Sociales, UNAM, México D.F.

Cammack, Paul. 1988. "The 'Brazilianization' of Mexico?" *Government and Opposition,* vol. 23, no. 3.

Camp, Roderic A. 1986a. "Overview." In *Mexico's Political Stability: the Next Five Years. See* Camp 1986c.

    1986b. "Potential Strengths of the Political Opposition and What It Means to the PRI." In *Mexico's Political Stability: the Next Five Years. See* Camp 1986c.

    ed. 1986c. *Mexico's Political Stability: the Next Five Years.* Westview Press, Boulder, Colo.

    1987. "Opposition in Mexico: a Comparison of Leadership." In *Mexican Politics in Transition. See* Gentleman 1987c.

Campa, Homero. 1987. "Ante la Indiferencia de la SEP, la Enseñanza Secundaria va en Retroceso." *Proceso,* no. 552, June 1.

Cano, Arturo, Luis Hernández, and Jesus Martín del Campo. 1990. *El Nuevo Sindicalismo.* Historias del Sindicalismo Mexicano, 15. Equipo Pueblo/Información Obrera, México D.F.

Carr, Barry. 1983. "The Mexican Economic Debacle and the Labor Movement: a New Era or More of the Same?" In *Mexico's Economic Crisis: Challenges and Opportunities. See* Wyman 1983.

    1985. *Mexican Communism, 1968–1983: Eurocommunism in the Americas?* Research Report Series, no. 42. Center for U.S.–Mexican Studies, University of California, San Diego.

    1986. "The Mexican Left, the Popular Movements, and the Politics of Austerity, 1982–85." In *The Mexican Left, the Popular Movements, and the Politics of Austerity. See* Carr and Montoya 1986.

    1987. "The PSUM: the Unification Process on the Mexican Left, 1981–1985." In *Mexican Politics in Transition. See* Gentleman 1987c.

Carr, B., and R. Montoya, eds. 1986. *The Mexican Left, the Popular Movements, and the Politics of Austerity.* Monograph Series, no. 18. Center for U.S.–Mexican Studies, University of California, San Diego.

Carrillo, Teresa. 1990. "Women and Independent Unionism in the Garment Industry." In *Popular Movements and Political Change in Mexico. See* Foweraker and Craig 1990.

Castellanos, Rosario. 1961. *Balún Canán.* Fondo de Cultura Económica, México D.F.

Castells, Manuel. 1982. "Squatters and Politics in Latin America." In Helen Safa, ed., *Toward a Political Economy of Urbanization in Third World Countries.* Oxford University Press, New Delhi.

    1983. *The City and the Grassroots.* Edward Arnold, London.

Cohen, Jean. 1985. "Strategy or Identity: New Theoretical Paradigms and Contemporary Social Movements." *Social Research,* vol. 52, no. 4.

Collier, George A. 1987. "Peasant Politics and the Mexican State: Indigenous Compliance in Highland Chiapas." *Mexican Studies,* 3 (1), Winter.

Cook, Maria Lorena. 1990. "Organizing Opposition in the Teachers' Movement Oaxaca." In *Popular Movements and Political Change in Mexico. See* Foweraker and Craig 1990.

Córdoba, Arnaldo. 1980. "La Dominación Corporativista." *La Política de Masas y el Futuro de la Izquierda en México.* Ediciones ERA, México D.F.

Cornelius, Wayne. 1986a. *The Political Economy of Mexico under de la Madrid: the Crisis Deepens, 1985–1986.* Center for U.S.–Mexican Studies, University of California, San Diego.

    1986b. "Political Liberalization and the 1985 Elections in Mexico." In *Elections and Democratization in Latin America, 1980–1985. See* Drake and Silva 1986.

    1987. "Political Liberalization in an Authoritarian Regime: Mexico, 1976–1985." In *Mexican Politics in Transition. See* Gentleman 1987c.

Cornelius, Wayne, and Ann Craig. 1984. *Politics in Mexico: An Introduction and Overview.* Reprint Series, no. 1. Center for U.S.–Mexican Studies, University of California, San Diego.

Cornelius, Wayne, Judith Gentleman, and Peter H. Smith, eds. 1989. *Mexico's Alternative*

*Political Futures.* Monograph Series, no. 30. Center for U.S.–Mexican Studies, University of California, San Diego.

Craig, Ann. 1990. "Institutional Context and Popular Strategies." In *Popular Movements and Political Change in Mexico. See* Foweraker and Craig 1990.

Craig, Ann, and Wayne Cornelius. 1980. "Political Culture in Mexico: Continuities and Revisionist Interpretations." In G. Almond and S. Verba, eds., *The Civic Culture Revisited.* Little, Brown & Co., Boston.

Craven, B. 1959. *La Carreta.* Vintage Press, New York.

De la Garza, Enrique. 1982. "Estructura Organizativa y Democracia en el SNTE." *Información Obrera,* num. 1, verano.

De los Reyes, Yolanda. 1986. "Decentralización de la Educación." In Blanca Torres, ed., *Decentralización y Democracia en México.* El Colegio de México, México D.F.

Drake, Paul, and Eduardo Silva, eds. 1986. *Elections and Democratization in Latin America, 1980–1985.* Center for Iberian and Latin American Studies and Center for U.S.–Mexican Studies, University of California, San Diego.

Elster, Jon. 1982. "Marxism, Functionalism, and Game Theory: the Case for Methodological Individualism." *Theory and Society,* vol. 11, no. 2.

Espinosa, Juan Antonio. 1982. "Los Maestros de los Maestros: Las Dirigencias Sindicales en la Historia del SNTE." *Historias,* num. 1, julio–septiembre. Instituto Nacional de Antropología e Historia, México D.F.

Evers, Tilman. 1985. "Identity: the Hidden Side of New Social Movements in Latin America." In D. Slater, ed., *New Social Movements and the State in Latin America.* CEDLA, Amsterdam.

Fagen, Richard, and William Tuohy. 1972. *Politics and Privilege in a Mexican City.* Stanford University Press, Stanford, Calif.

Feyerabend, Paul. 1978. *Against Method.* Verso, London.

Foucault, Michel. 1978. *The History of Sexuality, Volume 1: An Introduction.* Pantheon Books, New York.

Foweraker, Joe. 1988. "Transformism Transformed: the Nature of Mexico's Political Crisis." *Essex Papers in Politics and Government,* no. 46.

1989a. "Popular Movements and the Transformation of the System." In *Mexico's Alternative Political Futures. See* Cornelius, Gentleman, and Smith 1989.

1989b. *Making Democracy in Spain: Grass-roots Struggle in the South, 1955–1975.* Cambridge University Press, New York.

Foweraker, Joe, and Ann Craig, eds. 1990. *Popular Movements and Political Change in Mexico.* Lynne Reinner Publishers, Boulder, Colo.

Fox, Jonathan, and Gustavo Gordillo. 1989. "Between State and Market: the Campesinos Quest for Autonomy." In *Mexico's Alternative Political Futures. See* Cornelius, Gentleman, and Smith 1989.

Friedmann, John, and Mauricio Salguero. 1987. "The Barrio Economy and Collective Self Empowerment in Latin America." In Michael Peter Smith, ed., *Power, Community and the City.* Transaction Books, New Brunswick, N.J.

Fuentes Molinar, Olac. 1983. *Educación y Política en México.* Editorial Nueva Imagen, México D.F.

Gentleman, Judith. 1987a. "Political Change in Authoritarian Systems." In *Mexican Politics in Transition. See* Gentleman 1987c.

1987b. "Mexico after the Oil Boom: PRI Management of the Political Impact of National Disillusionment." In *Mexican Politics in Transition. See* Gentleman 1987c.

ed. 1987c. *Mexican Politics in Transition.* Westview Press, Boulder, Colo.

Germani, Gino. 1962. *Política y Sociedad en Una Época de Transición.* Eudeba, Buenos Aires.

Gómez Tagle, Silvia. 1987. "Democracy and Power in Mexico: the Meaning of Conflict in the 1979, 1982, and 1985 Federal Elections." In *Mexican Politics in Transition. See* Gentleman 1987c.

González Casanova, Pablo. 1970. *Democracy in México.* Oxford University Press, London.

1981. *El Estado y los Partidos Políticos en México.* Ediciones ERA, México D.F.

Gramsci, Antonio. 1971. *Selections from the Prison Notebooks of Antonio Gramsci.* Edited by Q. Hoare and G. N. Smith. Lawrence and Wishart, London.

Guadarrama, Rocío. 1987. "Elections in Sonora." In *Electoral Patterns and Perspectives in Mexico. See* Alvarado 1987.

Guillén López, Tonatiuh. 1987. "Political Parties and Political Attitudes in Chihuahua." In *Electoral Patterns and Perspectives in Mexico. See* Alvarado 1987.

Hamilton, Nora. 1982. *The Limits of State Autonomy: Post-Revolutionary Mexico.* Princeton University Press, Princeton, N.J.

Hansen, Roger. 1971. *The Politics of Mexican Development.* Johns Hopkins University Press, Baltimore.

Harvey, Neil. 1988. "Personal Networks and Strategic Choices in the Formation of an Independent Peasant Organization: the OCEZ of Chiapas, Mexico." *Bulletin of Latin American Research,* vol. 7, no. 2.

1990b. "Peasant Strategies and Corporatism in Chiapas." In *Popular Movements and Political Change in Mexico. See* Foweraker and Craig 1990.

Hellman, Judith. 1980. "Social Control in Mexico." *Comparative Politics,* vol. 12, no. 2.

1982. *Mexico in Crisis.* Holmes and Meier, New York.

Hernández, Luis. 1981. "Paciencia y acabamos con el Charrismo." *Cambio,* vol. 7, nos. 25–28. México D.F.

1982a. "México: Izquierda y Clase Obrera." *Información Obrera,* num. cero, primavera.

1982b. "Sobre el Grupo Vanguardia Revolucionaria" *Información Obrera,* num. 1, verano.

1982c. "Las Corrientes Político Sindicales dentro del SNTE." *Información Obrera,* num. 1, verano.

1983a. *Viva la CNTE! Fuera los Charros!* Cuadernos de Insurgencia Sindical, Información Obrera y Editorial Extemporaneos, junio.

1983b. "La Fuerza Ambivalente de la CNTE para el Estado." *Punto,* 1, num. 41, 15–22, agosto.

1983c. "La Violencia Charra." *Siempre,* num. 1110, suplemento, 21 septiembre.

1985a. "Paro en Chiapas: Paro con Mayúsculas." *Información Obrera,* num. 55, marzo.

1985b. "Chiapas: Febrero Mes de Movilizaciones, Marzo Mes de los Chiapanecos." *Información Obrera,* no. 56, abril.

1985c. "Una Historia que es no Sólo para Recordar." *Cuadernos Educativos,* num. 1, octubre.

1986. "The SNTE and the Teachers' Movement, 1982–1984." In *The Mexican Left, the Popular Movements, and the Politics of Austerity. See* Carr and Montoya 1986.

1987a. "Los Protagonistas del Golpe." *Siempre,* suplemento, 9 abril.

1987b. *Información Obrera,* num. 65, abril.

Hernández, Luis, and Francisco Pérez Arce. 1982. *Las Luchas Magisteriales 1979/1981 (Documentos II).* Editorial Macehual, México D.F.

Hernández Aguilar, Jorge Enrique. 1986. *En Nombre del Maíz.* Noviembre. Ediciones Pueblo, México D.F.

Jessop, Bob. 1980. "The Political Indeterminacy of Democracy." In Alan Hunt, ed., *Marxism and Democracy.* Lawrence and Wishart, London.

1982. *The Capitalist State.* Martin Robertson, Oxford.

1985. "The State and Political Strategy." International Political Science Association Conference, Paris, July.

Jimenez, Edith. 1989. "A New Form of Government Control over *Colonos* in Mexico City." In Alan Gilbert, ed., *Housing and Land in Urban Mexico*. Monograph Series, no. 31. Center for U.S.–Mexican Studies, University of California, San Diego.

Kaufman, Robert. 1977. "Mexico and Latin American Authoritarianism." In *Authoritarianism in Mexico. See* Reyna and Weinert 1977.

Klandermans, Bert. 1986. "New Social Movements and Resource Mobilization: the European and the American Approach." *Comparative Perspectives and Research on Collective Behavior and Social Movements*, vol. 4.

Klandermans, Bert, and Sidney Tarrow. 1988. "Mobilization into Social Movements: Synthesizing European and American Approaches." *International Social Movement Research*, vol. 1. JAI Press, Greenwich, Conn.

Knight, Alan. 1990. "Historical Continuities in Social Movements." In *Popular Movements and Political Change in Mexico. See* Foweraker and Craig 1990.

Kowarick, Lucio. 1985. "The Pathways to Encounter: Reflections on the Social Struggle in São Paulo." In D. Slater, ed., *New Social Movements and the State in Latin America*. CEDLA, Amsterdam.

Labastida, Julio. 1972. "El Régimen de Echeverría; perspectivas de cambio en la estrategia de desarrollo y en la estructura de poder." *Revista Mexicana de Sociología*, num. 3–4, julio.

Laclau, Ernesto. 1977. *Politics and Ideology in Marxist Theory*. New Left Books, London.

1985. "New Social Movements and the Plurality of the Social." In D. Slater, ed., *New Social Movements and the State in Latin America*. CEDLA, Amsterdam.

Laclau, E., and C. Mouffe. 1985. *Hegemony and Socialist Strategy*. Verso, London.

Leal, Juan Felipe. 1986. *México: Estado, Burocracia y Sindicatos*. Ediciones El Caballito, México D.F.

Lechner, Norberto. 1986. *La Conflictiva y Nunca Acabada Construcción del Orden Deseado*. Centro de Investigaciones Sociológicas, Madrid.

Lenin, V. I. 1970. *Two Tactics of Social Democracy in the Democratic Revolution*. Foreign Language Press, Peking.

1972. *The State and Revolution*. Progress Publishers, Moscow.

Levitt, Barbara, and James G. March. 1988. "Organizational Learning." *Annual Review of Sociology*, vol. 14.

Levy, Daniel, and Gabriel Szekely. 1987. *Mexico: Paradoxes of Stability and Change*. Westview, Boulder, Colo.

Linz, J. J. 1964. "An Authoritarian Regime: Spain." In E. Allardt and Y. Littunen, eds. *Cleavages, Ideologies and Party Systems*. The Academic Bookstore, New York.

Logan, Kathleen. 1990. "Women's Participation in Urban Protest." In *Popular Movements and Political Change in Mexico. See* Foweraker and Craig 1990.

Lomnitz, Larissa. 1982. "Horizontal and Vertical Relations in the Social Structures of Urban Mexico." *Latin American Research Review*, vol. 17, no. 2.

Loyo Brambila, Aurora. 1979. *El Movimiento Magisterial de 1958 en Mexico*. Ediciones ERA, México D.F.

Luna Jurado, Rogelio. 1977. "Los Maestros y la Democracia Sindical." *Cuadernos Políticos*, num. 14, octubre–diciembre.

Mao Ze-dong. 1965. "Report on an Investigation of the Peasant Movement in Hunan." *Selected Works of Mao Tse-Tung*, vol. 1. Foreign Languages Press, Peking.

Mainwaring, Scott. 1987. "Urban Popular Movements, Identity, and Democratization in Brazil." *Comparative Political Studies*, vol. 20, no. 2, July.

Marion S., Marie-Odile. 1987. "Pueblos de Chiapas: una Democracia a la Defensiva." *Revista Mexicana de Sociología*, vol. 49, num. 4, octubre.

Márquez, Enrique. 1987. "Political Anachronisms: the *navista* Movement and Political Processes in San Luis Potosí, 1958–1985. In *Electoral Patterns and Perspectives in Mexico. See* Alvarado 1987.

Martínez Assad, Carlos. 1987. "State Elections in Mexico." In *Electoral Patterns and Perspectives in Mexico. See* Alvarado 1987.

Martínez Hernández, David. 1987. "Los Maestros de Chiapas y Oaxaca Enfrentan el Cacicazgo Vanguardista." *Perfil del Sureste,* vol. 1, num. 3, marzo-abril.

Marván L., Ignacio, and J. Aurelio Cuevas. 1987. "El Movimiento de Damnificados de Tlatelolco." *Revista Mexicana de Sociología,* vol. 49, num. 4.

McCarthy, John, and Mayer Zald. 1973. *The Trends of Social Movements.* General Learning, New York.

1977. "Resource Mobilization and Social Movements." *American Journal of Sociology,* vol. 82.

eds. 1979. *The Dynamics of Social Movements.* Winthrop, Cambridge, Mass.

Medina, Luis. 1978. *Del Cardenismo al Avilacamachismo (Historia de la Revolución Mexicana 18).* El Colegio de México, México D.F.

Melucci, Alberto. 1988. "Getting Involved: Identity and Mobilization in Social Movements." *International Social Movement Research,* vol. 1, JAI Press, Greenwich, Conn.

1989. *Nomads of the Present: Social Movements and Individual Needs in Contemporary Society.* Temple University Press, Philadelphia.

Meyer, Lorenzo. 1983. "Mexico: the Political Problems of Economic Stabilization." In *Mexico's Economic Crisis: Challenges and Opportunities. See* Wyman 1983.

1985. "La Democracia Política: Esperando a Godot." *Nexos,* num. 117.

Michels, Robert. 1949. *Political Parties.* Free Press, Glencoe, Ill.

Middlebrook, Kevin. 1985. *Political Liberalization in an Authoritarian Regime.* Research Report Series, no. 41. Center for U.S.–Mexican Studies, University of California, San Diego.

Molinar, Juan. 1986. "The Mexican Electoral System: Continuity by Change." In *Elections and Democratization in Latin America, 1980–1985. See* Drake and Silva 1986.

1987. "The 1985 Federal Elections in Mexico: the Product of a System." In *Electoral Patterns and Perspectives in Mexico. See* Alvarado 1987.

Monsiváis, Carlos. 1981. "Los Apóstoles se cansaron de serlo y el SNTE se fracciona." *Proceso,* 9 febrero.

1987a. "Los Maestros de Chiapas pagan caro el intento de escapar al poder de Jonguitud." *Proceso,* num. 544, 6 abril.

1987b. *Entrada Libre (Crónicas de la Sociedad que Se Organiza).* Ediciones ERA, México D.F.

Montes, Eduardo. 1975. *Como Combatir al Charrismo.* Ediciones de Cultura Popular, México D.F.

Mora Forero, Jorge. 1979. "Los Maestros y la Práctica de la Educación Socialista." *Historia Mexicana,* 113, vol. 29, julio–septiembre.

Mouffe, Chantal. 1989. "Radical Democracy: Modern or Postmodern?" In Andrew Ross, ed., *Universal Abandon? The Politics of Postmodernism.* University of Minnesota Press, Minneapolis.

Munck, Gerardo. 1990. "Identity and Ambiguity in Democratic Struggles." In *Popular Movements and Political Change in Mexico. See* Foweraker and Craig 1990.

Murmis, M., and J. C. Portantiero. 1971. *Estudios sobre los Orígenes del Peronismo.* Siglo XXI, Buenos Aires.

Needler, Martin C. 1987. "The Significance of Recent Events for the Mexican Political System." In *Mexican Politics in Transition. See* Gentleman 1987c.

Obserschall, A. 1973. *Social Conflict and Social Movements.* Prentice Hall, Englewood Cliffs, N.J.

O'Donnell, Guillermo. 1978. "Reflections on the Pattern of Change in the Bureaucratic-Authoritarian State." *Latin American Research Review*, vol. 13, no. 1.

    1979. "Tensions in the Bureaucratic-Authoritarian State and the Question of Democracy." In D. Collier, ed., *The New Authoritarianism in Latin America*. Princeton University Press, Princeton, N.J.

O'Donnell, Guillermo, Philippe C. Schmitter, and Lawrence Whitehead. 1986. *Transitions from Authoritarian Rule*. Johns Hopkins University Press, Baltimore.

Offe, C. 1985. "New Social Movements: Challenging the Boundaries of Institutional Politics." *Social Research*, vol. 52, no. 4, Winter.

Olson, Mancur. 1965. *The Logic of Collective Action*. Harvard University Press, Cambridge, Mass.

Osorio, Ruben. 1976. *El Linchamiento de "San Miguel Canoa."* Sociedad Chihuahuense de Estudios Históricos, Chihuahua, Chihuahua, julio.

Palomino, Teodoro. 1983a. "Coordinadora Nacional de Trabajadores de la Educación (CNTE)." *Espacios*, num. 1, abril–junio.

    1983b. "La CNTE ante la Crisis." *Espacios*, num. 2, julio–septiembre.

Parsons, Talcott. 1960. *Structure and Process in Modern Societies*. Free Press, Glencoe, Ill.

Paz, Octavio. 1985. *The Labyrinth of Solitude/The Other Mexico*. Grove Press, New York.

Peláez, Gerardo. 1980. *Insurgencia Magisterial*. EDISA, México D.F., julio.

    1984a. *Historia del Sindicato Nacional de Trabajadores de la Educación*. Ediciones de Cultura Popular, México D.F.

    1984b. *Las Luchas Magisteriales de 1956–1960*. Ediciones de Cultura Popular, México D.F.

    1989. "El Movimiento Magisterial se Demuestra Andando." *Socialismo*, Ano 1, num. 2, agosto.

Pérez Arce, Francisco. 1982a. "Itinerario de las Luchas Magisteriales." *Información Obrera*, num. 1, verano.

    1982b. "Los Maestros Vinieron del Sur." *Siempre*, suplemento, 22 diciembre.

    1987. "Chiapas: 8 Años de Rebeldía." *Siempre*, suplemento, 9 abril.

    1988. *A Muchas Voces: Testimonios de la Lucha Magisterial*. Universidad Autónoma de Sinaloa/Praxis/Información Obrera, México.

    1990. "The Enduring Union Struggle for Legality and Democracy." In *Popular Movements and Political Change in Mexico. See* Foweraker and Craig 1990.

Perlo, Manuel, and Martha Schteingart. 1984. "Movimiento Sociales Urbanos en México." *Revista Mexicana de Sociología*, vol. 46, num. 4, octubre.

Piven, Frances Fox, and Richard Cloward. 1979. *Poor People's Movements: Why They Succeed, How They Fail*. Vintage Books, New York.

Pizzorno, A. 1985. "On the Rationality of Democratic Choice." *Telos*, no. 63, Spring.

Prieto, Ana. 1986. "Mexico's National *Coordinadoras* in a Context of Economic Crisis." In *The Mexican Left, the Popular Movements, and the Politics of Austerity. See* Carr and Montoya 1986.

Przeworski, Adam. 1977. "Proletariat into a Class: the Process of Class Formation from Karl Kautsky's *The Class Struggle* to Recent Controversies." *Politics and Society*, vol. 7, no. 4.

Purcell, S., and J. Purcell. 1980. "State and Society in Mexico: Must a Stable Polity Be Institutionalized?" *World Politics*, vol. 32, no. 2.

Raby, David. 1974. *Educación y Revolución Social en Mexico, 1921–1940*. Secretaría de Educación Pública, México D.F.

Ramírez Saiz, Juan Manuel. 1987. "Para Comprender el 'Movimiento Urbano Popular.'" *Tiempos de Ciencia*, num. 9, septiembre–diciembre, Universidad de Guadalajara.

    1990. "Urban Struggles and Their Political Consequences." In *Popular Movements and Political Change in Mexico. See* Foweraker and Craig 1990.

Reyna, J. L., and R. S. Weinert, eds. 1977. *Authoritarianism in Mexico*. ISHI, Philadelphia.

Riding, Alan. 1985. *Distant Neighbors: a Portrait of the Mexicans.* Alfred A. Knopf, New York.

Romero, Laura. 1985. "El Movimiento Fascista en Guadalajara." In Jaime Tamayo, ed., *Perspectivas de los Movimientos Sociales en la Región Centro-Occidente.* Editorial Línea, México D.F.

Ronfeldt, David. 1973. *Atencingo: the Politics of Agrarian Struggle in a Mexican Ejido.* Stanford University Press, Stanford, Calif.

Roxborough, Ian. 1981. "The Analysis of Labour Movements in Latin America: Typologies and Theories." *Bulletin of Latin American Research,* vol. 1, no. 1, October.

——— 1984. *Unions and Politics in Mexico.* Cambridge University Press, London.

Roxborough, Ian, and Ilan Bizberg. 1983. "Union Locals in Mexico: the 'New Unionism' in Steel and Automobiles." *Journal of Latin American Studies,* vol. 15, no. 1.

Rubin, Jeffrey W. 1987. "State Policies, Leftist Oppositions, and Municipal Elections: the case of the COCEI in Juchitan." In *Electoral Patterns and Perspectives in Mexico. See* Alvarado 1987.

——— 1990. "Popular Mobilization and the Myth of State Corporatism." In *Popular Movements and Political Change in Mexico. See* Foweraker and Craig 1990.

Salazar C., Luis. 1989. "Aplausos y Chiflados." *Cuadernos de Nexos,* marzo.

Salinas Alvarez, Samuel. 1983. *Aulas de Emergencia.* Editorial Oasis, México D.F.

Salinas Alvarez, Samuel, and Carlos Imaz Gispert. 1984. *Maestros y Estado: Estudio de las Luchas Magisteriales 1979 a 1982.* Dos tomos. Editorial Línea, México D.F.

Salinas de Gortari, Carlos. 1982. *Political Participation, Public Investment, and Support for the System: a Comparative Study of Rural Communities in Mexico.* Research Report Series, no. 35. Center for U.S.–Mexican Studies, University of California, San Diego.

Salinas Domínguez, Carlos F. 1987. "Tamaulipas: Mafias, Caciques, and Civic-Political Culture." In *Electoral Patterns and Perspectives in Mexico. See* Alvarado 1987.

Sanderson, Steven. 1981. *Agrarian Populism and the Mexican State.* University of California Press, Berkeley.

Sandoval Flores, Etelvina. 1987. "Los Supervisores: Una de las Formas de la Presencia del Sindicato en la Vida Cotidiana del Maestro." *Cuadernos Educativos,* nums. 3/4, primavera.

Sección XXII (SNTE). 1986. *Ataca Oaxaca: los 60 días de Lucha de los Maestros de la Sección 22* (Textos de Carlos Monsiváis, Luis Hernández, Paco Ignacio Taibo II, Adolfo Gilly, Gaston García Cantú, Sección XXII). Equipo Pueblo-Información Obrera. Editorial Leega.

Semo, Enrique. 1986. "The Mexican Left and the Economic Crisis." In *The Mexican Left, the Popular Movements, and the Politics of Austerity. See* Carr and Montoya 1986.

Simpson, Lesley Byrd. 1962. *Many Mexicos.* University of California Press, Berkeley.

Sirvent Gutiérrez, Carlos. 1973. Burocracia y Clases Sociales." In C. Sirvent Gutiérrez et al., eds., *Las Clases Dirigentes en México.* Cuadernos FCPS, UNAM, México D.F.

——— 1985. "Apuntes para el estudio de la burocracia mexicana." *Revista Mexicana de Ciencias Políticas y Sociales,* num. 119, enero–marzo.

Slater, David. 1985. "Social Movements and a Recasting of the Political." In D. Slater, ed., *New Social Movements and the State in Latin America.* CEDLA, Amsterdam.

Smith, Peter. 1979. *Labyrinths of Power: Political Recruitment in 20th c. Mexico.* Princeton University Press, Princeton, N.J.

——— 1986. "Leadership and Change, Intellectuals and Technocrats in Mexico." In *Mexico's Political Stability: the Next Five Years. See* Camp 1986c.

Soares, Glaucio Ary Dillon. 1986. "Elections and the Redemocratization of Brazil." In *Elections and Democratization in Latin America, 1980–1985. See* Drake and Silva 1986.

Stepan, Alfred. 1988. *Rethinking Military Politics.* Princeton University Press, Princeton, N.J.

Stevens, Evelyn. 1970. "Legality and Extra-Legality in Mexico." *Journal of Inter-American Studies & World Affairs,* vol. 12, no. 1, January.

——— 1974. *Protest and Response in Mexico,* M.I.T. Press, Cambridge, Mass.

Story, Dale. 1987. "The PAN, the Private Sector, and the Future of the Mexican Opposition." In *Mexican Politics in Transition*. *See* Gentleman 1987c.

Street, Susan. 1983. "Burocracia y Educación: Hacia un Análisis Político de la Desconcentración Administrativa en la Secretaría de Educación Pública." *Estudios Sociológicos*, vol. 1, num. 2, mayo–agosto.

———. 1984. "Los Distintos Proyectos para la Transformación del Aparato Burocrático de la SEP." *Perfiles Educativos*, num. 7, octubre–diciembre. UNAM, Mexico D.F.

———. 1987d. "Las Luchas Magisteriales del Sur de Mexico." *Perfil del Sureste*, vol. 1, num. 3, marzo–abril.

———. 1987e. "Vuelven Los Maestros Chiapanecos." *Siempre*, suplemento, 5 marzo.

———. 1989b. "El Magisterio Democrático y el Aparato Burocrático del Estado." *Foro Universitario*, epoca 3, num. 11, enero–abril.

Tamayo, Jaime. 1990. "Neoliberalism encounters *Neocardenismo*." In *Popular Movements and Political Change in Mexico*. *See* Foweraker and Craig 1990.

Tarrow, Sidney. 1986. "Comparing Social Movement Participation in Western Europe and the United States." *Comparative Perspectives and Research on Collective Behavior and Social Movements*, vol. 4.

———. 1988. "National Politics and Collective Action: Recent Theory and Research in Western Europe and the United States." *Annual Review of Sociology*, vol. 14.

Tilly, Charles. 1978. *From Mobilization to Revolution*. Addison-Wesley, Reading, Mass.

Torres, David, ed. 1987. *Política y Partidos en las Elecciones Federales de 1985*. UNAM, México D.F.

Touraine, Alain. 1987. *Actores Sociales y Sistemas Políticos en América Latina*. PREALC, Santiago, Chile.

———. 1988. *The Return of the Actor: Social Theory in PostIndustrial Society*. University of Minnesota Press, Minneapolis.

Trejo Delarbe, Raul. 1989. "Maestros: De la Calle al Sindicato" *Cuadernos de Nexos*, junio.

Whitehead, Laurence. 1981. "On 'Governability' in Mexico." *Bulletin of Latin American Research*, vol. 1, no. 1, October.

Wilkinson, Paul. 1971. *Social Movement*. Pall Mall, London.

Wyman, Donald L., ed. 1983. *Mexico's Economic Crisis: Challenges and Opportunities*. Center for U.S.–Mexican Studies, University of California, San Diego.

Zald, Mayer, and John McCarthy. 1987. *Social Movements in an Organizational Society*. Transaction Books, New Brunswick, N.J.

Zermeño, Sergio. 1978. *México: Una Democracia Utópica*. Siglo Veintiuno, México, D.F.

———. 1982. "De Echeverría a de la Madrid: las Clases Altas y el Estado Mexicano en la Batalla por la Hegemonía. Working Papers, no. 18. Wilson Center, Washington, D.C.

———. 1987a. "La Democracia como Identidad Restringida." *Revista Mexicana de Sociología*, vol. 49, num. 4, octubre.

———. 1987b. "Ocoyoacác: triunfo de la política." *Revista Mexicana de Sociología*, vol. 49, num. 4, octubre.

———. 1990. "Crisis, Neoliberalism and Disorder." In *Popular Movements and Political Change in Mexico*. *See* Foweraker and Craig 1990.

Printed in the United Kingdom
by Lightning Source UK Ltd.
2192